THIS
IS
LIFE

FIRST PUBLISHED IN GREAT BRITAIN IN 2019

LIFE CHURCH
WAPPING ROAD
BRADFORD, BD3 0EQ
WWW.LIFECHURCHHOME.COM

ISBN 978-1-78972-500-1

IN PARTNERSHIP WITH COMPASSION UK.

Whoever you are, wherever you find yourself, one way or another; life happens to all of us. The good, the bad and everything in between. Life has the ability to throw up a whole heap of circumstances and emotions whenever it feels like it! Whilst we can't always determine what happens to us, we can determine how we respond.

Jesus is our help. He is our guide.

Psalm 119:105 says "Your word is a lamp for my feet, a light on my path."
God gave us His Word to help navigate our way round this complex and beautiful thing called life....
When life is great, dig deep into the Word and when life is not so great, learn to dig even deeper into the Word. It contains everything we need, it feeds our heart, teaches our mind and keeps our faith alive.

This book is a collection of some of the big things we face & how they meet with what the Bible says. It can be used to guide us in our journey with God and bring light to the path we are travelling on as we follow Him.

Do your best to commit to this book, keep going, discuss it with friends, pray about it and enjoy it! When you do, we truly believe your eyes and your heart will be opened to a whole new level of God's goodness in your life. We pray that through spending time in the Word of God you learn to hear the voice of God and always stay in the love of God. He loves you, He cares for you and He wants the best for you.

Go for it, let's go live this thing called LIFE.

Love, Rocknations

Rocknations is the youth & young adults movement of Life Church UK.

THIS
IS
LIFE

01 - GOD'S REAL LOVE
Week 01 — Love's Story   07
Week 02 — Real Love   11

02 - JESUS
Week 03 — Prediction and Prophecy   15
Week 04 — History of Jesus   19
Week 05 — Spiritual Life   24
Week 06 — Death and Resurrection   28
Week 07 — The 7 "I am's" of Jesus   33

03 - HOLY SPIRIT
Week 08 — Person, Role, Fruit and Gifts   37
Week 09 — Gifts and Work   41

04 - COMMUNICATING WITH GOD
Week 10 — Prayer and Hearing God   45
Week 11 — Value of God's Word   49
Week 12 — The Role of the Bible   53

05 - CHRISTIAN FOUNDATIONS
Week 13 — Creation   57
Week 14 — Humanity and our Sin   61
Week 15 — Foundations for Following Jesus   66
Week 16 — Baptism (Water and Spirit)   70

06 - THE KINGDOM OF GOD
Week 17 — Old vs. New Covenant   75
Week 18 — Advancing the Kingdom   80
Week 19 — Jesus' Example   85
Week 20 — Peter as an Example   89
Week 21 — Peter as an Example   94
Week 22 — The Parables   98

07 - JESUS' TEACHINGS
Week 23 — Sermon on the Mount   103
Week 24 — Sermon on the Mount   108
Week 25 — Sermon on the Mount   112

08 - HEROES OF THE FAITH
Week 26 — Heroes of Faith   117
Week 27 — Heroes of Faith   121
Week 28 — Heroes of Faith   125

09 - JESUS' MISSION

Week 29	–	Making Disciples	129
Week 30	–	Hallmarks of a Jesus Follower	133
Week 31	–	Hallmarks of a Jesus Follower	137

10 - CHURCH

Week 32	–	Value of God's house	141
Week 33	–	The First Church	145

11 - RELATIONSHIPS

Week 34	–	Deep Spiritual Friendships	149
Week 35	–	Relationships	154

12 - FAMILY

Week 36	–	Family	159

13 - SEX & SEXUALITY

Week 37	–	God's plan for blessing	163
Week 38	–	Live Pure	167
Week 39	–	Singleness, Sex & Marriage	171

14 - CHANGING WITH GOD'S HELP

Week 40	–	Overcome with God's Help	176
Week 41	–	Grace & Mercy with Jesus	182
Week 42	–	Forgiveness	188

15 - HOLISTIC HEALTH

Week 43	–	Cultivating a Healthy Mind	196
Week 44	–	Anxiety, Emotions, Body Image	200

16 - SCHOOL LIFE

Week 45	–	School Life	205

17 - FUTURE, CALLING & GIFTING

Week 46	–	The True You	210
Week 47	–	All About Inheritance	214
Week 48	–	Spiritual Gifts & the Body of Christ	218
Week 49	–	Calling & Gifting	222

18 - THIS IS LIFE

Week 50	–	Obedience & Denying Self	228
Week 51	–	Lifestyle	232
Week 52	–	Priorities	236

COPYRIGHT & ACKNOWLEDGEMENTS

241

MODULE 01
GOD'S REAL LOVE

Love is the most used hashtag in history with over 1.6 billion posts signed with the famous four letters L-O-V-E. Probably the biggest, most asked question in our world: What is love? Like REAL love? Society has always been searching for the answer to this question, so we look for it on the Internet, we create apps to find who we should love, we create tests to find out how compatible we are, and who we should expect to love us, we read books telling us how to find love, we enter competitions on TV programs in order to find love, we look for it in relationship after relationship and yet, for some reason none of these things seem to satisfy.

So what is REAL love or better yet, WHO is real love?

In the first two weeks of our devotional, we want to explore this question with you, the most defining question of your life. What we understand and encounter as real love shapes the way that we can give love to others and the way we can love ourselves. We will unpack a real love story between a God, who isn't just the author and creator of love, but whose whole being IS love. This real love is the love that keeps chasing after you, that meets you at your worst, and loves you to your best.

Get ready to encounter real love...

WEEK 01 | LOVE'S STORY

DAY 01
GOD'S LOVE THROUGH JESUS

JOHN 3:16 NIV

For God so loved the world that he gave his only Son,
that whoever believes in him should not perish but have eternal life.

THOUGHT

It's God's desire for everybody to have a relationship with him, so much so that He gave His Son as a sacrifice for 'whosoever'. Our life on earth is temporary; therefore we can live with an eternal perspective, knowing that one day we will live in Heaven forever with a God who loves us. That understanding helps bring purpose and perspective to our life here on earth.

ACTION

Reflect on a time when someone made a sacrifice for you and how this impacted you.

DAY 02

UNDESERVED LOVE

ROMANS 5:5-9 NIV

And this hope will not lead to disappointment. For we know how dearly God loves us, because he has given us the Holy Spirit to fill our hearts with his love. When we were utterly helpless, Christ came at just the right time and died for us sinners. Now, most people would not be willing to die for an upright person, though someone might perhaps be willing to die for a person who is especially good. But God showed his great love for us by sending Christ to die for us while we were still sinners. And since we have been made right in God's sight by the blood of Christ, he will certainly save us from God's condemnation.

THOUGHT

We often think that we need to earn God's love or that we don't deserve it. The truth is, God loves you so much more than you will ever comprehend. There is no need to strive for something we cannot earn as it was never meant to be worked for. Jesus died to set us free - so we can freely accept His love for us today.

ACTION

Think and reflect on when God has kept loving you during times when you felt that you didn't deserve it.

DAY 03

LOVE'S STORY PT. 1

1 JOHN 4:9-10 NLT

God showed how much he loved us by sending his one and only Son into the world so that we might have eternal life through him. This is real love – not that we loved God, but that he loved us and sent his son as a sacrifice to take away our sins.

THOUGHT

'Real love' is more than a song. It's the ridiculously amazing truth of a God who cares so deeply for His creation. He chose to suffer so we would have the chance to be reunited with Him, fully aware that many of His children would not respond to His love. Yet He loves us all despite often our lack of love back to Him. He forgave our sins because He loves us.

ACTION

How does this scripture challenge what the world says about love?

DAY 04

LOVE'S STORY PT. 2

1 JOHN 4:18-19 NLT

Such love has no fear, because perfect love expels all fear. If we are afraid, it is for fear of punishment, and this shows that we have not fully experienced his perfect love. We love each other because he loved us first.

THOUGHT

Accepting God's love means we don't need to live in the prison of our fear or our worries. This comes with a daily surrendering of our burdens and concerns to Jesus and trusting that we can live in the freedom He died to give us. You are loved, therefore you can be courageous, confident and secure knowing He first loved you.

ACTION

Have you fully accepted God's love for you? What does this mean for areas in your life in which you feel afraid?

DAY 05

LOVE'S STORY PT. 3

1 JOHN 4:11-17 NLT

Dear friends, since God loved us that much, we surely ought to love each other. No one has ever seen God. But if we love each other, God lives in us, and his love is brought to full expression in us. And God has given us his Spirit as proof that we live in him and he in us. Furthermore, we have seen with our own eyes and now testify that the Father sent his Son to be the Savior of the world. All who declare that Jesus is the Son of God have God living in them, and they live in God. We know how much God loves us, and we have put our trust in his love. God is love, and all who live in love, live in God, and God lives in them. As we live in God, our love grows more perfect. So we will not be afraid on the day of judgment, but we can face him with confidence because we live like Jesus here in this world.

THOUGHT

Once we truly receive God's love, there is a change that occurs both internally and externally. This is because we have His Spirit dwelling within us. Our focus, desires and priorities are transformed when we truly experience His love in our lives. The love God has for us then overflows into our love for each other.

ACTION

How can you practically allow God's love to be fully expressed in your life?

DAY 06

LOVE'S STORY PT. 4

1 JOHN 4:7-8 NLT

Dear friends, let us continue to love one another, for love comes from God. Anyone who loves is a child of God and knows God. But anyone who does not love does not know God, for God is love.

THOUGHT

Love is foundational to our identity as children of God. Loving God means we know Him; His character, desires, likes and dislikes. Knowing God and living in relationship with Him every day is our life goal. The full outworking of knowing God is expressed primarily in our love for one another.

ACTION

How does this scripture encourage you in your understanding of being a child of God?

DAY 07

LOVE'S STORY PT. 5

1 JOHN 4:20-21 NLT

If someone says, "I love God," but hates a fellow believer, that person is a liar; for if we don't love people we can see, how can we love God, whom we cannot see? And he has given us this command: Those who love God must also love their fellow believers.

THOUGHT

"I love God" needs to be more than a phrase; it needs to become a way of life. Our love for God needs to be reflected in our love for each other. Can we truly say that we love God if we have bitterness and unforgiveness in our heart towards His children? We can love them with our feelings, but we choose to love them with our actions.

ACTION

Who are your fellow believers? How can you put this kind of love into action?

DAY 01

THIS IS REAL LOVE

1 CORINTHIANS 13:4-8 NLT

Love is patient and kind. Love is not jealous or boastful or proud or rude. It does not demand its own way. It is not irritable, and it keeps no record of being wronged. It does not rejoice about injustice but rejoices whenever the truth wins out. Love never gives up, never loses faith, is always hopeful, and endures through every circumstance. Prophecy and speaking in unknown languages and special knowledge will become useless. But love will last forever!

THOUGHT

When everything in this world is said and done - it is love that will remain. Love is described as an action rather than a passive thought or feeling. It is something we receive, share and give to one another. Love is so powerful that when you feel at the end of yourself, love can keep you going and going! It never fails.

ACTION

Paul is describing love as action rather than just a thought. With people that you love, such as family and friends, how do you actually action that love rather than just saying it to them?

DAY 02

REAL LOVE IS THE MOST SPIRITUAL THING

1 CORINTHIANS 13:1-3 NLT

If I could speak all the languages of earth and of angels, but didn't love others, I would only be a noisy gong or a clanging cymbal. If I had the gift of prophecy, and if I understood all of God's secret plans and possessed all knowledge, and if I had such faith that I could move mountains, but didn't love others, I would be nothing. If I gave everything I have to the poor and even sacrificed my body, I could boast about it; but if I didn't love others, I would have gained nothing.

THOUGHT

God has placed so many gifts in all of us - we all have an incredible purpose in this world which is connected to the Spirit of God within us. But these mean nothing if they are not centred around God's love. Our accomplishments in life mean nothing if they aren't done with the love for God and others in mind.

ACTION

Where in your life do you think love needs to be refocused? Are you valuing your gifts and talents over your love?

DAY 03

REAL LOVE IS GOD'S GREATEST COMMANDMENT PT. 1

MATTHEW 22:36-38 NLT

"Teacher, which is the most important commandment in the law of Moses?" Jesus replied, "'You must love the Lord your God with all your heart, all your soul, and all your mind.' This is the first and greatest commandment."

THOUGHT

Loving God is what our whole life is all about, it has to be our greatest priority. Jesus teaches us that loving God first and foremost from our whole being is the best way to live our lives. Everything in life flows from this one command.

ACTION

What does it look like for you to love God with all your heart, soul and mind?

DAY 04

REAL LOVE IS GOD'S GREATEST COMMANDMENT PT. 2

MATTHEW 22:39-40 NLT

A second is equally important: 'Love your neighbor as yourself.' The entire law and all the demands of the prophets are based on these two commandments.

THOUGHT

Everything we are in Christ is underpinned by love. All the laws and commandments of Christ were forged out of love - if God is real to our lives, this will be shown by the love we have for God and for others. Jesus also teaches us that our love for our neighbour stems out of receiving God's love for ourselves.

ACTION

How can you start loving your neighbours as you grow in your understanding of God's love for you?

DAY 05

LOVE EVEN YOUR ENEMIES PT.1

LUKE 6:27-31 NLT

But to you who are willing to listen, I say, love your enemies! Do good to those who hate you. Bless those who curse you. Pray for those who hurt you. If someone slaps you on one cheek, offer the other cheek also. If someone demands your coat, offer your shirt also. Give to anyone who asks; and when things are taken away from you, don't try to get them back. Do to others as you would like them to do to you.

THOUGHT

Loving your enemies is one of the hardest things to do. Many people may have wronged you but the reality is that we have also wronged and caused hurt to others. Jesus is the greatest example of someone who loved people who did not love Him. That is why we need the supernatural love of God to bless, pray and give to others as He has done for us.

ACTION

Who in your life could you start to love differently today? How?

DAY 06

LOVE EVEN YOUR ENEMIES PT. 2

LUKE 6:32-36 NLT

If you love only those who love you, why should you get credit for that? Even sinners love those who love them! And if you do good only to those who do good to you, why should you get credit? Even sinners do that much! And if you lend money only to those who can repay you, why should you get credit? Even sinners will lend to other sinners for a full return. Love your enemies! Do good to them. Lend to them without expecting to be repaid. Then your reward from heaven will be very great, and you will truly be acting as children of the Most High, for he is kind to those who are unthankful and wicked. You must be compassionate, just as your Father is compassionate.

THOUGHT

Loving our enemies in Jesus' eyes isn't just thinking nice thoughts, it involves a shift in our hearts. Jesus even says that people will know that we are His disciples by the way we love, forgive and treat others (John 13:34-36). Just as Jesus displayed love - even to those whom we would say don't deserve it - as Christ's followers we are called to do the same. When we see the world through the lens of Christ's love, it helps us to love everyone the same.

ACTION

Why don't you spend some time praying for people that right now you find it hard to show love to?

DAY 07

LOVE IS A DAILY CHOICE & A LONG TERM COMMITMENT

JOHN 15:9-11 NLT

I have loved you even as the Father has loved me. Remain in my love. When you obey my commandments, you remain in my love, just as I obey my Father's commandments and remain in his love. I have told you these things so that you will be filled with my joy. Yes, your joy will overflow!

THOUGHT

God will always love us. To remain in His love means to walk in His ways, acknowledge Him with our life and follow His commandments. Remaining in God's love is not His way of controlling us, it is God's way of ensuring we have deep joy through every season. The willingness to remain in God's love pleases Him far more than us "getting it right" all the time. Love and obedience go beyond just a feeling, it is often a choice. But even on our toughest days we can be assured that God remains with us.

ACTION

How do you think loving people will bring you joy?

MODULE 02

JESUS

A man starring in hundreds of famous paintings; the WWJD bracelets that became fashion (thanks again Kanye); the inspiration for YEEZY; a wooden cross or a golden statue hanging in a church; lyrics in Jay-Z, Kendrick Lemar, Phil Collins, Justin Bieber, Alicia Keys songs (to name a few); a viral hype on a slice of toast (#jesustoast); a bearded man in an R.E. textbook... these are things that our generation thinks of when we hear the name "Jesus". He is arguably the most loved and most hated man in history, and definitely the most talked about man, but WHO IS JESUS?

A question that seems so simple and yet a question that has divided humanity like nothing else.
Is he a moral teacher? A good man? A great prophet? The son of God?
Or is he a freak? A religious leader that tragically failed his mission? A fake?
In the next 5 weeks we will be looking at who Jesus really is. We will have a look at what the bible tells us about him, how he lived his life on earth, and what the purpose of him coming to earth and dying on a cross was. Open your mind and your heart to experience the truth and reality of who Jesus is to you.

WEEK 03 | PREDICTION AND PROPHECY

DAY 01

JESUS WOULD COME REPRESENTING MANKIND & GOD PT. 1

ISAIAH 9:6-7 NIV

For to us a child is born, to us a son is given, and the government will be on his shoulders. And he will be called Wonderful Counselor, Mighty God, Everlasting Father, Prince of Peace. Of the greatness of his government and peace there will be no end. He will reign on David's throne and over his kingdom establishing and upholding it with justice and righteousness from that time on and forever. The zeal of the Lord Almighty will accomplish this.

THOUGHT

Jesus is described in this passage as the child who would be born as the wonderful counsellor, mighty God, everlasting Father and prince of peace. We see this prophecy fulfilled in the book of Matthew, approximately 700 years after it was written. We are often impatient to see God fulfil the word that he has spoken, but this scripture is a powerful reminder to wait patiently and to believe in every word that is spoken by God.

ACTION

How has Jesus been a Wonderful Counsellor, Mighty God, Everlasting Father and Prince of Peace to you?

DAY 02

JESUS WOULD COME REPRESENTING MANKIND & GOD PT. 1

DANIEL 7:13-14 NIV

In my vision at night I looked, and there before me was one like a son of man, coming with the clouds of heaven. He approached the Ancient of Days and was led into his presence. He was given authority, glory and sovereign power; all nations and peoples of every language worshiped him. His dominion is an everlasting dominion that will not pass away, and his kingdom is one that will never be destroyed.

THOUGHT

This passage in Daniel is a prediction of Jesus yet to come to earth once again, as described in the book of Revelation. It talks about Jesus approaching God the Father also known as the Ancient of days. Jesus has the authority, the glory and the power. Today we worship Him from all over the world, in all nations and languages. This is a great reminder to remain in awe and wonder of Jesus. To worship Him is to put Him first and foremost in our lives above everything.

ACTION

Take time to meditate on His authority, His glory and His power.

DAY 03

JESUS WOULD BE A DESCENDANT OF KING DAVID

2 SAMUEL 7:12-16 NIV

When your days are over and you rest with your ancestors, I will raise up your offspring to succeed you, your own flesh and blood, and I will establish his kingdom. He is the one who will build a house for my Name, and I will establish the throne of his kingdom forever. I will be his father, and he will be my son. When he does wrong, I will punish him with a rod wielded by men, with floggings inflicted by human hands. But my love will never be taken away from him, as I took it away from Saul, whom I removed from before you. Your house and your kingdom will endure forever before me; your throne will be established forever.

THOUGHT

In this passage of scripture, we see how God has been shaping and ordaining key events behind the scenes to ensure that Jesus would come from the lineage of David, from one King of Israel to another whose reign would never end. David was praised for being a great earthly king, but Jesus would later be praised for being our Saviour King. This passage is a great reminder, that when God makes a promise, as he did to David, He will work behind the scenes to fulfil it.

ACTION

What are some of the promises that God has spoken over you, which are yet to be fulfilled?

DAY 04

JESUS WILL BE BORN TO A VIRGIN

ISAIAH 7:14 NIV

*Therefore the Lord himself will give you a sign: The virgin will conceive
and give birth to a son, and will call him Immanuel.*

THOUGHT

The miracle of Jesus' birth came out of an extraordinary experience, a circumstance which was impossible. He was birthed by a virgin and from a small clan of Judah, and yet Jesus has become known as the Lord of Lords and the King of Kings. God desires to use you, despite the impossible situations in your life. Jesus is called 'Immanuel' which means 'God with us'. When God is with us, anything is possible.

ACTION

What impossibilities in your life right now do you believe God can turn around?

DAY 05

HE WILL COME ON A MISSION FROM GOD TO SAVE HUMANITY

ISAIAH 42:1-7 NIV

"Here is my servant, whom I uphold, my chosen one in whom I delight; I will put my Spirit on him, and he will bring justice to the nations. He will not shout or cry out, or raise his voice in the streets. A bruised reed he will not break, and a smoldering wick he will not snuff out. In faithfulness he will bring forth justice; he will not falter or be discouraged till he establishes justice on earth. In his teaching, the islands will put their hope." This is what God the Lord says— the Creator of the heavens, who stretches them out, who spreads out the earth with all that springs from it, who gives breath to its people, and life to those who walk on it: "I, the Lord, have called you in righteousness; I will take hold of your hand. I will keep you and will make you to be a covenant for the people and a light for the Gentiles, to open eyes that are blind, to free captives from prison and to release from the dungeon those who sit in darkness."

THOUGHT

The first part of this scripture is a prophecy about Jesus' faithfulness and humility and what He would do on the earth, which we see fulfilled in Matthew 12. Jesus was a servant and He desires to partner with us to serve people and to help bring people freedom, justice, hope and healing.

ACTION

From reading this scripture, name a few ways that you can you walk in humility and faithfulness.

DAY 06
HE WILL BE PUNISHED ON OUR BEHALF

ISAIAH 53:4-6 NIV

Surely he took up our pain and bore our suffering, yet we considered him punished by God, stricken by him, and afflicted. But he was pierced for our transgressions, he was crushed for our iniquities; the punishment that brought us peace was on him, and by his wounds we are healed. We all, like sheep, have gone astray, each of us has turned to our own way; and the Lord has laid on him the iniquity of us all.

THOUGHT

Despite humanity's tendency to go astray from His ways and follow our own ways - which has led us into many difficult places - Jesus doesn't punish us, He instead takes our punishment on Him. It is His punishment and His wounds that bring us peace and healing.

ACTION

In what areas of your life have you gone your own way? Commit these to God and ask Him to lead you on the right path.

DAY 07
HE IS RIGHT BESIDE YOU

PSALM 16:8-11 NIV

I keep my eyes always on the Lord. With him at my right hand, I will not be shaken. Therefore my heart is glad and my tongue rejoices; my body also will rest secure, because you will not abandon me to the realm of the dead, nor will you let your faithful one see decay. You make known to me the path of life; you will fill me with joy in your presence, with eternal pleasures at your right hand.

THOUGHT

Jesus is right beside us. He never leaves us nor forsakes us. He intercedes on our behalf in prayer at the right hand of the Father. This truth helps us know that we don't have to go through life being shaken by the things that crumble around us, as that Jesus fills us with joy and pleasure as we trust in Him.

ACTION

Name three things to be joyful about today.

DAY 01

JESUS' STORY PT. 1

JOHN 1: 1–8 ESV

In the beginning was the Word, and the Word was with God, and the Word was God. He was in the beginning with God. All things were made through him, and without him was not any thing made that was made. In him was life, and the life was the light of men. The light shines in the darkness, and the darkness has not overcome it. There was a man sent from God, whose name was John. He came as a witness, to bear witness about the light, that all might believe through him. He was not the light, but came to bear witness about the light.

THOUGHT

Jesus is the Alpha and the Omega (the beginning and the end). Genesis starts with 'in the beginning' and so does this passage, to help reinforce that at the start of anything great, Jesus was there. He is the Word personified. In the Old Testament, God revealed His word through the prophets, while in the New Testament the Word of God was revealed in a person - God the Son.

John encourages us that no matter how dark the world gets, there is a light that has been lit since time began and now He brings His shining light to earth. John was simply a witness of that light, a witness of the life-changing power of Jesus.

ACTION

How could you be like John today and bear witness about the light of Jesus?

DAY 02

JESUS' STORY PT. 2

JOHN 1: 9–13 ESV

The true light, which gives light to everyone, was coming into the world. He was in the world, and the world was made through him, yet the world did not know him. He came to his own, and his own people did not receive him. But to all who did receive him, who believed in his name, he gave the right to become children of God, who were born, not of blood nor of the will of the flesh nor of the will of man, but of God.

THOUGHT

Many times in life, our opinions and beliefs are shaped and influenced by others around us. John helps us know that the light of Jesus is more than an opinion, it is the truth. The whole world has the opportunity to welcome the light into their world and yet many still choose not to because they don't recognise the need for the light of Jesus in their world. Let us make a daily decision to receive Jesus in our life and allow His light to flood our lives. When people see the light of Jesus in you, they will be attracted to the light because the light will always overcome darkness.

ACTION

How can you shine the light of Jesus to everyone today?

DAY 03

JESUS' STORY PT. 3

JOHN 1:14–18 ESV

And the Word became flesh and dwelt among us, and we have seen his glory, glory as of the only Son from the Father, full of grace and truth. (John bore witness about him, and cried out, "This was he of whom I said, 'He who comes after me ranks before me, because he was before me.'") For from his fullness we have all received, grace upon grace. For the law was given through Moses; grace and truth came through Jesus Christ. No one has ever seen God; the only God, who is at the Father's side, he has made him known.

THOUGHT

Jesus was God on earth. He wrapped himself in skin and came to earth to dwell among us. To dwell means to live and be settled in. Jesus was full of an abundance of grace and truth and that grace comes to live with you daily. If you want to know what God is like, look at the life of Jesus. We know God because we know Jesus. When Jesus came to earth, He didn't come as superman, He came in normal human 'flesh'. He experienced what we experienced, and felt what we felt. He connected with humanity in such a powerful way and He still connects with us today. God knew humanity's greatest need was grace and truth. That's why Jesus came in physical, tangible form.

ACTION

When you think of the life of Jesus, what are the characteristics that you most admire?

DAY 04

JESUS' HUMAN FAMILY ORIGINS

MATTHEW 1:1–17 ESV

The book of the genealogy of Jesus Christ, the son of David, the son of Abraham: Abraham was the father of Isaac, and Isaac the father of Jacob, and Jacob the father of Judah and his brothers, and Judah the father of Perez and Zerah by Tamar, and Perez the father of Hezron, and Hezron the father of Ram, and Ram the father of Amminadab, and Amminadab the father of Nahshon, and Nahshon the father of Salmon, and Salmon the father of Boaz by Rahab, and Boaz the father of Obed by Ruth, and Obed the father of Jesse, and Jesse the father of David the king. And David was the father of Solomon by the wife of Uriah, and Solomon the father of Rehoboam, and Rehoboam the father of Abijah, and Abijah the father of Asaph, and Asaph the father of Jehoshaphat, and Jehoshaphat the father of Joram, and Joram the father of Uzziah, and Uzziah the father of Jotham, and Jotham the father of Ahaz, and Ahaz the father of Hezekiah, and Hezekiah the father of Manasseh, and Manasseh the father of Amos, and Amos the father of Josiah, and Josiah the father of Jechoniah and his brothers, at the time of the deportation to Babylon. And after the deportation to Babylon: Jechoniah was the father of Shealtiel, and Shealtiel the father of Zerubbabel, and Zerubbabel the father of Abiud, and Abiud the father of Eliakim, and Eliakim the father of Azor, and Azor the father of Zadok, and Zadok the father of Achim, and Achim the father of Eliud, and Eliud the father of Eleazar, and Eleazar the father of Matthan, and Matthan the father of Jacob, and Jacob the father of Joseph the husband of Mary, of whom Jesus was born, who is called Christ.

DAY 04

THOUGHT

These may seem like purposeless verses yet they have a profound deeper meaning. There is a clear path between Jesus and Abraham and despite many generations they are still linked. Jesus was planned by God all along the genealogy and every single person may seem like just another name, but each name had a significant part to play. We understand that God has a plan for each and every one of us. There is an important role for all of us and despite sometimes being unable to see the bigger picture, we have to trust God that He is working everything together for the good of those who love Him. Many of the people listed above were considered 'normal people' and yet they were carrying the bloodline of the saviour! Never underestimate the normality of your life - you also carry greatness!

ACTION

Understand your significance today and think about how your normal daily routines can have a great impact in the kingdom of God.

DAY 05

JESUS' HEAVENLY FAMILY ORIGINS

LUKE 6:32-36 NLT

Now the birth of Jesus Christ took place in this way. When his mother Mary had been betrothed to Joseph, before they came together she was found to be with child from the Holy Spirit. And her husband Joseph, being a just man and unwilling to put her to shame, resolved to divorce her quietly. But as he considered these things, behold, an angel of the Lord appeared to him in a dream, saying, "Joseph, son of David, do not fear to take Mary as your wife, for that which is conceived in her is from the Holy Spirit. She will bear a son, and you shall call his name Jesus, for he will save his people from their sins." All this took place to fulfill what the Lord had spoken by the prophet: "Behold, the virgin shall conceive and bear a son and they shall call his name Immanuel" (which means, God with us). When Joseph woke from sleep, he did as the angel of the Lord commanded him: he took his wife, but knew her not until she had given birth to a son. And he called his name Jesus.

THOUGHT

The birth of Jesus was a miracle. It was prophesied that it would happen and because God said it, it happened! God always follows through on what He says. A young, faithful couple who lived righteously and followed God were about to give birth to the saviour of the world. Imagine the emotions they would have faced internally, and the challenges externally. Yet during the whole process, they trusted God, believed what He said and lived right. Jesus isn't looking for fame or prominence. He is looking for young people who trust Him and choose to follow Him no matter what comes their way. They had faith! Faith is one of the most crucial aspects of our relationship with God. When we live like Mary and Joseph did - obedient to God - the impossible becomes possible!

ACTION

In which aspects of our life could we trust God more?

DAY 06
JESUS' EARLY YEARS

MATTHEW 2:1–23 NIV

After Jesus was born in Bethlehem in Judea, during the time of King Herod, Magi from the east came to Jerusalem and asked, "Where is the one who has been born king of the Jews? We saw his star when it rose and have come to worship him." When King Herod heard this he was disturbed, and all Jerusalem with him. When he had called together all the people's chief priests and teachers of the law, he asked them where the Messiah was to be born. "In Bethlehem in Judea," they replied, "for this is what the prophet has written: 'But you, Bethlehem, in the land of Judah, are by no means least among the rulers of Judah for out of you will come a ruler who will shepherd my people Israel.' Then Herod called the Magi secretly and found out from them the exact time the star had appeared. He sent them to Bethlehem and said, "Go and search carefully for the child. As soon as you find him, report to me, so that I too may go and worship him." After they had heard the king, they went on their way, and the star they had seen when it rose went ahead of them until it stopped over the place where the child was. When they saw the star, they were overjoyed. On coming to the house, they saw the child with his mother Mary, and they bowed down and worshiped him. Then they opened their treasures and presented him with gifts of gold, frankincense and myrrh.

THOUGHT

Whenever God establishes something, it is often met with opposition. Herod was fearful that his reign as king was under threat from an unknown baby born in a manger. He sent a group of wise men to report back on what they saw, and they were guided to Jesus by a star that shone in the sky. In a world of much opposition to what the Bible and the Church stand for, we are now the stars that shine in the sky guiding people to Jesus. Like the famous nursery rhyme says:

Twinkle, twinkle, little star, how I wonder what you are! Up above the world so high, like a diamond in the sky. Twinkle, twinkle, little star, how I wonder what you are! Then the traveller in the dark, thanks you for your tiny spark, he could not see which way to go, if you did not twinkle so. Twinkle, twinkle, little star, how I wonder what you are!

ACTION

What opposition are you facing today? Make a decision and take a stand to keep shining in the dark.

DAY 07
JESUS' LIFE AGED 12-30 YEARS

LUKE 2:42-52 ESV

And when he was twelve years old, they went up according to custom. And when the feast was ended, as they were returning, the boy Jesus stayed behind in Jerusalem. His parents did not know it, but supposing him to be in the group they went a day's journey, but then they began to search for him among their relatives and acquaintances, and when they did not find him, they returned to Jerusalem, searching for him. After three days they found him in the temple, sitting among the teachers, listening to them and asking them questions. And all who heard him were amazed at his understanding and his answers. And when his parents saw him, they were astonished. And his mother said to him, "Son, why have you treated us so? Behold, your father and I have been searching for you in great distress." And he said to them, "Why were you looking for me? Did you not know that I must be in my Father's house?" And they did not understand the saying that he spoke to them. And he went down with them and came to Nazareth and was submissive to them. And his mother treasured up all these things in her heart. And Jesus increased in wisdom and in stature and in favor with God and man.

THOUGHT

We are never too young to be passionate about the things of God! Jesus was so hungry to engage with the scriptures and conversations with leaders about the kingdom of God. He had a humble spirit and desired to ask questions and increase His knowledge. His parents didn't understand and often people don't 'get it' when you are so passionate about God. Jesus models to us in His response to be respectful but He maintains His hunger for wisdom. His desire was to be in His Father's house and about His Father's business, because He understood His purpose. When we start to connect with our purpose, it determines our priorities and where we spend our time. Our job is not to please people but to please God. (Note, we please God when we honour our parents!) Putting God first never leaves us second.

ACTION

Begin to ask questions from people of greater spiritual maturity and start stretching yourself in your understanding of God and His kingdom.

DAY 01

THREE STATEMENTS ABOUT JESUS

MATTHEW 3:13-17 NIV

Then Jesus came from Galilee to the Jordan to be baptised by John. But John tried to deter him, saying, "I need to be baptised by you, and do you come to me?" Jesus replied, "Let it be so now; it is proper for us to do this to fulfill all righteousness." Then John consented. As soon as Jesus was baptised, he went up out of the water. At that moment heaven was opened, and he saw the spirit of God descending like a dove and alighting on him. And a voice from heaven said, "This is my son, whom I love and with him I am well pleased."

THOUGHT

In this passage, Jesus leads by example by immersing Himself into water. Jesus didn't need to, but He chose to reveal His humility. God affirms Jesus' divine identity by calling Him 'Son'. Likewise, we all need to remind ourselves daily that we are sons and daughters of the King through our faith in Jesus. Let's carry this affirmation with us!

ACTION

What are the three statements God makes over Jesus, and how do these apply to you?

DAY 02

TEMPTATIONS & SATISFACTION

MATTHEW 4:1-4 NIV

Then Jesus was led by the Spirit into the wilderness to be tempted by the devil. After fasting for forty days and forty nights he was hungry. The tempter came to him and said, "If you are the Son of God, tell these stones to become bread." Jesus answered, "It is written: 'Man shall not live on bread alone, but on every word that comes from the mouth of God".

THOUGHT

Jesus said we shouldn't rely on worldly things to live on, but we should hang on to every word God says. Don't be distracted by what others around you are doing! Focus on yourself and developing your own relationship with God - your identity comes from Him. God has given you the strength to overcome temptation that comes your way. His word is food to make you strong to follow God's way rather than the world's way.

ACTION

Jesus knew He didn't need to prove His identity to the tempter. Do you ever feel like you need to prove yourself?

DAY 03

ME & MYSELF

MATTHEW 4:5-7 NIV

Then the devil took him to the holy city and had him stand on the highest point of the temple. "If you are the Son of God, he said, throw yourself down. For it is written: He will command his angels concerning you, and they will lift you up in their hands, so that you will not strike your foot against a stone". Jesus answered him, "It is also written, do not put the Lord your God to the test".

THOUGHT

Let's not take advantage of God's grace and salvation in our life! Be intentional about having an attitude of gratitude when you're facing temptation and seasons of testing. God sends angels to help you and protect you even when you are totally unaware. No weapon formed against you shall prosper!

ACTION

Do you find yourself 'testing' God? If so, under what circumstances?

DAY 04

MATERIALISM

MATTHEW 4:8-11 NIV

Again, the devil took him to a very high mountain and showed him all the kingdoms of the world and their splendor. "All this I will give you", he said, "if you will bow down and worship me." Jesus said to him, "Away from me, Satan! For it is written: Worship the Lord your God and serve him only". Then the devil left him, and angels came and attended him.

THOUGHT

When you're in situations when people are challenging you and temptation comes, don't forget who you are, who you serve and who you are called to be. You're called for greater things than the challenges in front of you. Worshipping God is the best thing you can do when you face challenges. Worship lifts your head and changes your perspective. The devil flees when we lift up Jesus' name in worship.

ACTION

How does worship help you in your daily challenges?

DAY 05

JESUS BEGINS TO PREACH

MATTHEW 4:12-17 NIV

When Jesus heard that John had been put in prison, he withdrew to Galilee. Leaving Nazareth, he went and lived in Capernaum, which was by the lake in the area of Zebulun and Naphtali to fulfill what was said through the prophet Isaiah: Land of Zebulun and land of Naphtali, the way of the sea, beyond the Jordan, Galilee of the Gentiles the people living in darkness have seen a great light; on those living in the land of the shadow of death a light has dawned. From that time on Jesus began to preach "Repent, for the kingdom of heaven has come near."

THOUGHT

Knowing what you're called to can seem quite scary and intimidating, and you might not feel worthy of it, but always remember God will equip you to do whatever you're called to. There is no 'Plan B' when it comes to God's plan for your life. His gifting and His call on your life are irrevocable (Romans 11:29) - that means you can't escape it. He has purposed you for great things!

ACTION

Have you ever been in a position of moving away from something to fulfill something bigger? How did you feel?

DAY 06

JESUS CALLS HIS DISCIPLES

MATTHEW 4:18-22 NIV

As Jesus was walking beside the Sea of Galilee, he saw two brothers, Simon called Peter and his brother Andrew. They were casting a net into the lake, for they were fishermen. "Come, follow me," Jesus said, "and I will send you out to fish for people." At once they left their nets and followed him. Going on from there, he saw two other brothers, James son of Zebedee and his brother John. They were in a boat with their father Zebedee, preparing their nets. Jesus called them, and immediately they left the boat and their father and followed him.

THOUGHT

Leaving everything you know behind is hard, but knowing that you are following someone whose plans are far greater than anything you could dream, imagine or create for yourself will give you the courage to step into the next thing! Sometimes you need to leave the familiar to experience the extraordinary. What Jesus did with Peter and Andrew was miraculous and He can do the same with you when you choose to follow Him wholeheartedly.

ACTION

All of the people Jesus called dropped what they were doing instantly to follow Him. How would you respond if you were in their situation?

DAY 07

JESUS HEALS THE SICK

MATTHEW 4:23-25 NIV

Jesus went throughout Galilee, teaching in their synagogues, proclaiming the good news of the kingdom, and healing every disease and sickness among the people. News about him spread all over Syria, and people brought to him all who were ill with various diseases, those suffering severe pain, the demon-possessed, those having seizures, and the paralyzed; and he healed them. Large crowds from Galilee, the Decapolis, Jerusalem, Judea and the region across the Jordan followed him.

THOUGHT

People followed Jesus because they weren't just amazed by what He could do, but who He was. He was and is the God who can heal all diseases with a single touch - let's believe that He can bring the breakthroughs we are praying and believing for! News spread about Him everywhere because He was a man who stood out and gave His life to serve others. He brought good news everywhere - let's also be consistent bringers of the good news.

ACTION

Why do you think so many people began following Jesus at this time?

DAY 01

JESUS' FIRST SERMON

MATTHEW 5:1-12 NIV

Now when Jesus saw the crowds, he went up on a mountainside and sat down. His disciples came to him, and he began to teach them. He said: "Blessed are the poor in spirit, for theirs is the kingdom of heaven. Blessed are those who mourn, for they will be comforted. Blessed are the meek, for they will inherit the earth. Blessed are those who hunger and thirst for righteousness, for they will be filled. Blessed are the merciful, for they will be shown mercy. Blessed are the pure in heart, for they will see God. Blessed are the peacemakers, for they will be called children of God. Blessed are those who are persecuted because of righteousness, for theirs is the kingdom of heaven. Blessed are you when people insult you, persecute you and falsely say all kinds of evil against you because of me. Rejoice and be glad, because great is your reward in heaven, for in the same way they persecuted the prophets who were before you."

THOUGHT

The beatitudes are the beginning of Jesus' teachings of the sermon on the mount that He gave to His followers to describe the attributes of the character we should possess as believers, and the rewards that we will gain in return. What keeps recurring is that God desires to bless you. His blessing is His favour and protection over your life.

ACTION

What does the word 'blessed' mean to you? What do you look for in a 'blessed' life?

DAY 02

JESUS DID A LOT OF GOOD THINGS

JOHN 21:25 NIV

Jesus did many other things as well. If every one of them were written down, I suppose that even the whole world would not have room for the books that would be written.

THOUGHT

Jesus did so much within His lifetime that couldn't be accounted for, and we have the same power to do so. He used every day to do good and be good. He never missed or wasted an opportunity to love, serve and help people. Let's use that power to see change in our world.

ACTION

When reflecting upon all that Jesus has done for you, is there a significant moment in your life where you have seen Him move miraculously?

DAY 03

THE DEATH OF JESUS PT. 1

MATTHEW 26:36–50 NIV

Then Jesus went with his disciples to a place called Gethsemane, and he said to them, "Sit here while I go over there and pray." He took Peter and the two sons of Zebedee along with him, and he began to be sorrowful and troubled. Then he s aid to them, "My soul is overwhelmed with sorrow to the point of death. Stay here and keep watch with me." Going a little farther, he fell with his face to the ground and prayed, "My Father, if it is possible, may this cup be taken from me. Yet not as I will, but as you will." Then he returned to his disciples and found them sleeping. "Couldn't you men keep watch with me for one hour?" he asked Peter. "Watch and pray so that you will not fall into temptation. The spirit is willing, but the flesh is weak." He went away a second time and prayed, "My Father, if it is not possible for this cup to be taken away unless I drink it, may your will be done." When he came back, he again found them sleeping, because their eyes were heavy. So he left them and went away once more and prayed the third time, saying the same thing. Then he returned to the disciples and said to them, "Are you still sleeping and resting? Look, the hour has come, and the Son of Man is delivered into the hands of sinners. Rise! Let us go! Here comes my betrayer!" While he was still speaking, Judas, one of the Twelve, arrived. With him was a large crowd armed with swords and clubs, sent from the chief priests and the elders of the people. Now the betrayer had arranged a signal with them: "The one I kiss is the man; arrest him." Going at once to Jesus, Judas said, "Greetings, Rabbi!" and kissed him. Jesus replied, "Do what you came for, friend." Then the men stepped forward, seized Jesus and arrested him.

THOUGHT

When Jesus was arrested He stayed so calm as He knew that He was fulfilling the will of His Father. If we live in the will of God, we know that He gives us the strength we need to endure every season and emerge victorious. All we have to do is cry out to our Father and He will strengthen us. Gethsemane was the 'place of crushing' and Jesus fully feels the weight upon His shoulders. In that time He chose to pray and give His burdens to God.

ACTION

What do you think Jesus was feeling when He prayed to His Father?

DAY 04

THE DEATH OF JESUS PT. 2

MATTHEW 27:32-37 NIV

As they were going out, they met a man from Cyrene, named Simon, and they forced him to carry the cross. They came to a place called Golgotha (which means "the place of the skull"). There they offered Jesus wine to drink, mixed with gall; but after tasting it, he refused to drink it. When they had crucified him, they divided up his clothes by casting lots. And sitting down, they kept watch over him there. Above his head they placed the written charge against him: THIS IS JESUS, THE KING OF THE JEWS.

THOUGHT

It's crazy to think that Jesus went through all this to save us and make a way for us back to our Father. We should be so thankful that this happened so we don't have to carry the weight of our sins anymore. They mocked Him and abused Him, unaware that He wasn't only the King of the Jews, but in fact the King of the world.

ACTION

How do you feel knowing Jesus died for your sins?

DAY 05

THE DEATH OF JESUS PT. 3

MATTHEW 27:45-53 NIV

From noon until three in the afternoon darkness came over all the land. About three in the afternoon Jesus cried out in a loud voice, "Eli, Eli, lema sabachthani?" (which means "My God, my God, why have you forsaken me?"). When some of those standing there heard this, they said, "He's calling Elijah." Immediately one of them ran and got a sponge. He filled it with wine vinegar, put it on a staff, and offered it to Jesus to drink. The rest said, "Now leave him alone. Let's see if Elijah comes to save him." And when Jesus had cried out again in a loud voice, he gave up his spirit. At that moment the curtain of the temple was torn in two from top to bottom. The earth shook, the rocks split and the tombs broke open. The bodies of many holy people who had died were raised to life. They came out of the tombs after Jesus' resurrection and went into the holy city and appeared to many people.

THOUGHT

Jesus went through incredible pain and suffering within His last moments; however, He did it to save all of mankind. He did it to fulfil the will of His Father in heaven, and reunite creation with the Creator. The curtain in the temple, which was a barrier for people to access the presence of God, was torn in two. This was symbolic of the fact that Jesus opened up a free, unrestricted way to the Father.

ACTION

How do you feel when you read this passage of Jesus suffering?

DAY 06
THE BURIAL OF JESUS

MATTHEW 27:57-66 NIV

As evening approached, there came a rich man from Arimathea, named Joseph, who had himself become a disciple of Jesus. Going to Pilate, he asked for Jesus' body, and Pilate ordered that it be given to him. Joseph took the body, wrapped it in a clean linen cloth, and placed it in his own new tomb that he had cut out of the rock. He rolled a big stone in front of the entrance to the tomb and went away. Mary Magdalene and the other Mary were sitting there opposite the tomb. The next day, the one after Preparation Day, the chief priests and the Pharisees went to Pilate. "Sir," they said, "we remember that while he was still alive that deceiver said, 'After three days I will rise again.' So give the order for the tomb to be made secure until the third day. Otherwise, his disciples may come and steal the body and tell the people that he has been raised from the dead. This last deception will be worse than the first." "Take a guard," Pilate answered. "Go, make the tomb as secure as you know how." So they went and made the tomb secure by putting a seal on the stone and posting the guard.

THOUGHT

People were in disbelief that Jesus would ever return, but He did, and He showed us that He has beaten death so we don't have to die with our sin. He made a way so we could return to relationship with the Father. They were intent on shutting Jesus up, closing Him down. But when Jesus said "it is finished", death died, giving us all the chance to experience eternal life in Him.

ACTION

Do you believe that the same power that raised Jesus from the dead lives in you?

DAY 07

THE RESURRECTION OF JESUS

MATTHEW 28:1-10 NIV

After the Sabbath, at dawn on the first day of the week, Mary Magdalene and the other Mary went to look at the tomb. There was a violent earthquake, for an angel of the Lord came down from heaven and, going to the tomb, rolled back the stone and sat on it. His appearance was like lightning, and his clothes were white as snow. The guards were so afraid of him that they shook and became like dead men. The angel said to the women, "Do not be afraid, for I know that you are looking for Jesus, who was crucified. He is not here; he has risen, just as he said. Come and see the place where he lay. Then go quickly and tell his disciples: 'He has risen from the dead and is going ahead of you into Galilee. There you will see him.' Now I have told you." So the women hurried away from the tomb, afraid yet filled with joy, and ran to tell his disciples. Suddenly Jesus met them. "Greetings," he said. They came to him, clasped his feet and worshiped him. Then Jesus said to them, "Do not be afraid. Go and tell my brothers to go to Galilee; there they will see me."

THOUGHT

The death and resurrection of Jesus Christ is so much more than just a story, it is the greatest event that ever happened to mankind. Jesus Christ chose to meet us where we were, bridging the gap of the severed connection between us and God. As the tomb opened up, so did a whole new chapter for humanity. He was victorious over death and we share in that victory today. Because of the resurrection of Christ, you too are resurrected into the fulness of all you can be.

ACTION

How has knowing that Jesus died and rose again impacted your life today?

DAY 01

JESUS IS THE BREAD OF LIFE

JOHN 6:35 NIV

Then Jesus declared, "I am the bread of life. Whoever comes to me will never go hungry, and whoever believes in me will never be thirsty.

THOUGHT

Jesus is enough. We don't need to fill our lives with other things, because everything we need and desire in life is found in Jesus. Our response to our hunger and our thirst determines our ability to survive. Jesus is encouraging us that our sustenance in life comes from our relationship with Him. Bread and water are two basic essentials for everyday life and Jesus is essential to our life thriving everyday.

ACTION

How do you feed your soul with the "bread of life"?

DAY 02

JESUS IS THE LIGHT OF THE WORLD

JOHN 8:12 NIV

When Jesus spoke again to the people, he said, "I am the light of the world. Whoever follows me will never walk in darkness, but will have the light of life."

THOUGHT

Jesus overcomes darkness with His light. So often life can present dark situations that we have to face mentally, spiritually or physically. When it's dark we can easily lose our way and end up lost and in fear. If we choose to follow Jesus, He continues to light up the path for our lives. Be encouraged and follow the light!

ACTION

Do you have areas in your life that you need God's light to shine into?

DAY 03

JESUS IS THE GATE TO PASS THROUGH

JOHN 10:9 NIV

I am the gate; whoever enters through me will be saved. They will come in and go out, and find pasture.

THOUGHT

Jesus is the entry point for our freedom. Sheep would often leave the pasture and find themselves in trouble with wolves or other enemies. The job of the shepherd was to protect the sheep and provide access for them back into the pasture. We find our freedom and our salvation in the pastures of his love for us.

ACTION

What does freedom in Christ mean to you?

DAY 04

JESUS IS THE TRUE VINE

JOHN 15:1 NIV

"I am the true vine, and my Father is the gardener."

THOUGHT

Our connectedness to the vine who is Jesus is what enables us to flourish and grow. If the branch is disconnected from the vine, the branch withers and dies. God the Father often spends time pruning our lives - a cutting away of things that are dead or have no life source - so that we can focus our attention on Jesus and become fruitful.

ACTION

Where do you feel your life is being pruned so that you can become even more fruitful?

DAY 05

JESUS IS THE GOOD SHEPHERD

JOHN 10:11 NLT

"I am the good shepherd. The good shepherd sacrifices his life for the sheep."

THOUGHT

Jesus is the very best shepherd. He is the ultimate protector, provider, carer and guide for our lives. Shepherds care for their sheep because their sheep are valuable! Jesus is your shepherd and He places great value on you! He is protecting you, guiding you and maybe correcting you because He loves you and He knows it's very easy for sheep to go astray. But our best life is with the shepherd in His pasture.

ACTION

Understand your significance today and think about how your normal daily routines can have a great impact in the kingdom of God.

DAY 06

JESUS IS THE RESURRECTION & THE LIFE

JOHN 11:25 NIV

Jesus said to her, "I am the resurrection and the life. The one who believes in me will live, even though they die;"

THOUGHT

We have eternity with Jesus when we choose to believe in Him! Our life on earth is temporary but one day we will live forever in heaven. Thankfully, we don't need to wait till we get to heaven, and can experience true life in all its fullness here on earth. Jesus raises Lazarus to life in this passage and Martha has the belief that Jesus can do it - she experienced true life that day! Let's be like Martha today.

ACTION

Imagine if you truly believed all of whom Jesus is! What would our lives look like?

DAY 07

JESUS IS THE WAY, THE TRUTH & THE LIFE

JOHN 14:6 NIV

Jesus answered, "I am the way and the truth and the life. No one comes to the Father except through me."

THOUGHT

There is one way to the Father and that is through Jesus. He is the direction we should follow, He is the truth we should trust and He is the life we should receive. Thomas is unsure and troubled as to what will happen in the future. Jesus reassures him that the Father is ready and waiting for him but it starts by following Jesus here on earth. If you fear the future, stick to the ways of Jesus and stick to His truth.

ACTION

How can you make some choices to walk in His ways and trust in His truth today?

MODULE 03

HOLY SPIRIT

"Will God ever ask you to do something you are not able to do? The answer is yes - ALL THE TIME! It must be that way, for God's glory and kingdom. If we function according to our ability alone, we get the glory; if we function according to the power of the Spirit within us, God gets the glory. He wants to reveal Himself to a watching world."
- Henry Blackaby

We are called to live an extraordinary life. A life where we experience breakthroughs in areas that are too big for us to conquer on our own, where we see miracles that are beyond anything that we can dream, think of or imagine... Where we see the impossible, the unimaginable, the unworkable and the unthinkable come to life.
The problem is, we can't do it by ourselves. We are in desperate need of the power of the Holy Spirit in our lives, in order to live the life God has planned for us. Without it, living our lives to its fullest potential is impossible.

But the Holy Spirit is more than 'just' the activated power of God in our circumstances when we need it. The Holy Spirit is God himself, given to us as Jesus ascended into heaven as the direct route to a living and tangible relationship with God. It reveals God's love to us, it manifests the presence of God in our lives, it helps us grow in character and it helps us discern different situations. It reveals the light and darkness and gives us the tools to fight and the strength to stand in spiritual warfare. There are so many different facets to the Holy Spirit.

We are going to spend the next couple of weeks looking at together to discover who the Holy Spirit is, what it's purpose is, and how to have the Holy Spirit working in and through us.

WEEK 8 | PERSON, ROLE, FRUIT AND GIFTS

DAY 01
YOU PERSONALLY HAVE THE HOLY SPIRIT IN YOU

1 COR 6:19-20 NLT

Don't you realize that your body is the temple of the Holy Spirit, who lives in you and was given to you by God? You do not belong to yourself, for God bought you with a high price. So you must honour God with your body.

THOUGHT

The Holy Spirit isn't some spooky ghost that comes and goes. The Holy Spirit is the presence of God that dwells within you. God values you so much that He would deposit His Spirit to live in you and be a continual presence in your lives. That's why the body is called a temple of the Holy Spirit, because it is a physical dwelling place for the Spirit within. Therefore we honour our body as a temple for the Spirit who lives in us.

ACTION

How are you honouring God with your body?

DAY 02

WHAT JESUS SAID ABOUT THE HOLY SPIRIT

JOHN 14:15-17 NLT

If you love me, obey my commandments. And I will ask the Father, and he will give you another Advocate, who will never leave you. He is the Holy Spirit, who leads into all truth. The world cannot receive him, because it isn't looking for him and doesn't recognize him. But you know him, because he lives with you now and later will be in you.

THOUGHT

The Holy Spirit is the very presence of God within us, helping us to live as God wants and helping us build Christ's Church on earth. Many people are unaware of the Holy Spirit's involvement, but to those who hear Christ's words and understand the Spirit's power, He gives a whole new way to live our life. The Holy Spirit is our advocate, comforter, encourager and counsellor. He is our very present help in times of need.

ACTION

How are you relying on the Holy Spirit to build your life and build Christ's Church?

DAY 03

HOW THE HOLY SPIRIT HELPS US

ROMANS 8:26-27 NIV

In the same way, the Spirit helps us in our weakness. We do not know what we ought to pray for, but the Spirit himself intercedes for us through wordless groans. And he who searches our hearts knows the mind of the Spirit, because the Spirit intercedes for God's people in accordance with the will of God.

THOUGHT

As a child of God you are not left to your own resources to cope with problems. God is always just a prayer away. Even when you don't know the right words to say, the Holy Spirit prays with and for you, and God answers. With God helping you pray, you don't need to be afraid to come before Him. Often our understanding is weak, our desires are weak and our prayers are weak, but thank God that the Holy Spirit makes us strong even in our weakest moments.

ACTION

How are you allowing the Holy Spirit to intercede for you?

DAY 04

HOW WE WORK WITH THE HOLY SPIRIT

EPHESIANS 4:30-32 NLT

And do not bring sorrow to God's Holy Spirit by the way you live. Remember, he has identified you as his own, guaranteeing that you will be saved on the day of redemption. Get rid of all bitterness, rage, anger, harsh words, and slander, as well as all types of evil behavior. Instead, be kind to each other, tenderhearted, forgiving one another, just as God through Christ has forgiven you.

THOUGHT

The presence of the Holy Spirit in us demonstrates the genuineness of our faith, proves that we are God's children, and secures eternal life for us. His power works in us to transform us. Therefore what we experience now is a taste of the total transformation we will experience in eternity. Every day we should make a decision to be led by the Holy Spirit. We decide how we live our lives and we often have to get rid of ways of living that are not in step with the Spirit and instead follow the Spirit's way.

ACTION

What would be a good idea to get rid of in your daily way of doing things, and replace with the Spirit's way?

DAY 05

CONFLICT BETWEEN OUR FLESH & THE HOLY SPIRIT

1 JOHN 4:11-17 NLT

But I say, walk by the Spirit, and you will not gratify the desires of the flesh. For the desires of the flesh are against the Spirit, and the desires of the Spirit are against the flesh, for these are opposed to each other, to keep you from doing the things you want to do.

THOUGHT

Being led by the Holy Spirit involves the desire to hear, the readiness to obey God's Word and the sensitivity to differentiate between your feelings and His promptings. If we try to follow the Spirit by our own human effort, we will fail. Our only way to freedom from evil desires is through the empowering of the Holy Spirit. If we feed our flesh, it gets stronger but if we feed our spirit, it too gets stronger and can overcome the flesh

ACTION

How can you feed and strengthen your spirit today?

DAY 06

WHAT LIFE WITHOUT THE HOLY SPIRIT LOOKS LIKE

GALATIANS 5:19-21 ESV

Now the works of the flesh are evident: sexual immorality, impurity, sensuality, idolatry, sorcery, enmity, strife, jealousy, fits of anger, rivalries, dissensions, divisions, envy, drunkenness, orgies, and things like these. I warn you, as I warned you before, that those who do such things will not inherit the kingdom of God.

THOUGHT

We all have evil desires and we can't ignore them. Those who ignore such sin or refuse to deal with them reveal that they have not received the gift of the Spirit that will lead to a transformed life. Many of the troubles the world faces are because the works of the flesh are so evident. Jesus can change that and give us a different way. The Holy Spirit can help us surrender the desires of our flesh to God.

ACTION

How can you be more intentional about living each day submitted to and guided by the Holy Spirit?

DAY 07

WHAT LIFE WITH THE HOLY SPIRIT LOOKS LIKE

GALATIANS 5:22-26 ESV

But the fruit of the Spirit is love, joy, peace, patience, kindness, goodness, faithfulness, gentleness, self-control; against such things there is no law. And those who belong to Christ Jesus have crucified the flesh with its passions and desires. If we live by the Spirit, let us also keep in step with the Spirit. Let us not become conceited, provoking one another, envying one another.

THOUGHT

The fruit of the Spirit is the spontaneous work of the Holy Spirit in us. The Spirit produces these character traits that are found in the nature of Christ. Therefore as we live by the Holy Spirit's power, we need to submit every aspect of our lives to God. Like fruit grows from the branches of a tree and hangs, so the Spirit fruit grows from our lives and hangs off to provide enjoyment and nourishment for all who taste it. Fruit doesn't try to grow, it is a natural byproduct of being connected to the vine.

ACTION

Can you, and those around you, see the fruit of the Spirit in your life?

HOW THE HOLY SPIRIT FIRST CAME TO EARTH

ACTS 2:1-21 NLT

On the day of Pentecost all the believers were meeting together in one place. Suddenly, there was a sound from heaven like the roaring of a mighty windstorm, and it filled the house where they were sitting. Then, what looked like flames or tongues of fire appeared and settled on each of them. And everyone present was filled with the Holy Spirit and began speaking in other languages, as the Holy Spirit gave them this ability.

THOUGHT

The Holy Spirit came from heaven to earth with a mighty entrance. The Spirit rested on everyone present that day and filled them all to overflowing. They were so filled within that what came out of their mouths was the gift of speaking in tongues. Everyone who was filled then went out into Jerusalem and the power of God moved mightily through them as a result. People were saved and healed as the disciples ministered to them.

ACTION

Why do we need the Holy Spirit to work in our lives?

JESUS MINISTERS WITH THE HOLY SPIRIT

LUKE 4:14-21 NLT

When he came to the village of Nazareth, his boyhood home, he went as usual to the synagogue on the Sabbath and stood up to read the Scriptures. The scroll of Isaiah the prophet was handed to him. He unrolled the scroll and found the place where this was written: "The Spirit of the Lord is upon me, for he has anointed me to bring Good News to the poor. He has sent me to proclaim that captives will be released, that the blind will see, that the oppressed will be set free, and that the time of the Lord's favor has come." He rolled up the scroll, handed it back to the attendant, and sat down. All eyes in the synagogue looked at him intently. Then he began to speak to them. "The Scripture you've just heard has been fulfilled this very day!"

THOUGHT

When we accept Jesus as our Saviour, the Holy Spirit comes to live inside of us, giving us power to do what God called us to do. God + nothing = everything. If you have the Holy Spirit you have everything you need to do what God has created you to do. The Spirit of the Lord is upon you. Jesus said we would do even greater things than He did. This isn't possible because of our own strength, it is possible because of the Spirit working within us. You are anointed for a purpose.

ACTION

What does it mean to be anointed and how does it change how you live your life?

DAY 03

MINISTRY THROUGH THE HOLY SPIRIT

1 CORINTHIANS 2:4-5 NLT

And my message and my preaching were very plain. Rather than using clever and persuasive speeches, I relied only on the power of the Holy Spirit. I did this so you would trust not in human wisdom but in the power of God.

THOUGHT

When the power of God gets involved, everything changes. Nothing can stay the same.. We should sharpen our gifts and our skills, but without the work of the Holy Spirit within us, it's pointless. When God anoints you, you go from working in your own capacity to working within God's capacity. We bring our normal and the anointing of God makes it supernatural. The world has seen plenty of gifts, but imagine if it saw a demonstration of the Spirit's power.

ACTION

Where have you seen the evidence of the power of God?

DAY 04

GIFTS OF THE HOLY SPIRIT PT. 1

ROMANS 12:3-6 NLT

Because of the privilege and authority God has given me, I give each of you this warning: Don't think you are better than you really are. Be honest in your evaluation of yourselves, measuring yourselves by the faith God has given us. Just as our bodies have many parts and each part has a special function, so it is with Christ's body. We are many parts of one body, and we all belong to each other. In his grace, God has given us different gifts for doing certain things well. So if God has given you the ability to prophesy, speak out with as much faith as God has given you.

THOUGHT

We don't measure our lives in comparison to others. We measure our lives by the faith God has given us and what we do with it. God has gifted everyone differently for the purposes of His will. Think about this: God, the Creator of the heavens and earth, has gifted you! Therefore, let's use that gift for His glory. If we all use the different gifts within one body, the body of Christ will be so strong and so effective.

ACTION

What gifts do you bring to the body of Christ?

DAY 05

GIFTS OF THE HOLY SPIRIT PT. 2

ROMANS 12:6–8 NLT

In His grace, God has given us different gifts for doing certain things well. So if God has given you the ability to prophesy, speak out with as much faith as God has given you. If your gift is serving others, serve them well. If you are a teacher, teach well. If your gift is to encourage others, be encouraging. If it is giving, give generously. If God has given you leadership ability, take the responsibility seriously. And if you have a gift for showing kindness to others, do it gladly.

THOUGHT

Spiritual gifts are not like super powers given only to the people we look up to and respect. You have spiritual gifts too, and because they are gifts, you don't have to do anything to get them. All we need to do is ask God to give us the gifts He created us to use. Once God gives us these different gifts, it is our responsibility to use them well.

ACTION

Why did God give us spiritual gifts? What is the purpose of having them?

DAY 06

GIFTS OF THE HOLY SPIRIT PT. 3

1 CORINTHIANS 12:4–7 NLT

There are different kinds of spiritual gifts, but the same Spirit is the source of them all. There are different kinds of service, but we serve the same Lord. God works in different ways, but it is the same God who does the work in all of us. Spiritual gifts are given to each of us so we can help each other.

THOUGHT

The Holy Spirit is the distributor of the gifts that God has enabled us to use. He is the source of them all, despite each gift being different. He doesn't randomly allocate the gifts but gives them according to our skills and personality. The purpose of the gifts is not to show them off but to use them so that we can help each other.

ACTION

Why do you think the Holy Spirit chooses to give us gifts to use to help each other?

DAY 07

GIFTS OF THE HOLY SPIRIT PT. 4

1 CORINTHIANS 12:8-11 NLT

To one person the Spirit gives the ability to give wise advice; to another the same Spirit gives a message of special knowledge. The same Spirit gives great faith to another, and to someone else the one Spirit gives the gift of healing. He gives one person the power to perform miracles, and another the ability to prophesy. He gives someone else the ability to discern whether a message is from the Spirit of God or from another spirit. Still another person is given the ability to speak in unknown languages, while another is given the ability to interpret what is being said. It is the one and only Spirit who distributes all these gifts. He alone decides which gift each person should have.

THOUGHT

The gifts that the Holy Spirit gives us are awesome. We have the opportunity to use these gifts, such as healing and prophecy, on a daily basis. The purpose of the gifts isn't solely to be used at special church events but to be used in the normal everyday. In your school or college you can be naturally supernatural and allow the gifts of the Holy Spirit to flow through you.

ACTION

The challenge today is to find out your spiritual gifts (there are several online tests that you can use – ask your leaders for help) and to ask Jesus to help you to use one of the gifts today.

MODULE 04
COMMUNICATING WITH GOD

Due to the technology revolution, social media, and the many hundreds of apps that make it possible, this generation is the most communicative generation yet. The average person today sends 94 text messages a day, that is 33,834 text messages a year, not including mail, postcards or letters (does anyone still do that?). We live our lives constantly sharing and commenting, blogging and vlogging, texting and tweeting, and in 24/7 communication with the rest of the world. We should be the experts in communication however when it comes to communicating with God, if we're honest, it's become quite a complicated thing. There are lots of questions surrounding our communication with God like, "can God talk to me?", "can He hear me?", "does he care about what I have to say?", "how do I hear his voice?".

Don't leave these questions unanswered! It has been said that, "Communication is to a relationship, like oxygen is to life. Without it ….. it dies", which shows how important it is for us to learn how to really communicate with God, how to hear his voice and how to bring our thoughts to him, as it basically sets the tone of our whole relationship with God. In this next chapter, we want to look at answering some of these questions, and simplifying communicating with God. We want to get equipped to clearly hear his voice as it guides us on each step of the journey, and to feel confident in approaching him with our emotions, fears, desires and requests.

WEEK 10 | PRAYER AND HEARING GOD

DAY 01
START WITH PRAYER

MARK 1:35 NIV
*Very early in the morning, while it was still dark, Jesus got up, left the house
and went off to a solitary place, where he prayed.*

THOUGHT

This passage shows us the importance of prayer in our daily lives. We need to make time and remove ourselves from the world (even from our phones) to spend a bit of time with God, just as Jesus did. For Jesus, it wasn't an optional extra. It was His priority. First things first for Jesus! He made a decision to talk with His Father before the day even started. He knew this conversation would set Him up for the day ahead.

ACTION

What does spending time with God look like for you?

DAY 02

JESUS SHOWS US HOW TO PRAY

MATTHEW 6:9-13 NIV

This, then, is how you should pray: "Our Father in heaven, hallowed be your name, your kingdom come, your will be done, on earth as it is in heaven. Give us today our daily bread. And forgive us our debts, as we also have forgiven our debtors. And lead us not into temptation, but deliver us from the evil one."

THOUGHT

This prayer is how Jesus taught us to pray. God is holy, God is sovereign, God is your provider, God is your redeemer, God is your leader and He is your deliverer. This prayer presents God in all of these ways. The Lord's Prayer, as this passage is known, starts off with praise and adoration. 'Hallowed' means to be greatly revered and honoured. He is our Father and we honour Him for who He is.

ACTION

How can you improve your prayer life, and how can this prayer shape the way you pray today?

DAY 03

PRAYER FOR HELP, THANKFULNESS & HEALING

JAMES 5:13-15 NIV

Is anyone among you in trouble? Let them pray. Is anyone happy? Let them sing songs of praise. Is anyone among you sick? Let them call the elders of the church to pray over them and anoint them with oil in the name of the Lord. And the prayer offered in faith will make the sick person well; the Lord will raise them up. If they have sinned, they will be forgiven.

THOUGHT

God wants to be a part of your daily life. Go to Him with your problems and see them change. You are His child, He loves you and wants to help you - don't hide your sins and regrets from God. He is kind and forgiving. Whatever situation you find yourself in, good or bad, decide to make prayer a daily habit.

ACTION

Is there anything you feel you can't bring before God? Bring that to Him today.

DAY 04
PRAYER FOR SIN & POWER

JAMES 5:16 NIV

*Therefore confess your sins to each other and pray for each other so that you may be healed.
The prayer of a righteous person is powerful and effective.*

THOUGHT

Not only is prayer a way of building an intimate relationship with God, it's also one of the most powerful weapons in His kingdom. The prayers of the righteous can heal thousands and change nations. Notice how the scripture encourages us to confess our sins to each other and pray for each other. James had a revelation of the power of partnership in prayer. Healing flows in our honesty and our accountability.

ACTION

Who could you ask to become a great partner in prayer?

DAY 05
CONTINUING THE WORK OF JESUS THROUGH PRAYER

JOHN 14:12-14 NIV

Very truly I tell you, whoever believes in me will do the works I have been doing, and they will do even greater things than these, because I am going to the Father. And I will do whatever you ask in my name, so that the Father may be glorified in the Son. You may ask me for anything in my name, and I will do it

THOUGHT

Jesus is saying that the same power that conquered death lives inside of you - that you have the spiritual authority to advance the kingdom as Jesus did. Heaven on earth does not end with Jesus, it starts with Him. Our prayer can be limited by a worldly view but this passage encourages us to become bold and audacious in our prayers and ask for some of those 'whatevers' in His name!

ACTION

What do you think Jesus meant by "greater things than these"? Pray into these things today.

DAY 06

HEARING GOD'S VOICE PT. 1

1 KINGS 19:11-13 NIV

The Lord said, "Go out and stand on the mountain in the presence of the Lord, for the Lord is about to pass by." Then a great and powerful wind tore the mountains apart and shattered the rocks before the Lord, but the Lord was not in the wind. After the wind there was an earthquake, but the Lord was not in the earthquake. After the earthquake came a fire, but the Lord was not in the fire. And after the fire came a gentle whisper. When Elijah heard it, he pulled his cloak over his face and went out and stood at the mouth of the cave. Then a voice said to him, "What are you doing here, Elijah?"

THOUGHT

To hear God's voice clearly, you need to know God. You get to know Him by spending time with Him! Pray, worship and read your Bible. Learn what God is for and against - you should start hearing God's whisper, because He wants to talk to you. His voice can be heard through thousands at an event and also can be heard with just you alone. Be sensitive and alert to His voice.

ACTION

How can you create a time and space to hear God's still small voice?

DAY 07

HEARING GOD'S VOICE PT. 2

1 SAMUEL 3:1-11 NIV

Then Eli realized that the Lord was calling the boy. So Eli told Samuel, "Go and lie down, and if He calls you, say, 'Speak, Lord, for your servant is listening.'" So Samuel went and lay down in his place. The Lord came and stood there, calling as at the other times, "Samuel! Samuel!" Then Samuel said, "Speak, for your servant is listening." And the Lord said to Samuel: "See, I am about to do something in Israel that will make the ears of everyone who hears about it tingle."

THOUGHT

God isn't restricted to just speak in one way to you. Don't feel like He isn't talking to you because you can't hear Him literally speak with a voice to you, He might just be trying to contact you in a different way. We can learn to listen for His whisper and His shout! The reality is that God wants to communicate with His children. He wants to share great things with you. Our listening skills with God are equally as important as our speaking skills.

ACTION

How do you think God is trying to communicate with you? How can you improve your listening skills?

DAY 01

VALUE OF THE WORD OF GOD PT. 1

PSALM 119: 89-96 NIV

Your word, Lord, is eternal; it stands firm in the heavens. Your faithfulness continues through all generations; you established the earth, and it endures. Your laws endure to this day, for all things serve you. If your law had not been my delight, I would have perished in my affliction. I will never forget your precepts, for by them you have preserved my life. Save me, for I am yours; I have sought out your precepts. The wicked are waiting to destroy me, but I will ponder your statutes. To all perfection I see a limit, but your commands are boundless.

THOUGHT

Not only is prayer a way of building an intimate relationship with God, it's also one of the most powerful weapons in His kingdom. The prayers of the righteous can heal thousands and change nations. Notice how the scripture encourages us to confess our sins to each other and pray for each other. James had a revelation of the power of partnership in prayer. Healing flows in our honesty and our accountability.

ACTION

Reflect and think about how God's Word has helped you overcome challenges in your own life?

DAY 02

VALUE OF THE WORD OF GOD PT. 2

PSALM 119: 97-104 NIV

Oh, how I love your law! I meditate on it all day long. Your commands are always with me and make me wiser than my enemies. I have more insight than all my teachers, for I meditate on your statutes. I have more understanding than the elders, for I obey your precepts. I have kept my feet from every evil path so that I might obey your word. I have not departed from your laws, for you yourself have taught me. How sweet are your words to my taste, sweeter than honey to my mouth! I gain understanding from your precepts; therefore I hate every wrong path.

THOUGHT

Meditating on God's Word involves taking a passage of scripture, focusing on it and reflecting upon it repeatedly in our daily lives. Through meditating on the scriptures, the Holy Spirit gives us wisdom, insight and understanding. God's wisdom and insight gives us a different perspective on life compared to the world.

ACTION

Select a scripture that you have meditated on or would like to meditate on, and write down what you learnt from meditating on it.

DAY 03

VALUE OF THE WORD OF GOD PT. 3

PSALM 119: 105-120 NIV

Your word is a lamp for my feet, a light on my path. I have taken an oath and confirmed it, that I will follow your righteous laws. I have suffered much; preserve my life, Lord, according to your word. Accept, Lord, the willing praise of my mouth, and teach me your laws. Though I constantly take my life in my hands, I will not forget your law. The wicked have set a snare for me, but I have not strayed from your precepts. Your statutes are my heritage forever; they are the joy of my heart. My heart is set on keeping your decrees to the very end. I hate double-minded people, but I love your law. You are my refuge and my shield; I have put my hope in your word. Away from me, you evildoers, that I may keep the commands of my God! Sustain me, my God, according to your promise, and I will live; do not let my hopes be dashed. Uphold me, and I will be delivered; I will always have regard for your decrees. You reject all who stray from your decrees, for their delusions come to nothing. All the wicked of the Earth you discard like dross; therefore I love your statutes. My flesh trembles in fear of you; I stand in awe of your laws.

THOUGHT

God's Word is described as a lamp unto our feet and a light unto our path. This means clinging on to His Word for direction and clarity, especially when we are unsure. God's Word speaks to our immediate circumstances, helping us take our next steps. The Word of God also speaks to our future by teaching and building us up, strengthening us for the path ahead.

ACTION

What uncertainties are present in your life right now of which you need to ask God for His direction and clarity?

DAY 04

VALUE OF THE WORD OF GOD PT. 4

PSALM 119: 121-136 NIV

I have done what it righteous and just; do not leave me to my oppressors. Ensure your servant's well-being; do not let the arrogant oppress me. My eyes fail, looking for your salvation, looking for your righteous promise. Deal with your servant according to your love and teach me your decrees. I am your servant; give me discernment that I may understand your statutes. It is time for you to act, Lord; your law is being broken. Because I love your commands more than gold, more than pure gold, and because I consider all your precepts right, I hate every wrong path. Your statutes are wonderful; therefore I obey them. The unfolding of your words gives light; it gives understanding to the simple. I open my mouth and pant, longing for your commands. Turn to me and have mercy on me, as you always do to those who love your name. Direct my footsteps according to your word; let no sin rule over me. Redeem me from human oppression, that I may obey your precepts. Make your face shine on your servant and teach me your decrees. Streams of tears flow from my eyes, for your law is not obeyed.

DAY 04

THOUGHT

Life can throw many obstacles in our way, aiming to oppress us through robbing us of our hope, joy and peace. God's Word brings light to dark situations, strengthening us spiritually, mentally and physically. When we dwell on God's Word, we can exchange anything that appears to oppress us for the hope, love and peace that He gives us.

ACTION

Think about how God's Word has given you hope in the face of oppression in your own life?

DAY 05

VALUE OF THE WORD OF GOD PT. 5

PSALM 119: 137-152 NIV

You are righteous, Lord, and your laws are right. The statutes you have laid down are righteous; they are fully trustworthy. My zeal wears me out, for my enemies ignore your words. Your promises have been thoroughly tested, and your servant loves them. Though I am lowly and despised, I do not forget your precepts. Your righteousness is everlasting and your law is true. Trouble and distress have come upon me, but your commands give me delight. Your statutes are always righteous; give me understanding that I may live. I call with all my heart; answer me, Lord, and I will obey your decrees. I call out to you; save me and I will keep your statutes. I rise before dawn and cry for help; I have put my hope in your word. My eyes stay open through the watches of the night, that I may meditate on your promises. Hear my voice in accordance with your love; preserve my life, Lord, according to your laws. Those who devise wicked schemes are near, but they are far from your law. Yet you are near, Lord, and all your commands are true. Long ago I learned from your statutes that you established them to last forever.

THOUGHT

God's Word is the truth and His righteousness is everlasting. We often forget the promises written in His Word, and even the ones that He has spoken to us. The truth of God's Word is hope like an anchor for our soul; when we are distressed and cry for help, we are held steadfast by God.

ACTION

Recall a promise of God which you may have forgotten and remind yourself of the truth of that promise.

DAY 06

VALUE OF THE WORD OF GOD PT. 6

PSALM 119: 153-160 NIV

Look on my suffering and deliver me, for I have not forgotten your law. Defend my cause and redeem me; preserve my life according to your promise. Salvation is far from the wicked, for they do not seek out your decrees. Your compassion, Lord, is great; preserve my life according to your laws. Many are the foes who persecute me, but I have not turned from your statutes. I look on the faithless with loathing, for they do not obey your word. See how I love your precepts; preserve my life, Lord, in accordance with your love. All your words are true; all you righteous laws are eternal.

THOUGHT

God's Word speaks of His compassion. He is always defending and redeeming us. We often go through life trying to do everything on our own when we don't have to. We can call upon Him for help and He will surely answer us.

ACTION

Can you think of a situation in your life where you need to know God's compassion? How do you think God's Word will help you?

DAY 07

VALUE OF THE WORD OF GOD PT. 7

PSALM 119: 161-176 NIV

Rulers persecute me without cause, but my heart trembles at your word. I rejoice in your promise like one who finds great spoil. I hate and detest falsehood but I love your law. Seven times a day I praise you for your righteous laws. Great peace have those who love your law, and nothing can make them stumble. I wait for your salvation, Lord, and I follow your commands. I obey your statutes, for I love them greatly. I obey your precepts and your statutes, for all my ways are known to you. May my cry come before you, Lord; give me understanding according to your word. May my supplication come before you; deliver me according to your promise. May my lips overflow with praise, for you teach me your decrees. May my tongue sing of your word, for all your commands are righteous. May your hand be ready to help me, for I have chosen your precepts. I long for your salvation, Lord, and your law gives me delight. Let me live that I may praise you, and may your laws sustain me. I have strayed like a lost sheep. Seek your servant, for I have not forgotten your commands.

THOUGHT

Praising God is an expression of our admiration of who God is. We can sing and use our voice to glorify Him, and all the remarkable things that He has done for us. Praise brings a fulfillment and joy that sustains us. This then deepens our trust in Him, helping us to remain firm in God in our daily lives. Make praise a part of your daily walk with God.

ACTION

Pause and take a moment to praise God for who He is and for how He has shown up for you in your life

DAY 01
THE WORD CREATES

GENESIS 1:1-3, 6, 9, 14, 20, 24, 26 NIV

In the beginning God created the heavens and the earth. Now the earth was formless and empty, darkness was over the surface of the deep, and the Spirit of God was hovering over the waters. And God said, "Let there be light," and there was light. And God said, "Let there be a vault between the waters to separate water from water." And God said, "Let the water under the sky be gathered to one place, and let dry ground appear." And it was so. And God said, "Let there be lights in the vault of the sky to separate the day from the night, and let them serve as signs to mark sacred times, and days and years. And God said, "Let the water teem with living creatures, and let birds fly above the earth across the vault of the sky." And God said, "Let the land produce living creatures according to their kinds: the livestock, the creatures that move along the ground, and the wild animals, each according to its kind." And it was so. Then God said, "Let us make mankind in our image, in our likeness, so that they may rule over the fish in the sea and the birds in the sky, over the livestock and all the wild animals, and over all the creatures that move along the ground."

THOUGHT

Words are powerful! In the very first chapter of the Bible, God spoke and suddenly the Word came to life. His words have that same transforming power today. God has given us the authority to use our words to speak life or death, we can choose to speak God's Word and see lives transformed. What will you choose?

ACTION

What areas of your life, which appear to be dormant, could you speak life into?

DAY 02
THE WORD FULFILLED IN JESUS

JOHN 1:1-2, 14 NIV

In the beginning was the Word, and the Word was with God, and the Word was God. He was with God in the beginning. The Word became flesh and made his dwelling among us. We have seen his glory, the glory of the one and only Son, who came from the Father, full of grace and truth.

THOUGHT

The Old Testament talks about Jesus coming and the New Testament shows Jesus in action. When Jesus came He was the fulfilment of the Word - He became the Word. When we read His Word, we are in a conversation with Jesus. Think about what Jesus is speaking to you about today through His Word.

ACTION

Can you think of any examples of Jesus fulfilling predictions about His coming in the Old Testament?

DAY 03

THE WORD KEEPS US ALIVE

MATTHEW 4:4 NIV

Jesus answered, "It is written: 'Man shall not live on bread alone, but on every word that comes from the mouth of God.'"

THOUGHT

I'm sure you can think of many things you think you cannot live without, but the Word of God holds top priority in our lives. Leaning on His Word is what will sustain us. Go back to what He last said to you, and make it your priority to live accordingly.

ACTION

How can you feed yourself with the Word of God more regularly?

DAY 04

HOW THE ENEMY CHALLENGES THE WORD OF GOD

MATTHEW 13:1-23 NIV

Listen then to what the parable of the sower means: When anyone hears the message about the kingdom and does not understand it, the evil one comes and snatches away what was sown in their heart. This is the seed sown along the path. The seed falling on rocky ground refers to someone who hears the word and at once receives it with joy. But since they have no root, they last only a short time. When trouble or persecution comes because of the word, they quickly fall away. The seed falling among the thorns refers to someone who hears the word, but the worries of this life and the deceitfulness of wealth choke the word, making it unfruitful. But the seed falling on good soil refers to someone who hears the word and understands it. This is the one who produces a crop, yielding a hundred, sixty or thirty times what was sown.

THOUGHT

When we make a choice to prioritise our relationship with God by reading the Word and putting this into action, we can be certain that our roots will be able to sustain any struggles that we face. During our walk with Christ, the enemy plots to come against us by pinpointing our weaknesses, by throwing hardships and persecution our way and by planting worries into our minds. Choosing the Word of God over everything else in our lives will help us stand firm in our faith through all the struggles that we may face.

ACTION

Are you living a faith-driven life that bears godly fruit, or have you given into the enemy's lies as he brings hardships, persecution or worries to you?

DAY 05

THE POWER OF THE WORD

HEBREWS 4:12 NIV

For the Word of God is alive and active. Sharper than any double-edged sword, it penetrates even to dividing soul and spirit, joints and marrow; it judges the thoughts and attitudes of the heart. Nothing in all creation is hidden from God's sight. Everything is uncovered and laid bare before the eyes of him to whom we must give account.

THOUGHT

Knowing the Word of God is alive and active gives us the assurance that God will speak to us and that what He says will be relevant in every area of our lives. We can speak the Word of God over our lives knowing that our thoughts and attitudes can be challenged and changed by the Word.

ACTION

What is God challenging you about right now as you read this passage? How can you act on what He is saying?

DAY 06

THE WORD IS GOD-BREATHED

2 TIMOTHY 3:16-17 NIV

All Scripture is God-breathed and is useful for teaching, rebuking, correcting and training in righteousness, so that the servant of God may be thoroughly equipped for every good work.

THOUGHT

The scriptures continuously teach us how to be more Christ-like in a society which is godless. They rebuke and correct us when we are living a lifestyle that is not pleasing to Him and when we make decisions that are not in alignment with God's. They even train us to walk in right standing with Jesus, so that we can outwork every good work He has called us to. If there is any doubt about where we are at in our walk with Christ, reading the scriptures will help to examine ourselves.

ACTION

List the scriptures which are currently teaching, rebuking, correcting and training you to become the fully equipped servant of God whom God desires you to be.

DAY 07

TRUE DISCIPLES HOLD TO THE WORD

JOHN 8:31-32 NIV

To the Jews who had believed him, Jesus said, "If you hold to my teaching, you are really my disciples. Then you will know the truth, and the truth will set you free."

THOUGHT

Following Jesus requires us to abide to Jesus' Word; this makes us true disciples. The blessing that comes with following Jesus is that we can live in truth and freedom. Walking in the fullness of this truth and freedom will help us to take others on the journey of following Jesus.

ACTION

Are there any areas in your life where your actions do not line up with Jesus' teachings?

MODULE 05
CHRISTIAN FOUNDATIONS

Foundations are the unseen elements that are key to the outcome and success of something. For example, due to major construction failures in its foundation, the 2008 built, Millennium Tower in San Francisco will have to go through a massive makeover, to stop the building from sinking at a rate of 2 inches per year. The costs that engineers proposed for the renovation ($500 million) will almost double the initial costs it took to build the Tower in the first place ($350 million). This goes to show how costly it can be, when we try to build on poor, unstable, shallow foundations.

We are all looking for a strong outcome in life, striving to be successful and be the best that we can be, and each and every one of us is called for great things. But sometimes we neglect the hard, unseen, sometimes mundane, yet vital work of setting in solid foundations on which we can build our lives on. The next two weeks we will be looking at the foundations of our christian life, what makes them and shapes them. These foundations are the basis of a life with Jesus and it's time to set them right in your life. Let's commit to being a generation with deep roots founded in solid truths, that makes our lives unshakeable in the highs and lows, so that regardless of our situation, we can continue to grow and go for it in all that God has for us.

WEEK 13 | CREATION

DAY 01
CREATION: THE FIRST DAY

GENESIS 1:1-5 NIV

In the beginning God created the heavens and the earth. Now the earth was formless and empty, darkness was over the surface of the deep, and the Spirit of God was hovering over the waters. And God said, "Let there be light," and there was light. God saw that the light was good, and he separated the light from the darkness. God called the light "day" and the darkness he called "night." And there was evening, and there was morning – the first day.

THOUGHT

From the beginning, the Spirit of God was alive and active, bringing light into the darkness, bringing the words of God to life! God has that power to revive whatever may seem dead in our lives and bring it out for His purpose, just as He did by bringing light into the world.

ACTION

How does this scripture make you think about how God's almighty and sovereign power brings His words to life in your own life?

WEEK 13 | CREATION

DAY 02

CREATION: THE SECOND DAY

GENESIS 1:6-8 NIV

And God said, "Let there be a vault between the waters to separate water from water." So God made the vault and separated the water under the vault from the water above it. And it was so. God called the vault "sky." And there was evening, and there was morning - the second day.

THOUGHT

This scripture shows us how detailed God is about His creation, including ourselves. He has a plan for all the details of the earth, just as He does for our lives. God has thoroughly thought about our lives way more than we ever could know. So as tough as it can be to not to understand every detail of our lives, we can trust that His plans are way greater than our own.

ACTION

How does this scripture make you think about God's plan for your life?

DAY 03

CREATION: THE THIRD DAY

GENESIS 1:9-13 NIV

And God said, "Let the water under the sky be gathered to one place, and let dry ground appear." And it was so. God called the dry ground "land", and the gathered waters he called "seas". And God saw that it was good. Then God said, "Let the land produce vegetation: seed-bearing plants and trees on the land that bear fruit with seed in it, according to their various kinds." And it was so. The land produced vegetation: plants bearing seed according to their kinds and trees bearing fruit with seed in it according to their kinds. And God saw that it was good. And there was evening, and there was morning - the third day.

THOUGHT

Sometimes we can take God's provision for granted, such as the fruits and crops He created for us to enjoy, the beauty of the ocean and the sun rising or setting. God created all these elements as a reflection of who He is. We should take more opportunities to pause and think about how His creation shows His characteristics.

ACTION

What do these scriptures communicate about God's characteristics?

DAY 04

CREATION: THE FOURTH DAY

GENESIS 1:14-19 NKJV

Then God said, "Let there be lights in the firmament of the heavens to divide the day from the night; and let them be for signs and seasons, and for days and years; and let them be for lights in the firmament of the heavens to give light on the earth"; and it was so. Then God made two great lights: the greater light to rule the day, and the lesser light to rule the night. He made the stars also. God set them in the firmament of the heavens to give light on the earth, and to rule over the day and over the night, and to divide the light from the darkness. And God saw that it was good. So the evening and the morning were the fourth day.

THOUGHT

God intentionally created lights for several purposes, one to signify the day and the night, another to be used as a sign, another to mark the seasons, days and years. Just as God has designed the sun, moon and stars with many purposes, He desires to use us all in many ways.

ACTION

How does this scripture make you reflect upon how God has designed you and the many purposes He has placed upon you?

DAY 05

CREATION: THE FIFTH DAY

GENESIS 1:20-23 NKJV

Then God said, "Let the waters abound with an abundance of living creatures, and let birds fly above the earth across the face of the firmament of the heavens." So God created great sea creatures and every living thing that moves, with which the waters abounded, according to their kind, and every winged bird according to its kind. And God saw that it was good. And God blessed them, saying, "Be fruitful and multiply, and fill the waters in the seas, and let birds multiply on the earth." So the evening and the morning were the fifth day.

THOUGHT

God's sovereignty is highlighted in this passage where we see living creatures as well as the waters obeying His commands. His command to them is to continue to produce an abundance of animals and to multiply. This reflects His power to be obeyed and His desire to see His creation in abundance and multiplication. There is always more with God, and so much more that we are yet to experience.

ACTION

Reflect and write about the countless ways God has blessed you. Write down some ways in which you would like to experience more of God.

DAY 06

CREATION: THE SIXTH DAY

GENESIS 1:27-2:1 NIV

So God created mankind in his own image in the image of God he created them; male and female he created them. God blessed them and said to them, "Be fruitful and increase in number; fill the earth and subdue it. Rule over the fish in the sea and the birds in the sky and over every living creature that moves on the ground." Then God said, "I give you every seed-bearing plant on the face of the whole earth and every tree that has fruit with seed in it. They will be yours for food. And to all the beasts of the earth and all the birds in the sky and all the creatures that move along the ground – everything that has the breath of life in it – I give every green plant for food." And it was so. God saw all that he had made, and it was very good. And there was evening, and there was morning – the sixth day. Thus the heavens and the earth were completed in all their vast array.

THOUGHT

This is the beginning of the picture of the love God has for us. His desire to be in relationship with us is seen from he beginning when He first envisions us in His image. This was the beginning of a partnership where He desired to have a part of Him in us and us in Him. His love for us is further seen when He gives us authority and power to rule over all the animals, fish and seed-bearing plants that He's just created and deemed them to be good. God has given us this freedomto rule from the beginning, and entrusts us to steward and outwork whatever He has placed in our hands.

ACTION

Thinking about this scripture. How do these verses make you realise how God sees you?

DAY 07

CREATION: THE SEVENTH DAY

GENESIS 2:2-3 NIV

By the seventh day God had finished the work he had been doing; so on the seventh day he rested from all his work. Then God blessed the seventh day and made it holy, because on it he rested from all the work of creating that he had done.

THOUGHT

God had finished His amazing work. He knew the importance of rest, so He rested on the seventh day. Sometimes we can get swamped by the busyness of life, but God, who is a lot busier than ourselves, who created the whole earth in six days, rested on the seventh day. We too need to take a day out to rest and embrace the work that God is doing in our own lives.

ACTION

Take time out to pause from your busy schedule, rest and make a note of what God is doing in you and through you.

DAY 01

THE GARDEN

GENESIS 2:4-14 NIV

This is the account of the heavens and the earth when they were created, when the Lord God made the earth and the heavens. Now no shrub had yet appeared on the earth and no plant had yet sprung up, for the Lord God had not sent rain on the earth and there was no one to work the ground, but streams came up from the earth and watered the whole surface of the ground. Then the Lord God formed a man from the dust of the ground and breathed into his nostrils the breath of life, and the man became a living being. Now the Lord God had planted a garden in the east, in Eden; and there he put the man he had formed. The Lord God made all kinds of trees grow out of the ground - trees that were pleasing to the eye and good for food. In the middle of the garden were the tree of life and the tree of the knowledge of good and evil. A river watering the garden flowed from Eden; from there it was separated into four headwaters. The name of the first is the Pishon; it winds through the entire land of Havilah, where there is gold. (The gold of that land is good; aromatic resin and onyx are also there.) The name of the second river is the Gihon; it winds through the entire land of Cush. The name of the third river is the Tigris; it runs along the east side of Ashur. And the fourth river is the Euphrates.

THOUGHT

Out of all creation, God chose to make us in His image, placing man in the garden of Eden where life was great and full of abundance. From the beginning, man was living in paradise and enjoyed everything the garden had to offer. This is a humbling thought, as we realise God could have decided to leave us out of His plan, but He decided to include us and breathe life into our beings. In His love He was willing to give us the choice on how we live the lives He has given us.

ACTION

Reflect and think about how God is blessing you with a life of abundance.

DAY 02

MAN & WOMAN

GENESIS 2:15-25 NIV

The Lord God took the man and put him in the Garden of Eden to work it and take care of it. And the Lord God commanded the man, "You are free to eat from any tree in the garden; but you must not eat from the tree of the knowledge of good and evil, for when you eat from it you will certainly die." The Lord God said, "It is not good for the man to be alone. I will make a helper suitable for him." Now the Lord God had formed out of the ground all the wild animals and all the birds in the sky. He brought them to the man to see what he would name them; and whatever the man called each living creature, that was its name. So the man gave names to all the livestock, the birds in the sky and all the wild animals. But for Adam no suitable helper was found. So the Lord God caused the man to fall into a deep sleep; and while he was sleeping, he took one of the man's ribs and then closed up the place with flesh. Then the Lord God made a woman from the rib he had taken...

DAY 02

out of the man, and he brought her to the man. The man said, "This is now bone of my bones and flesh of my flesh she shall be called 'woman, for she was taken out of man." That is why a man leaves his father and mother and is united to his wife, and they become one flesh. Adam and his wife were both naked, and they felt no shame.

THOUGHT

God brings the right people into our lives at the right time. God saw that the man was alone and needed a helper, so He created a woman to help the man. God's desire for man and woman was and still is to be in unity with each other. He breathed this unique and special relationship into existence as one which brings strength and has no shame.

ACTION

Reflecting upon this scripture, think of some people who have come into your life at the right time and how they have made a difference in your life.

DAY 03

THE FALL (FIRST SIN)

GENESIS 3:1-7 NIV

Now the serpent was more crafty than any of the wild animals the Lord God had made. He said to the woman, "Did God really say, 'You must not eat from any tree in the garden'?" The woman said to the serpent, "We may eat fruit from the trees in the garden, but God did say, 'You must not eat fruit from the tree that is in the middle of the garden, and you must not touch it, or you will die.'" "You will not certainly die," the serpent said to the woman. "For God knows that when you eat from it your eyes will be opened, and you will be like God, knowing good and evil." When the woman saw that the fruit of the tree was good for food and pleasing to the eye, and also desirable for gaining wisdom, she took some and ate it. She also gave some to her husband, who was with her, and he ate it. Then the eyes of both of them were opened, and they realized they were naked; so they sewed fig leaves together and made coverings for themselves.

THOUGHT

"Did God really say?" The serpent exists in our lives as the enemy, who constantly fills our minds up with partial truths, making us forget or not trust the Word that God spoke out. The woman recalled what God said, but she chose to listen to a partial truth. Standing firm on the Word of God requires us not to compromise on His truths and to be aware of any partial truths we may be believing.

ACTION

What partial truths are you believing? Now replace these with God's truth.

DAY 04

THE CONSEQUENCES OF SIN FOR SATAN & WOMAN

GENESIS 3:8-16 NIV

Then the man and his wife heard the sound of the Lord God as he was walking in the garden in the cool of the day, and they hid from the Lord God among the trees of the garden. But the Lord God called to the man, "Where are you?" He answered, "I heard you in the garden, and I was afraid because I was naked; so I hid." And he said, "Who told you that you were naked? Have you eaten from the tree that I commanded you not to eat from?" The man said, "The woman you put here with me — she gave me some fruit from the tree, and I ate it." Then the Lord God said to the woman, "What is this you have done?" The woman said, "The serpent deceived me, and I ate." So the Lord God said to the serpent, "Because you have done this, Cursed are you above all livestock and all wild animals! You will crawl on your belly and you will eat dust all the days of your life. And I will put enmity between you and the woman, and between your offspring and hers; he will crush your head and you will strike his heel." To the woman he said, "I will make your pains in childbearing very severe; with painful labour you will give birth to children. Your desire will be for your husband, and he will rule over you."

THOUGHT

The moment Eve stepped away from God's truth, which is sin, she became aware of how her disobedience opened her eyes to her nakedness. This feeling of shame, is what tries to get in the way of our intimacy with God. Although Adam and Eve were attempting to hide from God, He knew where they were in the garden, He was waiting for them to come out of hiding and bring themselves to Him.

The same goes for our relationship with God, He waits for us to bring our sin and shame to Him in order for Him to heal us and set us free.

ACTION

What sin is currently causing you to hide away from God? Confess your sins, and walk in the freedom that He desires for you.

DAY 05

THE CONSEQUENCES OF SIN FOR MAN

GENESIS 3:17-19 NIV

To Adam he said, "Because you listened to your wife and ate fruit from the tree about which I commanded you, 'You must not eat from it,' "Cursed is the ground because of you; through painful toil you will eat food from it all the days of your life. It will produce thorns and thistles for you and you will eat the plants of the field. By the sweat of your brow you will eat your food until you return to the ground, since from it you were taken for dust you are and to dust you will return."

THOUGHT

God is explaining the consequences of Adam's sin, for example that human beings would have to work hard to earn the food they need to survive all the days of their lives. The bottom line is all sin has consequences and the consequence of sin is death. God's love and grace for us is so great that He would later pay for our sins by dying on the cross, that we would have eternal life in exchange for our sins.

ACTION

Have you ever been negatively influenced by someone or something you felt you shouldn't have been? Confess this to a well trusted friend, and stay accountable.

DAY 06

HOW HUMANITY WENT FROM THERE

GENESIS 3:20-24 NIV

Adam named his wife Eve, because she would become the mother of all the living. The Lord God made garments of skin for Adam and his wife and clothed them. And the Lord God said, "The man has now become like one of us, knowing good and evil. He must not be allowed to reach out his hand and take also from the tree of life and eat, and live forever." So the Lord God banished him from the Garden of Eden to work the ground from which he had been taken. After he drove the man out, he placed on the east side of the Garden of Eden cherubim and a flaming sword flashing back and forth to guard the way to the tree of life.

THOUGHT

Although Adam and Eve chose to disobey God which led to them being banished from the Garden of Eden, God still chose to clothe them, meet them where they were at and put them elsewhere to start afresh. This choice led to the beginning of humans living outside of paradise, in a life where they had to work hard. This led to rivalry between siblings and the distance between God and humans grew. But God's desire was always to restore Eden, by leading people to life and life to the full through Jesus.

ACTION

Reflect and remember a time when you have felt God pick you up and clothe you in something new again?

THE NEXT GENERATION

GENESIS 4:1-2 NIV

Adam made love to his wife Eve, and she became pregnant and gave birth to Cain. She said, "With the help of the Lord I have brought forth a man." Later she gave birth to his brother Abel. Now Abel kept flocks, and Cain worked the soil.

THOUGHT

God commanded us to be fruitful and multiply, and this is continuously outworked today. Even in the midst of hopeless situations, God can turn them around and make them new again, just as we see with Adam and Eve bearing their sons. A God encounter leads to the rebirth of what we thought was lost and turns it around for the good of those who love Him. In the end, even Jesus would be a descendant of Adam, restoring what was lost back to life.

ACTION

Reflect and think about the new things that God has birthed in your heart.

DAY 01

REGRET

LUKE 19:5-8 NIV

To Adam he said, "Because you listened to your wife and ate fruit from the tree about which I commanded you, 'You must When Jesus reached the spot, he looked up and said to him, "Zacchaeus, come down immediately. I must stay at your house today." So he came down at once and welcomed him gladly. All the people saw this and began to mutter, "He has gone to be the guest of a sinner." But Zacchaeus stood up and said to the Lord, "Look, Lord! Here and now I give half of my possessions to the poor, and if I have cheated anybody out of anything, I will pay back four times the amount." It will produce thorns and thistles for you and you will eat the plants of the field. By the sweat of your brow you will eat your food until you return to the ground, since from it you were taken for dust you are and to dust you will return."

THOUGHT

When you understand that the choice or choices you have made are not good, the first thing you feel is regret. This means you identify with and understand the negative impact of those choices on your life. But don't stop here, take the next step!

ACTION

What are the areas in my life in which I can identify the negative impact of my choices?

DAY 02

REMORSE

LUKE 19:8-10 NIV

But Zacchaeus stood up and said to the Lord, "Look, Lord! Here and now I give half of my possessions to the poor, and if I have cheated anybody out of anything, I will pay back four times the amount." Jesus said to him, "Today salvation has come to this house, because this man, too, is a son of Abraham. For the Son of Man came to seek and to save the lost."

THOUGHT

Remorse is the next step. Regret helps you identify the impact of your choices on your own world, while remorse helps you understand the impact of your choices on other people and their worlds. It's the damage we do to others in our disobedience to God. But don't stop here - take the next step!

ACTION

What are the areas in my life where I can identify the negative impact of my choices on others? Like Zacchaeus, is there anything I can do today to put that right?

DAY 03

REPENTANCE TO BELIEVE

MARK 1:14-15 NIV

After John was put in prison, Jesus went into Galilee, proclaiming the good news of God. "The time has come," he said. "The kingdom of God has come near. Repent and believe the good news!"

THOUGHT

Repentance is the next step. Repentance is identifying with and understand the impact of your bad choices on your relationship with God. Repentance means to turn and go in the opposite direction, to walk away from our bad choices and towards God, believing and trusting in His power to help us. But don't stop here, take the next step!

ACTION

Is there any area of my life that I am withholding from God, where I don't believe He is willing to help me?

DAY 04

REPENTANCE TO WIPE AWAY SIN IN JESUS

ACTS 3:19 NIV

Repent, then, and turn to God, so that your sins may be wiped out, that times of refreshing may come from the Lord,

THOUGHT

Repentance restores our relationship with God, but in choosing to turn away from our sin through Jesus (or the Lord as He is referred to in these verses) it also wipes out the bad between you and God, and refreshes you.

ACTION

Are there areas where you feel disconnected from God? Can you link this disconnection back to your mistakes? Bring these to God and allow Him to restore you.

DAY 05

REPENTANCE TO RECEIVE FORGIVENESS

ACTS 2:38-39 NIV

Peter replied, "Repent and be baptized, every one of you, in the name of Jesus Christ for the forgiveness of your sins. And you will receive the gift of the Holy Spirit. The promise is for you and your children and for all who are far off — for all whom the Lord our God will call."

THOUGHT

Repentance is closely linked to baptism, as both signify a fresh start with God and a complete forgiveness of sins through what Jesus has done.

ACTION

Are there any areas of your life where you need complete forgiveness? Have you been baptised in water?

DAY 06

FORGIVENESS OF OTHERS & YOURSELF

MATTHEW 6:14 NIV

For if you forgive other people when they sin against you, your heavenly Father will also forgive you.

THOUGHT

Forgiveness comes in two parts. Part one is that forgiveness is something you will always require from God. Part 2 is that forgiveness is something people will always require from you. Here, God is clear if you freely receive forgiveness from God, He expects that you freely give forgiveness to others.

ACTION

Ask Jesus if there is anyone who you need to forgive. Wait and see if anyone comes to mind.

DAY 07
BELIEF & PUBLIC CONFESSION

ROMANS 10:9-10 NIV

If you declare with your mouth, "Jesus is Lord," and believe in your heart that God raised him from the dead, you will be saved. For it is with your heart that you believe and are justified, and it is with your mouth that you profess your faith and are saved.

THOUGHT

So far a lot of what we have covered has discussed our belief and how we internally work things out with God. However, there should also be a public announcement that Jesus is Lord, that you have chosen to live by Him and for Him. This is the moment we call salvation.

ACTION

Have you ever publicly said that you are following Jesus? Maybe you prayed a prayer in youth or church? If not, and you believe in your heart, right now speak out, "Jesus is Lord of my life", then let someone you trust (a friend or youth leader) know that you've made this decision to follow Jesus.

DAY 01

A NEW LIFE

2 CORINTHIANS 5:17-18 NIV

Therefore, if anyone is in Christ, the new creation has come: the old has gone, the new is here! All this is from God, who reconciled us to himself through Christ and gave us the ministry of reconciliation.

THOUGHT

This scripture reminds us to embrace our new reality in Jesus. The moment we accept Jesus, we are no longer the old version of ourselves, we have been made new. We become one with Christ, so we immediately intertwine with who He is, making us a whole new individual. This means we no longer need to dwell on who we were, and can step into who God is calling us to be.

ACTION

How does this scripture help you see yourself as a new creation in Christ?

DAY 02

THE IMPORTANCE OF BAPTISM

MARK 1:1-5 NIV

The beginning of the good news about Jesus the Messiah, the Son of God, as it is written in Isaiah the prophet: "I will send my messenger ahead of you, who will prepare your way" - "a voice of one calling in the wilderness, 'Prepare the way for the Lord, make straight paths for him.'" And so John the Baptist appeared in the wilderness, preaching a baptism of repentance for the forgiveness of sins. The whole Judean countryside and all the people of Jerusalem went out to him. Confessing their sins, they were baptized by him in the Jordan River.

THOUGHT

We are called to be 'John the Baptists' by leading others into repentance and forgiveness. Repentance requires us to confess our sins, completely turning away from them, asking God for forgiveness. It also means forgiving ourselves of our mistakes. Baptism is an outward display of an internal decision to repent and walk in forgiveness. We can show others the way of true repentance and forgiveness by teaching them this message and baptising them.

ACTION

Have you repented and asked God for forgiveness of your sins?

DAY 03
JESUS' BAPTISM

MATTHEW 3:16-17 NIV

As soon as Jesus was baptised, he went up out of the water. At that moment heaven was opened, and he saw the Spirit of God descending like a dove and alighting on him. And a voice from heaven said, "This is my Son, whom I love; with him I am well pleased."

THOUGHT

After Jesus' baptism, the Spirit of God descends upon Him, followed by Jesus beginning His ministry and performing many miracles. This is such a significant moment in Jesus' ministry, and sets an example to us to get baptised. This is a divine, life changing moment, an encounter like no other.

ACTION

Recall the moment you were baptised. How did your life change? If you haven't been baptised, inform your youth leader and go for it!

DAY 04
REPENTANCE & BAPTISM IN WATER: THE FIRST CHRISTIANS

ACTS 3:19 NIV

"Therefore let all Israel be assured of this: God has made this Jesus, whom you crucified, both Lord and Messiah." When the people heard this, they were cut to the heart and said to Peter and the other apostles, "Brothers, what shall we do?" Peter replied, "Repent and be baptised, every one of you, in the name of Jesus Christ for the forgiveness of your sins. And you will receive the gift of the Holy Spirit.

THOUGHT

A few characteristics of true repentance as seen in this scripture include: an internal realisation that Jesus died for you, and a desire to change and become more Christ-like. This is good news for everyone! When people hear good news, they too want to receive it. We can be the bringer of good news to the people we meet daily.

ACTION

Examine your heart. Do you realise Jesus died for you and do you want to change and become more Christ like?

DAY 05

THE EFFECTS OF BAPTISM

ROMANS 6:3-6 NIV

Or don't you know that all of us who were baptized into Christ Jesus were baptized into his death? We were therefore buried with him through baptism into death in order that, just as Christ was raised from the dead through the glory of the Father, we too may live a new life. For if we have been united with him in a death like His, we will certainly also be united with Him in a resurrection like his. For we know that our old self was crucified with Him so that the body ruled by sin might be done away with, that we should no longer be slaves to sin.

THOUGHT

Baptism gives us the fresh start that we need after we have acknowledged our need for Jesus. The moment we acknowledge Jesus as our Lord and Saviour and turn away from our sins, we are forgiven and saved. This truth is further outworked when we get baptised. Baptism is a new beginning, where our old nature is put to death and our new nature arises with Christ. We don't have to strive to be made new; we are automatically renewed when we are baptised.

ACTION

Think about the new characteristics of Christ that are now being outworked in you, after being baptised.

DAY 06

REPENTANCE TO RECEIVE THE HOLY SPIRIT

ACTS 2:38-39 NIV

Peter replied, "Repent and be baptized, every one of you, in the name of Jesus Christ for the forgiveness of your sins. And you will receive the gift of the Holy Spirit. The promise is for you and your children and for all who are far off - for all whom the Lord our God will call."

THOUGHT

When we repent, we turn away from our sin and allow room in our hearts for Jesus to come in and transform us by the power of the Holy Spirit. In this moment, we surrender our lives to Christ, knowing we cannot do life our way, and desiring to live life according to the Holy Spirit. This is a gift that God wants to give us, to strengthen other believers and to lead unbelievers to Christ. We are also reminded that this gift is not for any selective set of people, it is for everyone.

ACTION

What is the Holy Spirit prompting you to do in this moment?

DAY 07

THE EFFECTS OF SALVATION, BAPTISM & THE HOLY SPIRIT

ROMANS 7:4-6 NIV

So, my brothers and sisters, you also died to the law through the body of Christ, that you might belong to another, to Him who was raised from the dead, in order that we might bear fruit for God. For when we were in the realm of the flesh, the sinful passions aroused by the law were at work in us, so that we bore fruit for death. But now, by dying to what once bound us, we have been released from the law so that we serve in the new way of the Spirit, and not in the old way of the written code.

THOUGHT

Following Jesus means that we are forgiven, set free and can walk in partnership with God through the power of the Holy Spirit. We no longer live our lives for ourselves, but we live our lives for God! Prior to following Jesus, our lives were ruled by placing our sinful desires above God's great desires for us. Living our lives for God means we are made new and can live the lives that we've been called to live!

ACTION

Considering this new way of life by the Holy Spirit, write down the ways God wants you to live for Him.

MODULE 06

THE KINGDOM OF GOD

If you have been in church for longer than a month you will have heard the phrase 'the kingdom of God' being used quite often. It's in the worship songs we sing, the preaches we preach, and the bible is full of teaching about the kingdom. Whenever we hear or read about the kingdom of God, we get introduced to something that is constantly growing and expanding, no matter the circumstance. It is something powerful. It is something Jesus spoke about most and that is represented by Him. But what actually is the kingdom of God, and how on earth (excuse the pun) does it relate to me today in 2019?

There has been a lot of misunderstanding and miscommunication about what the kingdom of God is (and what it isn't), so in the next couple of weeks, we want to get back to basics and look at what did Jesus say the kingdom of God is, and how can I apply that and be part of building something bigger than myself?

WEEK 17 | OLD VS. NEW COVENANT

DAY 01

GOD GAVE STANDARDS FOR HUMANITY TO LIVE BY

DEUTERONOMY 4:44–5:1–5 NIV

This is the law Moses set before the Israelites. Moses summoned all Israel and said: Hear, Israel, the decrees and laws I declare in your hearing today. Learn them and be sure to follow them. The Lord our God made a covenant with us at Horeb. It was not with our ancestors that the Lord made this covenant, but with us, with all of us who are alive here today. The Lord spoke to you face to face out of the fire on the mountain. (At that time I stood between the Lord and you to declare to you the word of the Lord, because you were afraid of the fire and did not go up the mountain.)

THOUGHT

God wants us to be free. His laws were meant to reveal evil; that we would know right from wrong, hence walk in righteousness. They were not meant to keep us in captivity. God is simply looking for our obedience and for us to put our trust in him.

ACTION

Write down ways of how you can maintain the standard in today's world even when it proves difficult?

DAY 02
THE STANDARDS (10 COMMANDMENTS) PT. 1

DEUTERONOMY 5:6-15 NIV

"I am the Lord your God, who brought you out of Egypt, out of the land of slavery.

"You shall have no other gods before me.

"You shall not make for yourself an image in the form of anything in heaven above or on the earth beneath or in the waters below. You shall not bow down to them or worship them; for I, the Lord your God, am a jealous God, punishing the children for the sin of the parents to the third and fourth generation of those who hate me, but showing love to a thousand generations of those who love me and keep my commandments.

"You shall not misuse the name of the Lord your God, for the Lord will not hold anyone guiltless who misuses his name.

"Observe the Sabbath day by keeping it holy, as the Lord your God has commanded you. Six days you shall labour and do all your work, but the seventh day is a sabbath to the Lord your God. On it you shall not do any work, neither you, nor your son or daughter, nor your male or female servant, nor your ox, your donkey or any of your animals, nor any foreigner residing in your towns, so that your male and female servants may rest, as you do. Remember that you were slaves in Egypt and that the Lord your God brought you out of there with a mighty hand and an outstretched arm. Therefore the Lord your God has commanded you to observe the Sabbath day.

THOUGHT

Our God is a Holy God but also a jealous God, meaning He desires your attention alone, He doesn't desire to be in competition with the other things that you put before God. Therefore, as His children, we should strive to live a holy life and honour him and him alone. There is nothing you need that you'll find outside of Him.

ACTION

Why do you think God stresses the point that we should not serve other gods or put anything or anyone else above him? In what ways do you put other things before God?

DAY 03

THE STANDARDS (10 COMMANDMENTS) PT. 2

DEUTERONOMY 5:16-22 NIV

"Honour your father and your mother, as the Lord your God has commanded you, so that you may live long and that it may go well with you in the land the Lord your God is giving you. "You shall not murder. You shall not commit adultery. You shall not steal. You shall not give false testimony against your neighbor. You shall not covet your neighbor's wife. You shall not set your desire on your neighbor's house or land, his male or female servant, his ox or donkey, or anything that belongs to your neighbor." These are the commandments the Lord proclaimed in a loud voice to your whole assembly there on the mountain from out of the fire, the cloud and the deep darkness; and he added nothing more. Then he wrote them on two stone tablets and gave them to me.

THOUGHT

These commandments are still relevant to us today and can be summed up into love the Lord your God with all your heart, soul, mind and strength and love your neighbour as you love yourself. These commandments help us to check the condition of our heart, if we love God with all of our heart, we will find it easy to love our neighbours through our generosity and not expect anything in return. These commandments enable us to be more like Christ and to please Him.

ACTION

Are you outworking these commandments and how can you outwork them this week?

DAY 04

INSTRUCTIONS FOR COMMANDMENTS

DEUTERONOMY 6:1-19 NIV

… Hear, Israel, and be careful to obey so that it may go well with you and that you may increase greatly in a land flowing with milk and honey, just as the Lord, the God of your ancestors, promised you. Hear, O Israel: The Lord our God, the Lord is one. Love the Lord your God with all your heart and with all your soul and with all your strength. These commandments that I give you today are to be on your hearts. Impress them on your children. Talk about them when you sit at home and when you walk along the road, when you lie down and when you get up. Tie them as symbols on your hands and bind them on your foreheads. Write them on the doorframes of your houses and on your gates…

THOUGHT

Everything God does, he does simply out of His love for you. He demands your heart, mind and soul and desires to be in relationship with you. Making God our priority, helps us to not become consumed by the ways of society, and helps us to strengthen our identity in Christ as opposed to following what others in society want to do. Walking strongly in your identity attracts others to desire God too.

ACTION

Do you keep your priorities in alignment with Loving God? What obstacles tend to get in your way of doing so?

DAY 05

HUMANITY FAILS & GOD MAKES A NEW PLAN

JEREMIAH 31:31-34 NIV

"The days are coming," declares the Lord, "when I will make a new covenant with the people of Israel and with the people of Judah. It will not be like the covenant I made with their ancestors when I took them by the hand to lead them out of Egypt, because they broke my covenant, though I was a husband to them," declares the Lord. "This is the covenant I will make with the people of Israel after that time," declares the Lord. "I will put my law in their minds and write it on their hearts. I will be their God, and they will be my people. No longer will they teach their neighbour or say to one another, 'Know the Lord,' because they will all know me, from the least of them to the greatest," declares the Lord. "For I will forgive their wickedness and will remember their sins no more."

THOUGHT

How great is God that even after the first covenant was broken, that he would make a new covenant and still call us his own. How much greater that he would also forgive us and say he would remember our sins no more.

ACTION

How has God's forgiveness made a difference in your life?

DAY 06

GOD IMPLEMENTS HIS NEW PLAN THROUGH JESUS PT. 1

DEUTERONOMY 6:1-19 NIV

But in fact the ministry Jesus has received is as superior to theirs as the covenant of which he is mediator is superior to the old one, since the new covenant is established on better promises. For if there had been nothing wrong with that first covenant, no place would have been sought for another. But God found fault with the people and said: "The days are coming, declares the Lord, when I will make a new covenant with the people of Israel and with the people of Judah. It will not be like the covenant I made with their ancestors when I took them by the hand to lead them out of Egypt, because they did not remain faithful to my covenant, and I turned away from them", declares the Lord.

THOUGHT

God made the new covenant, so that we could walk out our faith in Jesus through His Grace. This new covenant involves Jesus being the mediator between God and humanity, allowing us to have a direct relationship with Him and to obtain the free gift of salvation without works but by believing that Jesus died for our sins and to set us free.

ACTION

What impact does the new covenant have on our lives today in comparison to the old testament?

DAY 07

GOD IMPLEMENTS HIS NEW PLAN THROUGH JESUS PT. 2

HEBREWS 8:10-13 NIV

"This is the covenant I will establish with the people of Israel after that time", declares the Lord. "I will put my laws in their minds and write them on their hearts. I will be their God, and they will be my people. No longer will they teach their neighbor, or say to one another, 'Know the Lord,' because they will all know me, from the least of them to the greatest. For I will forgive their wickedness and will remember their sins no more." By calling this covenant "new," he has made the first one obsolete; and what is obsolete and outdated will soon disappear.

THOUGHT

When we have God's word written in our heart and know him as OUR God; our natural response will be to put him first and to abide by His laws. We won't kill, nor steal, nor lie, nor covet, nor disrespect our mothers and fathers. We will see radical change from the inside out.

ACTION

How can we practically outwork His law in our hearts of loving God and others?

DAY 01

WHAT GOD'S PLAN THROUGH JESUS MEANS FOR US PT. 1

HEBREWS 7:18-22 NIV

The former regulation is set aside because it was weak and useless (for the law made nothing perfect), and a better hope is introduced, by which we draw near to God. And it was not without an oath! Others became priests without any oath, but he became a priest with an oath when God said to him: "The Lord has sworn and will not change his mind: 'You are a priest forever.' Because of this oath, Jesus has become the guarantor of a better covenant.

THOUGHT

In the Old Testament, God's people had to connect with Him through seeking God's Word through a priest. The priest would have been a specific individual who was deemed closest to God. However, God has always desired to bridge the gap between humanity and Himself. The way in which He could do this was by sending Himself to Earth as a human being - Jesus, to be the ultimate Priest forever. This meant we could relate with Him directly where we no longer have to draw near to God by finding a priest. We can simply talk to Him in prayer and tune into His Holy Spirit dwelling within us. In other words, God has made it so easy for us to relate to Him through sending Jesus!

ACTION

How does this scripture influence how you now view your relationship with God? And how does it encourage you to want to pursue Jesus more?

DAY 02

WHAT GOD'S PLAN THROUGH JESUS MEANS FOR US PT. 2

DEUTERONOMY 6:1-19 NIV

Now there have been many of those priests, since death prevented them from continuing in office; but because Jesus lives forever, he has a permanent priesthood. Therefore he is able to save completely those who come to God through him, because he always lives to intercede for them. Such a high priest truly meets our need—one who is holy, blameless, pure, set apart from sinners, exalted above the heavens. Unlike the other high priests, he does not need to offer sacrifices day after day, first for his own sins, and then for the sins of the people. He sacrificed for their sins once for all when he offered himself. For the law appoints as high priests men in all their weakness; but the oath, which came after the law, appointed the Son, who has been made perfect forever.

DAY 02

THOUGHT

Jesus' sacrifice on the cross for humanity, means that we no longer have to offer animal sacrifices, without any blemishes, to God for our sins. This was the custom in the days before Jesus came to cleanse us of our sins. Jesus is holy, blameless, pure and fully sinless so by dying for us it means that we can all approach God with a heart full of repentance and walk free from our sins. Jesus offered himself, holy and sanctified so that our sins yesterday, today and for the rest of our days are covered by Jesus' death on the cross. Sin has been replaced by forgiveness.

ACTION

How does this verse make you re-evaluate the power of what God did for us, so that we could walk in the full realisation of the power of Jesus' death on the cross for us?

DAY 03

JESUS' PERSONAL EXAMPLE OF RESCUING HUMANITY PT. 1

LUKE 5:31-32 NIV

Jesus answered them, "It is not the healthy who need a doctor, but the sick. I have not come to call the righteous, but sinners to repentance."

THOUGHT

Jesus was on a rescue mission to help us become whole through Him. All of us have fallen short of the glory of God. None of us come close to how perfect God is; He is sinless. Although we continuously sin, the moment we accept that we have sinned, and need Jesus to save us, we are then completely forgiven. Jesus makes us righteous! We need to ask Jesus for forgiveness. He desires to bring us into wholeness and to draw us closer to Him.

ACTION

Have you repented of your sins? Call upon Jesus and repent today.

DAY 04

JESUS PERSONAL EXAMPLE OF RESCUING HUMANITY PT. 2

LUKE 19:9-10 NIV

Jesus said to him, "Today salvation has come to this house, because this man, too, is a son of Abraham. For the Son of Man came to seek and to save the lost."

THOUGHT

Have you ever lost something important to you? When you lose something valuable you look everywhere until you find it. We are so valuable to Jesus that He perseveres with us so that we can be saved from our sins and selfish ways. He wants to rescue us from ourselves and help us to discover our true identity so that we can be all we were created to be.

ACTION

Jesus came to seek and save the lost: who are the people in your life you can reach out to?

DAY 05

JESUS CALLS PEOPLE TO FOLLOW HIS EXAMPLE

DEUTERONOMY 6:1-19 NIV

As Jesus walked beside the Sea of Galilee, he saw Simon and his brother Andrew casting a net into the lake, for they were fishermen. "Come, follow me," Jesus said, "and I will send you out to fish for people." At once they left their nets and followed him.

THOUGHT

A true encounter with Jesus changes you. It's radical! After an encounter with Jesus you will never be the same. You will feel desperate to want what He desires for you and live a life full of purpose. He is calling us to be more like Him. This is where our true fulfilment is found. As we find fulfilment in following Jesus, we cannot keep it to ourselves. He sends us out to others so that they can also find their fulfilment in Jesus.

ACTION

Have you had an encounter with Jesus? What is He asking you to leave behind to follow Him?

DAY 06

JESUS SHOWS THAT HE HAS POWER WHERE THE OLD LAW DOESN'T

MARK 1:21-27 NIV

They went to Capernaum, and when the Sabbath came, Jesus went into the synagogue and began to teach. The people were amazed at his teaching, because he taught them as one who had authority, not as the teachers of the law. Just then a man in their synagogue who was possessed by an impure spirit cried out, "What do you want with us, Jesus of Nazareth? Have you come to destroy us? I know who you are—the Holy One of God!" "Be quiet!" said Jesus sternly. "Come out of him!" The impure spirit shook the man violently and came out of him with a shriek. The people were all so amazed that they asked each other, "What is this? A new teaching—and with authority! He even gives orders to impure spirits and they obey him."

THOUGHT

In the Old Testament, we see the old law didn't have the authority or power to set people free. However here in Mark, we can see Jesus has that authority to save us from our sins and to save us from bondage, in order to give us freedom. He speaks power and releases freedom over the most difficult of circumstances!

ACTION

What areas of your life, do you need Jesus' authority to walk in your freedom and to set others free?

DAY 07

JESUS SHOWS THAT HE HAS POWER TO FORGIVE SINS & HEAL US

MARK 2:3-12 NIV

Some men came, bringing to him a paralyzed man, carried by four of them. Since they could not get him to Jesus because of the crowd, they made an opening in the roof above Jesus by digging through it and then lowered the mat the man was lying on. When Jesus saw their faith, he said to the paralyzed man, "Son, your sins are forgiven." Now some teachers of the law were sitting there, thinking to themselves, "Why does this fellow talk like that? He's blaspheming! Who can forgive sins but God alone?" Immediately Jesus knew in his spirit that this was what they were thinking in their hearts, and he said to them, "Why are you thinking these things? Which is easier: to say to this paralyzed man, 'Your sins are forgiven,' or to say, 'Get up, take your mat and walk'? But I want you to know that the Son of Man has authority on earth to forgive sins." So he said to the man, "I tell you, get up, take your mat and go home." He got up, took his mat and walked out in full view of them all. This amazed everyone and they praised God, saying, "We have never seen anything like this!"

DAY 07

THOUGHT

Jesus came not just to heal us, but to free us completely from the ultimate consequences of sin. When Jesus died on the cross He took our sins to the grave. Then, when He was resurrected, He broke the curse of sin and sickness on humanity. He now has the power over sickness and sin and He chooses to share that power with us!

ACTION

Can you think of areas in your life where you require Jesus' forgiveness and healing?

DAY 01
JESUS IS FOR ALL HUMANITY

MARK 2:14-17 NLT

As he walked along, he saw Levi son of Alphaeus sitting at the tax collector's booth. "Follow me," Jesus told him, and Levi got up and followed him. While Jesus was having dinner at Levi's house, many tax collectors and sinners were eating with him and his disciples, for there were many who followed him. When the teachers of the law who were Pharisees saw him eating with the sinners and tax collectors, they asked his disciples: "Why does he eat with tax collectors and sinners?" On hearing this, Jesus said to them, "It is not the healthy who need a doctor, but the sick. I have not come to call the righteous, but sinners."

THOUGHT

There can be a misconception that people are 'not good enough' for God. We may hear our friends say things like 'I'm too bad to go to church or be a Christian'. We can even fall into the trap of feeling like everybody else is a better person than us. Jesus shows that all of this is irrelevant. He doesn't judge people in the way that we do and His intention is to seek out all humanity; no matter how good or bad others perceive them to be.

ACTION

What can you do each day to remind yourself or someone else of the Good News about Jesus?

DAY 02
JESUS IS ALWAYS AVAILABLE TO US

MARK 3:1-6 NIV

"Another time Jesus went into the synagogue, and a man with a shriveled hand was there. Some of them were looking for a reason to accuse Jesus, so they watched him closely to see if he would heal on the Sabbath. Jesus said to the man with the shriveled hand, "Stand up in front of everyone." Then Jesus asked them, "Which is lawful on the Sabbath: to do good or to do evil, to save life or to kill?" But they remained silent. He looked around them in anger and, deeply distressed at their stubborn hearts, said to the man, "Stretch out your hand." He stretched it out, and his hand was completely restored. Then the Pharisees went out and began to plot with the Herodians how they might kill Jesus."

THOUGHT

When we boldly approach and reach out to Jesus with surrender and trust, He will always step in and help us. Following Jesus entails living a humble lifestyle, where we put our stubbornness and pride to the side and allow Him to correct us. This requires us to be willing and to make the space to listen to what He has to say.

ACTION

When was the last time you made yourself available to hear from God? Pause and listen to what He wants to say to you.

DAY 03

JESUS HAS CHOSEN US FOR THE PRIVILEGE OF ADVANCING GOD'S KINGDOM.

MARK 3:13-15 MSG

"He climbed a mountain and invited those he wanted with him. They climbed together. He settled on twelve, and designated them apostles. The plan was that they would be with him, and he would send them out to proclaim the Word and give them authority to banish demons."

THOUGHT

Jesus climbs with us through obstacles and aids us through life. He has chosen us to live a purpose greater than ourselves and to take responsibility for our generation - giving us power to overcome and be a solution.

ACTION

Do your day-to-day actions reflect that Jesus has chosen you, and do they advance and give glory to His kingdom?

DAY 04

JESUS HAS EQUIPPED US FOR THE COMMISION OF ADVANCING GOD'S KINGDOM

MARK 3:1-6 NIV

Calling the Twelve to him, he began to send them out two by two and gave them authority over impure spirits. These were his instructions: "Take nothing for the journey except a staff—no bread, no bag, no money in your belts. Wear sandals but not an extra shirt. Whenever you enter a house, stay there until you leave that town. And if any place will not welcome you or listen to you, leave that place and shake the dust off your feet as a testimony against them." They went out and preached that people should repent. They drove out many demons and anointed many sick people with oil and healed them.

THOUGHT

Jesus encourages us to not lean on the security of worldly things but let Him work through us for His Kingdom. He has already equipped us internally with the tools; we just need to act on our responsibility!

ACTION

Are you using your God given authority and power wisely in a way which has a positive impact on people's lives? What things in your life do you need to let go of to move forward into where Jesus is calling you to be?

DAY 05

CHOOSE TO USE WHAT YOU ALREADY HAVE

MARK 6:34-44 NIV

"When Jesus landed and saw a large crowd, he had compassion on them, because they were like sheep without a shepherd. So he began teaching them many things. By this time it was late in the day, so his disciples came to him. "This is a remote place," they said, "and it's already very late. Send the people away so that they can go to the surrounding countryside and villages and buy themselves something to eat." But he answered, "You give them something to eat." They said to him, "That would take more than half a year's wages! Are we to go and spend that much on bread and give it to them to eat?" "How many loaves do you have?" he asked. "Go and see." When they found out, they said, "Five—and two fish." Then Jesus directed them to have all the people sit down in groups on the green grass. So they sat down in groups of hundreds and fifties. Taking the five loaves and the two fish and looking up to heaven, he gave thanks and broke the loaves. Then he gave them to his disciples to distribute to the people. He also divided the two fish among them all. They all ate and were satisfied, and the disciples picked up twelve basketfuls of broken pieces of bread and fish. The number of the men who had eaten was five thousand."

THOUGHT

Walking wisely and following Jesus means choosing to live a life of generosity and sacrifice with what God has given us. God desires to partner with us in our daily lives, He wants to use us to see His name glorified, He wants to see miracles done through us!

ACTION

Have you ever doubted if what God has given you is enough? List the skills and gifts God has given you to advance the Kingdom.

DAY 06

CHOOSE COURAGE OVER FEAR

MARK 6:45-51 NIV

Immediately Jesus made his disciples get into the boat and go on ahead of him to Bethsaida, while he dismissed the crowd. After leaving them, he went up on a mountainside to pray. Later that night, the boat was in the middle of the lake, and he was alone on land. He saw the disciples straining at the oars, because the wind was against them. Shortly before dawn he went out to them, walking on the lake. He was about to pass by them, but when they saw him walking on the lake, they thought he was a ghost. They cried out, because they all saw him and were terrified. Immediately he spoke to them and said, "Take courage! It is I. Don't be afraid." Then he climbed into the boat with them, and the wind died down. They were completely amazed.

DAY 06

THOUGHT

Our choice to focus on Jesus instead of fear allows us to rest in His peace, knowing that it's not confidence in our actions that expands the Kingdom, but our courage to give everything for God's will. Jesus went aside to pray, He came back to help lead the disciples in the midst of the storms. There is a spiritual strength that occurs when we make a decision to set time aside to pray. Our prayers are powerful and effective, they have the power to bring peace amidst the stress and worry of our lives.

ACTION

Can you name an area of your life where you are relying on your own abilities instead of God's abilities?

DAY 07
CHOOSE TO COMMIT TO HIM

MATTHEW 4:18-20 MSG

Walking along the beach of Lake Galilee, Jesus saw two brothers: Simon (later called Peter) and Andrew. They were fishing, throwing their nets into the lake. It was their regular work. Jesus said to them, "Come with me. I'll make a new kind of fisherman out of you. I'll show you how to catch men and women instead or perch and bass." They didn't ask questions, but simply dropped their nets and followed.

THOUGHT

Through every aspect of our lives we must choose to live for Jesus and give Him our all without question. Don't doubt the God who made you. Even with nothing, He will take care of you if you trust him.

ACTION

What "regular work" do you need to drop to follow Jesus more intentionally?

DAY 01

PETER'S JOURNEY: BRINGING JESUS & HIS POWER TO HIS HOUSEHOLD

MATTHEW 8:14–16 NIV

When Jesus came into Peter's house, he saw Peter's mother-in-law lying in bed with a fever. He touched her hand and the fever left her, and she got up and began to wait on him. When evening came, many who were demon-possessed were brought to him, and he drove out the spirits with a word and healed all the sick.

THOUGHT

Here we see the supernatural power attained by Jesus to heal and perform miracles. We are reminded of the true extent of God's power as we were created by Him. The moment we believe in Jesus, we receive this same power to heal and perform miracles in the world around us through the power of the Holy Spirit that dwells within us.

ACTION

Do you know someone who needs healing? Find someone in your school or church who wants to be healed, and pray for their healing.

DAY 02

PETER'S JOURNEY: GREAT FAITH IN JESUS

MATTHEW 14:23–29 NIV

After he had dismissed them, he went up on a mountainside by himself to pray. Later that night, he was there alone, and the boat was already a considerable distance from land, buffeted by the waves because the wind was against it. Shortly before dawn Jesus went out to them, walking on the lake. When the disciples saw him walking on the lake, they were terrified. "It's a ghost," they said, and cried out in fear. But Jesus immediately said to them: "Take courage! It is I. Don't be afraid." "Lord, if it's you," Peter replied, "tell me to come to you on the water." "Come," he said. Then Peter got down out of the boat, walked on the water and came toward Jesus.

THOUGHT

In this scripture, we observe that Peter puts his entire trust in Jesus and gives Him complete control. Like the fearful disciples, many of us at times are scared to fully submit to God's will for our lives as it doesn't fit society's view of what is possible. The disciples believed it was impossible to walk on water, but it still happened! God exceeds our expectations as his thoughts are higher than our thoughts and his ways are higher than our ways. To be a true disciple and commit fully to God's will, we need faith in God rather than in the world.

ACTION

Are you living in faith or fear? Ask God to fill you up with faith in this moment.

DAY 03

PETER'S JOURNEY: STILL STRUGGLING WITH HIS HUMANITY

MATTHEW 14:30-32 NIV

But when he saw the wind, he was afraid and, beginning to sink, cried out, "Lord, save me!" Immediately Jesus reached out his hand and caught him. "You of little faith," he said, "why did you doubt?" And when they climbed into the boat, the wind died down.

THOUGHT

As we explored yesterday, faith is the answer, but Peter reminds us that as humans we are not perfect. He begins to doubt and this is a perfectly natural human emotion. As you go through your journey and explore who God is, you're not always going to understand or have full conviction about what you're doing. However, God will always catch you and uphold you, even in times of doubt.

ACTION

In what areas of your life are you doubting God's ability to show up? Submit those areas to God in prayer.

DAY 04

PETER'S JOURNEY: PETER PROCLAIMS JESUS

MATTHEW 16:13-19 NIV

When Jesus came to the region of Caesarea Philippi, he asked his disciples, "Who do people say the Son of Man is?" They replied, "Some say John the Baptist; others say Elijah; and still others, Jeremiah or one of the prophets." "But what about you?" he asked. "Who do you say I am?" Simon Peter answered, "You are the Messiah, the Son of the living God." Jesus replied, "Blessed are you, Simon son of Jonah, for this was not revealed to you by flesh and blood, but by my Father in heaven. And I tell you that you are Peter, and on this rock I will build my church, and the gates of Hades will not overcome it. I will give you the keys of the kingdom of heaven; whatever you bind on earth will be bound in heaven, and whatever you loose on earth will be loosed in heaven."

THOUGHT

Peter lived in a time of conflicting beliefs. Judaism and Christianity were at odds. Many pharisees and scribes saw Jesus as a threat as many Jews were becoming followers (disciples) of Jesus. By declaring Jesus to be the Messiah, Peter was going against many others' beliefs. As disciples we may have to overcome contrary opinions to our faith. The way we live and worship God may go against society's views, but we will overcome through the boldness and courage that God has given us.

ACTION

Have you ever spoken about your belief in Jesus Christ? Share with somebody, how Jesus has changed your life.

DAY 05

PETER'S JOURNEY: PETER MISUNDERSTANDS JESUS

MATTHEW 16:21-28 NIV

From that time on Jesus began to explain to his disciples that he must go to Jerusalem and suffer many things at the hands of the elders, the chief priests and the teachers of the law, and that he must be killed and on the third day be raised to life. Peter took him aside and began to rebuke him. "Never, Lord!" he said. "This shall never happen to you!" Jesus turned and said to Peter, "Get behind me, Satan! You are a stumbling block to me; you do not have in mind the concerns of God, but merely human concerns." Then Jesus said to his disciples, "Whoever wants to be my disciple must deny themselves and take up their cross and follow me. For whoever wants to save their life will lose it, but whoever loses their life for me will find it. What good will it be for someone to gain the whole world, yet forfeit their soul? Or what can anyone give in exchange for their soul? For the Son of Man is going to come in his Father's glory with his angels, and then he will reward each person according to what they have done. "Truly I tell you, some who are standing here will not taste death before they see the Son of Man coming in his kingdom."

THOUGHT

Peter, like many of us misunderstood Jesus' role on Earth. Jesus didn't come to take revenge on people, He came to serve and guide his people on earth and His greatest act of service was dying on the cross. Jesus' death paid for our sins. Peter saw this as inconceivable - the son of God dying on a cross! But Jesus urges us to take up our own cross and serve others as vengeance is not ours. He wants us to sacrifice our own selfish desires and show people who he is through our actions.

ACTION

What do you think Jesus meant by 'take up their cross'? What are some practical ways you can 'deny' yourself?

DAY 06

PETER'S JOURNEY: KNOWN BY JESUS

MATTHEW 26:31-35 NIV

Then Jesus told them, "This very night you will all fall away on account of me, for it is written: "I will strike the shepherd, and the sheep of the flock will be scattered.' But after I have risen, I will go ahead of you into Galilee." Peter replied, "Even if all fall away on account of you, I never will." "Truly I tell you," Jesus answered, "this very night, before the rooster crows, you will disown me three times." But Peter declared, "Even if I have to die with you, I will never disown you." And all the other disciples said the same.

THOUGHT

Despite Peter's mistakes, we see his triumphs as well as his downfalls. This reminds us that we will also have our triumphs and downfalls. As disciples, we can be fully genuine in our attempts to do good and serve God, but should also recognise that though we may make mistakes, this does not have to stop us from being all God has called us to be.

ACTION

Have you ever done something you told yourself you would never do? Have you forgiven yourself for this, if not, ask God for forgiveness.

DAY 07

PETER'S JOURNEY: PETER FAILS JESUS

MATTHEW 26:36-46 NIV

Then Jesus went with his disciples to a place called Gethsemane, and he said to them, "Sit here while I go over there and pray." He took Peter and the two sons of Zebedee along with him, and he began to be sorrowful and troubled. Then he said to them, "My soul is overwhelmed with sorrow to the point of death. Stay here and keep watch with me." Going a little farther, he fell with his face to the ground and prayed, "My Father, if it is possible, may this cup be taken from me. Yet not as I will, but as you will." Then he returned to his disciples and found them sleeping. "Couldn't you men keep watch with me for one hour?" he asked Peter. "Watch and pray so that you will not fall into temptation. The spirit is willing, but the flesh is weak." He went away a second time and prayed, "My Father, if it is not possible for this cup to be taken away unless I drink it, may your will be done." When he came back, he again found them sleeping, because their eyes were heavy. So he left them and went away once more and prayed the third time, saying the same thing. Then he returned to the disciples and said to them, "Are you still sleeping and resting? Look, the hour has come, and the Son of Man is delivered into the hands of sinners. Rise! Let us go! Here comes my betrayer!"

THOUGHT

Often, our desire to please God is present but our feelings, emotions and physical being can stop us from outworking God's will. Recognising that our flesh is weak, but our Spirit is willing, can help us to put practical things into place to help us pursue God. When we pray, it is important to set aside the distractions, and to focus on Him. For example, we can do this through writing our prayers in our journals, or even by praying when we're physically awake.

ACTION

Where do you like to pray? Find a time and a place where you can pray without distractions.

DAY 01

PETER'S JOURNEY: HE DISOWNS JESUS

MATTHEW 26:69-75 NIV

Now Peter was sitting out in the courtyard, and a servant girl came to him. "You also were with Jesus of Galilee," she said. But he denied it before them all. "I don't know what you're talking about," he said. Then he went out to the gateway, where another servant girl saw him and said to the people there, "This fellow was with Jesus of Nazareth." He denied it again, with an oath: "I don't know the man!" After a little while, those standing there went up to Peter and said, "Surely you are one of them; your accent gives you away." Then he began to call down curses, and he swore to them, "I don't know the man!" Immediately a rooster crowed. Then Peter remembered the word Jesus had spoken: "Before the rooster crows, you will disown me three times." And he went outside and wept bitterly.

THOUGHT

In this scripture, Peter, the mighty man of God, puts his own desire to fit in above Jesus. As we follow Peter's life as an example this week, know that just as Jesus had grace for Peter even after Peter denied Him, so He has grace for us! Peter had a willingness both before and after this moment to work with Jesus and walk with Him into all that he was called to.

ACTION

Is there something in your life right now you want to turn from to follow Jesus?

DAY 02

PETER'S JOURNEY: IT'S NOT OVER

JOHN 20:1-9 NIV

Early on the first day of the week, while it was still dark, Mary Magdalene went to the tomb and saw that the stone had been removed from the entrance. So she came running to Simon Peter and the other disciple, the one Jesus loved, and said, "They have taken the Lord out of the tomb, and we don't know where they have put him!" [Simon Peter] went straight into the tomb. He saw the strips of linen lying there, as well as the cloth that had been wrapped around Jesus' head. The cloth was still lying in its place, separate from the linen. Finally the other disciple, who had reached the tomb first, also went inside. He saw and believed. (They still did not understand from Scripture that Jesus had to rise from the dead.)

THOUGHT

Peter did not hesitate to run to see where Jesus was, even after denying Him. In your life, you have the chance to run back to Jesus without hesitation. Even if, like Peter, you thought Jesus was dead in your life, you can still run to find Him - alive! You don't need to understand this fully, you just need to run to Jesus.

ACTION

Is there an area in your life which you thought your faith was dead in? Run back to Jesus in prayer today.

DAY 03

PETER'S JOURNEY: NEW BEGINNINGS WITH JESUS & THE HOLY SPIRIT

JOHN 20:19-22 NIV

On the evening of that first day of the week, when the disciples were together, with the doors locked for fear of the Jewish leaders, Jesus came and stood among them and said, "Peace be with you!" After he said this, he showed them his hands and side. The disciples were overjoyed when they saw the Lord. Again Jesus said, "Peace be with you! As the Father has sent me, I am sending you." And with that he breathed on them and said, "Receive the Holy Spirit."

THOUGHT

Although some of the disciples lived in fear and doubt when Jesus had risen, He still chose to seek them out and reveal His risen form to them. When Jesus reveals His sacrifice to us and the scars He bore for us, He doesn't leave us confused and anxious. He sends us out into life with His peace and the great gift of the Holy Spirit - our constant companion.

ACTION

How can what God has equipped you with (peace and the Holy Spirit) help you to advance the Kingdom of God on earth?

DAY 04

PETER'S JOURNEY: JESUS REINSTATES HIM

JOHN 21:15-21 NIV

*When they had finished eating, Jesus said to Simon Peter, "Simon son of John, do you love me more than these?" "Yes, Lord,"
he said, "you know that I love you." Jesus said, "Feed my lambs." Again Jesus said, "Simon son of John, do you love me?" He answered, "Yes, Lord, you know that I love you." Jesus said, "Take care of my sheep." The third time he said to him, "Simon son of John, do you love me?" Peter was hurt because Jesus asked him the third time, "Do you love me?" He said, "Lord, you know all things; you know that I love you." Jesus said, "Feed my sheep. Very truly I tell you, when you were younger you dressed yourself and went where you wanted; but when you are old you will stretch out your hands, and someone else will dress you and lead you where you do not want to go." Jesus said this to indicate the kind of death by which Peter would glorify God. Then he said to him, "Follow me!"*

THOUGHT

Jesus responds to our slip ups with open arms by not only forgiving us but by reconnecting with us and reinstating us to where He intended us to be. Through this act of love Jesus eliminates the walls of guilt and shame which we put up around our hearts.

No matter what, we're never too far gone for Jesus. His love surpasses everything (Romans 8:38-39).

ACTION

Think and reflect on times you've felt God's call even if you didn't believe you deserved it.

DAY 05

PETER'S JOURNEY: THE HOLY SPIRIT WORKS THROUGH PETER TO PROCLAIM JESUS

ACTS 2:1-36 NIV

Then Peter stood up with the Eleven, raised his voice and addressed the crowd… "Fellow Israelites, listen to this: Jesus of Nazareth was a man accredited by God to you by miracles, wonders and signs, which God did among you through him, as you yourselves know. This man was handed over to you by God's deliberate plan and foreknowledge; and you, with the help of wicked men, put him to death by nailing him to the cross. But God raised him from the dead, freeing him from the agony of death, because it was impossible for death to keep its hold on him… God has raised this Jesus to life, and we are all witnesses of it. Exalted to the right hand of God, he has received from the Father the promised Holy Spirit and has poured out what you now see and hear… "Therefore let all Israel be assured of this: God has made this Jesus, whom you crucified, both Lord and Messiah."

THOUGHT

As you can read in the beginning of this scripture, Peter is speaking to the crowd after being filled with the Holy Spirit. We can now see the contrast between the Peter who denied Jesus to this Peter who boldly proclaims the Gospel of Jesus to 'Jews from every nation under heaven' (Acts 2:5). Like He did with Peter, God can turn your messiest moments into a masterpiece when you choose to partner with Him.

ACTION

How do you believe the Holy Spirit can work in and through you to affect the world around you?

DAY 06

PETER'S JOURNEY: HE STARTS THE EARLY CHURCH

ACTS 2:37-41 NIV

When the people heard this, they were cut to the heart and said to Peter and the other apostles, "Brothers, what shall we do?" Peter replied, "Repent and be baptized, every one of you, in the name of Jesus Christ for the forgiveness of your sins. And you will receive the gift of the Holy Spirit. The promise is for you and your children and for all who are far off—for all whom the Lord our God will call." With many other words he warned them; and he pleaded with them, "Save yourselves from this corrupt generation." Those who accepted his message were baptized, and about three thousand were added to their number that day.

DAY 06

THOUGHT

The early church began not with a building but with a group of people who believed in Jesus, chose to follow Him and were filled with the Holy Spirit. How amazing is it to know that you don't need anything else to be part of God's Church except to follow Him among other believers? The Holy Spirit gives us a next level relationship with God which can fill us with a boldness to share the gospel and grow the Church just like He did with Peter!

ACTION

Pray and ask God to receive the gift of the Holy Spirit.

DAY 07

PETER'S JOURNEY: MINISTRY OF POWER IN THE HOLY SPIRIT

ACTS 5:12-16 NIV

The apostles performed many signs and wonders among the people. And all the believers used to meet together in Solomon's Colonnade. No one else dared join them, even though they were highly regarded by the people. Nevertheless, more and more men and women believed in the Lord and were added to their number. As a result, people brought the sick into the streets and laid them on beds and mats so that at least Peter's shadow might fall on some of them as he passed by. Crowds gathered also from the towns around Jerusalem, bringing their sick and those tormented by impure spirits, and all of them were healed.

THOUGHT

Peter's life took a complete U-turn from what it was in Matthew 26. Through partnership with the Holy Spirit, humility and a willingness to be used by God, Peter's life began to mirror the life of Jesus - our ultimate example. People followed Christ and were healed through the life Peter led with the Holy Spirit, just as they can through our lives when we partner with God. Follow Peter's example - you are never too far gone, run after Jesus, let Him love you and work through you then tell the world about it.

ACTION

How can we be more like Peter, to have the Holy Spirit radiate off us so much that it can help those around us?

DAY 01

PARABLE OF THE SOWER

MATTHEW 13:1-9 NIV

That same day Jesus went out of the house and sat by the lake. Such large crowds gathered around him that he got into a boat and sat in it, while all the people stood on the shore. Then he told them many things in parables, saying: "A farmer went out to sow his seed. As he was scattering the seed, some fell along the path, and the birds came and ate it up. Some fell on rocky places, where it did not have much soil. It sprang up quickly, because the soil was shallow. But when the sun came up, the plants were scorched, and they withered because they had no root. Other seed fell among thorns, which grew up and choked the plants. Still other seed fell on good soil, where it produced a crop—a hundred, sixty or thirty times what was sown. Whoever has ears, let them hear."

THOUGHT

The way Jesus speaks to us is so important. Back in His time on earth, Jesus chose to speak to the people in ways they could easily comprehend. Speaking about such things as farmers & seeds ensured that everyone was able to hear, understand and have the opportunity to accept the message He was proclaiming. The Kingdom of God is available to everyone and spread to all, but only few will hear and accept it.

ACTION

How can you position yourself to hear and understand God's word?

DAY 02

PARABLE OF THE SOWER EXPLAINED

MATTHEW 13:10-23 NIV

… Listen then to what the parable of the sower means: When anyone hears the message about the kingdom and does not understand it, the evil one comes and snatches away what was sown in their heart. This is the seed sown along the path. The seed falling on rocky ground refers to someone who hears the word and at once receives it with joy. But since they have no root, they last only a short time. When trouble or persecution comes because of the word, they quickly fall away. The seed falling among the thorns refers to someone who hears the word, but the worries of this life and the deceitfulness of wealth choke the word, making it unfruitful. But the seed falling on good soil refers to someone who hears the word and understands it. This is the one who produces a crop, yielding a hundred, sixty or thirty times what was sown."

THOUGHT

The culture of God's kingdom is to understand the Word so that we can bear fruit in our lives. The fruit is the evidence to us and to others that our lives have been changed by God. Hearing God's Word is great! However, are we receiving and applying that Word? We are in control of the condition of our heart and that, like the different types of soil, determines how we receive God's Word.

ACTION

Who are the people in your world that you can go to if you need help understanding the Word of God (The Bible)?

DAY 03

PARABLE OF THE WEEDS

MATTHEW 13:24–30 NIV

Jesus told them another parable: "The kingdom of heaven is like a man who sowed good seed in his field. But while everyone was sleeping, his enemy came and sowed weeds among the wheat, and went away. When the wheat sprouted and formed heads, then the weeds also appeared. The owner's servants came to him and said, 'Sir, didn't you sow good seed in your field? Where then did the weeds come from?' 'An enemy did this,' he replied. The servants asked him, 'Do you want us to go and pull them up?' 'No,' he answered, 'because while you are pulling the weeds, you may uproot the wheat with them. Let both grow together until the harvest. At that time I will tell the harvesters: First collect the weeds and tie them in bundles to be burned; then gather the wheat and bring it into my barn.'

THOUGHT

Once again Jesus speaks in a way that is relevant, understandable and relatable to His audience. Through this parable we can be comforted by the knowledge that the 'bad seeds' and 'weeds' that spring up in our lives are not plans by God to hurt us but an attack from an enemy. As plans of the enemy grow alongside you, fix your eyes on Jesus so that you can grow for Him. You are good seed.

ACTION

Pause and reflect on what is growing in your life. Ask God to help you separate the wheat from the weeds.

DAY 04

PARABLE OF THE WEEDS EXPLAINED

MATTHEW 13:36–43 NIV

… "Explain to us the parable of the weeds in the field." He answered, "The one who sowed the good seed is the Son of Man. The field is the world, and the good seed stands for the people of the kingdom. The weeds are the people of the evil one, and the enemy who sows them is the devil. The harvest is the end of the age, and the harvesters are angels. As the weeds are pulled up and burned in the fire, so it will be at the end of the age. The Son of Man will send out his angels, and they will weed out of his kingdom everything that causes sin and all who do evil. They will throw them into the blazing furnace, where there will be weeping and gnashing of teeth. Then the righteous will shine like the sun in the kingdom of their Father. Whoever has ears, let them hear.

THOUGHT

God sows only good seed, that way we can know that anything that is not good seed is not from God. The people in your life who are from God should lead you closer to him rather than draw you away. And when time comes to an end, you have the promise of being amongst those other 'good seeds' in the Kingdom of God.

ACTION

Who are the people in your life that are encourage you to draw closer to God? Can you be that to someone else?

DAY 05

PARABLE OF THE MUSTARD SEED & YEAST

MATTHEW 13:31-35 NIV

He told them another parable: "The kingdom of heaven is like a mustard seed, which a man took and planted in his field. Though it is the smallest of all seeds, yet when it grows, it is the largest of garden plants and becomes a tree, so that the birds come and perch in its branches." He told them still another parable: "The kingdom of heaven is like yeast that a woman took and mixed into about sixty pounds of flour until it worked all through the dough." Jesus spoke all these things to the crowd in parables; he did not say anything to them without using a parable. So was fulfilled what was spoken through the prophet: "I will open my mouth in parables: I will utter things hidden since the creation of the world."

THOUGHT

Don't underestimate the significance of your "little". Whatever it is, it can be used in the great expansion and multiplication of the Kingdom of God. As this parable shows, when you take what you have and 'plant' it with God or 'work it through' what God has placed around you - it can so vastly expand from what it was. God can take your 'little' and build it beyond anything you can imagine.

ACTION

What is your "little" that seems unimportant and insignificant? How can you use that thing to be a blessing to others?

DAY 06

PARABLE OF HIDDEN TREASURE & THE PEARL

MATTHEW 13:44-46 NIV

The kingdom of heaven is like treasure hidden in a field. When a man found it, he hid it again, and then in his joy went and sold all he had and bought that field. Again, the kingdom of heaven is like a merchant looking for fine pearls. When he found one of great value, he went away and sold everything he had and bought it.

THOUGHT

Being God's child and serving Him should be celebrated! You may have an expensive item you value but living for God is worth far more than that item and it gives you more pleasure than anything ever could. It's worth pursuing with all you have. Find God's love for you, accept it and do everything in your power to chase after it all the days of your life.

ACTION

What would it look like for you to pursue Jesus with your whole life?

DAY 07
PARABLE OF THE NET

MATTHEW 13:47-52 NIV

Once again, the kingdom of heaven is like a net that was let down into the lake and caught all kinds of fish. When it was full, the fishermen pulled it up on the shore. Then they sat down and collected the good fish in baskets, but threw the bad away. This is how it will be at the end of the age. The angels will come and separate the wicked from the righteous and throw them into the blazing furnace, where there will be weeping and gnashing of teeth. "Have you understood all these things?" Jesus asked. "Yes," they replied. He said to them, "Therefore every teacher of the law who has become a discile in the kingdom of heaven is like the owner of a house who brings out of his storeroom new treasures as well as old."

THOUGHT

Relationship with God is so important because it determines your destination both while you are here on earth and when your time here ends. Don't get carried away following people or just "attending church', it's all about knowing God and having a relationship with Him. This parable alongside many others is very clear that in the Kingdom of God you are either in or you are out. Choose God.

ACTION

Take time to think about what your personal relationship with God looks like. Take whatever steps you need to today to move closer to Him.

MODULE 07

JESUS' TEACHING

"Give a man a fish, and he will be full for a day, TEACH him how to fish and he will be full forever."

Most of us have a weird relationship with teaching. It's mostly linked to our experience in school, where teaching can be boring, uninteresting or leave you wondering why you are even learning these things (give me one place/scenario that I will ever need to use Pythagoras' theorem in??). That's mainly because we don't relate to the subjects that we are taught or we don't seem to understand and cherish their worth for our life. Teaching (when done right and when approachable for your life) is something absolutely life giving. It's something that can revolutionize your life and bring it to a new level.

Jesus spent most of his public years going through Israel from town to town, teaching and proclaiming the Gospel of the kingdom of God. His main goal was to show God's will on earth and to impart a relevant and practical wisdom for people to build their lives on. There are numerous parables, sermons and illustrations throughout the gospels that note Jesus' teachings and are all worth looking at to learn more about life in the Kingdom of God. Probably the most known of all Jesus' teachings is the Sermon on the Mount and that's the one we want to primarily focus on over the next three weeks. We will have a closer look at the sermon and unveil what Jesus said, and what it actually means so we can apply it in our lives today.

WEEK 23 | SERMON ON THE MOUNT

DAY 01

THE BEATITUDES

MATTHEW 5:3-12 NIV

Blessed are the poor in spirit, for theirs is the kingdom of heaven. Blessed are those who mourn, for they will be comforted. Blessed are the meek, for they will inherit the earth. Blessed are those who hunger and thirst for righteousness, for they will be filled. Blessed are the merciful, for they will be shown mercy. Blessed are the pure in heart, for they will see God. Blessed are the peacemakers, for they will be called children of God. Blessed are those who are persecuted because of righteousness, for theirs is the kingdom of heaven. Blessed are you when people insult you, persecute you and falsely say all kinds of evil against you because of me. Rejoice and be glad, because great is your reward in heaven, for in the same way they persecuted the prophets who were before you.

THOUGHT

Jesus speaks of blessings in abundance for all types of people who might not typically seem 'blessed'. This passage shows blessings as a direct result of actions, character and circumstance in life. These blessings are a declaration of God's love for us. When faced with affliction we must trust in God, for we can know His blessing is upon us, even when it doesn't feel like it.

ACTION

Are there any areas in your life where you think God wants you to recognise His blessing above your current circumstance?

DAY 02

SALT & LIGHT

MATTHEW 5:13-16 NIV

You are the salt of the earth. But if the salt loses its saltiness, how can it be made salty again? It is no longer good for anything, except to be thrown out and trampled underfoot. You are the light of the world. A town built on a hill cannot be hidden. Neither do people light a lamp and put it under a bowl. Instead they put it on its stand, and it gives light to everyone in the house. In the same way, let your light shine before others, that they may see your good deeds and glorify your Father in heaven.

THOUGHT

You are the way that the world can see and taste God. Jesus describes us as salt and light, two of the most essential things in our world. We have been gifted with the ingredients to influence our peers, and given the light to brighten areas where darkness lingers. So there is no use in hiding all that God has created you to be or in being ashamed of the Gospel - it is good news! Share it out and light up the world around you with Jesus.

ACTION

How can you use your life to brighten your community, allowing others to discover God?

DAY 03

THE FULFILMENT OF THE LAW

MATTHEW 5:17-20 NIV

Do not think that I have come to abolish the Law or the Prophets; I have not come to abolish them but to fulfil them. For truly I tell you, until heaven and earth disappear, not the smallest letter, not the least stroke of a pen, will by any means disappear from the Law until everything is accomplished. Therefore, anyone who sets aside one of the least of these commands and teaches others accordingly will be called least in the kingdom of heaven, but whoever practices and teaches these commands will be called great in the kingdom of heaven. For I tell you that unless your righteousness surpasses that of the Pharisees and the teachers of the law, you will certainly not enter the kingdom of heaven.

THOUGHT

Jesus has asked us to live a life that is centred around Him, for everything we have comes from Him. When referencing the 'pharisees and the teachers of the law' Jesus was making the point that while those people 'appeared' righteous by following the law as far as anyone could see, they were unwilling to submit to true righteousness by accepting the grace and forgiveness of Jesus. He is not asking us to become like the pharisees by practising religion, but to instead follow Him. Only the forgiveness of our sins can make us truly righteous. The sacrifice Jesus made for our sins is not an excuse for us to disregard the law, but as He says, He came to fulfill the law, to show it in all of its grace and fullness.

ACTION

Pause and reflect on what it means to be righteous in Christ.

DAY 04

MURDER

MATTHEW 5:21-26 NLT

You have heard that our ancestors were told, "You must not murder. If you commit murder, you are subject to judgment." But I say, if you are even angry with someone, you are subject to judgment! If you call someone an idiot, you are in danger of being brought before the court. And if you curse someone, you are in danger of the fires of hell. So if you are presenting a sacrifice at the altar in the Temple and you suddenly remember that someone has something against you, leave your sacrifice there at the altar. Go and be reconciled to that person. Then come and offer your sacrifice to God. When you are on the way to court with your adversary, settle your differences quickly. Otherwise, your accuser may hand you over to the judge, who will hand you over to an officer, and you will be thrown into prison. And if that happens, you surely won't be free again until you have paid the last penny.

THOUGHT

Anger may block us from fully receiving God's gifts. Jesus teaches that reconciliation takes precedence over our offering to God and urges us to forgive those who have offended us. You might understand the feeling when there is someone you really dislike around you and you can't concentrate on anything else except the fact that they are there. God knows how powerful and distracting anger towards others can be! He also know that anger is no light issue (even comparable to murder!). We must come to God as an empty vessel, free from distractions, in order to be filled by Him.

ACTION

When we hold onto past hurts, we allow them to interfere with our communication with God. If you are holding onto any offence or hurt that someone caused you, take this time to begin to forgive them and trust in God.

DAY 05

ADULTERY

MATTHEW 5:27-30 NLT

You have heard the commandment that says, "You must not commit adultery." But I say, anyone who even looks at a woman with lust has already committed adultery with her in her heart. So if your eye – even your good eye – causes you to lust, gouge it out and throw it away. It is better for you to lose one part of your body than for your whole body to be thrown into hell. And if your hand – even your stronger hand – causes you to sin, cut it off and throw it away. It is better for you to lose one part of your body than for your whole body to be thrown into hell.

DAY 05

THOUGHT

We have control over our thoughts and actions. As followers of Christ we need to know that our actions have consequences, even if we think they aren't affecting other people. The state of our heart and its submission to the will of God is so important. Jesus even uses the overstatements of removing the body parts that cause us to sin, in order to magnify the consequences of our sinful nature - death. Anything that draws us into sin and away from God is not worth it, and cutting it out of our lives is a great solution.

ACTION

When we allow lustful thoughts to occupy our mind, sin is manifested. Where do you find yourself being ambushed by temptation and what steps can you take in order to cut out lustful desires that linger in your mind?

DAY 06

DIVORCE

MATTHEW 5:31-32 NIV

It has been said, "Anyone who divorces his wife must give her a certificate of divorce." But I tell you that anyone who divorces his wife, except for sexual immorality, makes her the victim of adultery, and anyone who marries a divorced woman commits adultery.

THOUGHT

Jesus encourages us to not seek divorce as an easy way out of a commitment. We are taught that marriage should be a permanent union of two becoming one flesh (Mark 10:8). All throughout the Word of God you can see how highly God favours faithfulness and hates disloyalty, from Adam and Eve with the fruit, to Moses with the Israelites, all the way through to the teachings of Jesus! God values and honours commitment and loyalty, especially within the covenant of marriage.

ACTION

Think about the relationship between Jesus and the Church when it is described as the 'bride of Christ' - how does this set an example for marriage?

DAY 07

OATHS

MATTHEW 5:33-37 MSG

And don't say anything you don't mean. This counsel is embedded deep in our traditions. You only make things worse when you lay down a smoke screen of pious talk, saying, "I'll pray for you," and never doing it, or saying, "God be with you," and not meaning it. You don't make your words true by embellishing them with religious lace. In making your speech sound more religious, it becomes less true. Just say "yes" and "no." When you manipulate words to get your own way, you go wrong.

THOUGHT

Jesus urges us to possess a character of integrity. We must not make empty oaths, and should carry ourselves in an honest manner. Just as was said yesterday, we know how highly God values commitment and faithfulness. He urges us to keep our oaths and respect the words that come out of our mouths as promises to one another. Let us walk with such integrity that our words carry the weight of truth without the need for an oath.

ACTION

What area of your life do you want to work with God to be more faithful in?

DAY 01

EYE FOR AN EYE

MATTHEW 5:38-42 NCV

You have heard that it was said, "An eye for an eye, and a tooth for a tooth." But I tell you, don't stand up against an evil person. If someone slaps you on the right cheek, turn to him the other cheek also. If someone wants to sue you in court and take your shirt, let him have your coat also. If someone forces you to go with him one mile, go with him two miles. If a person asks you for something, give it to him. Don't refuse to give to someone who wants to borrow from you.

THOUGHT

God urges us to forgive one another just as He forgives us for our sins. God is constantly forgiving us! This means we should follow in His footsteps and do what God created us to do, to help support each other and forgive people's mistakes. This passage shows us how pointless holding grudges is, encouraging us to live in a way which is counter-cultural but that makes the world a better place.

ACTION

Name a person you can go the extra mile for today and explain how you would do that.

DAY 02

LOVE FOR ENEMIES

MATTHEW 5:43-48 NCV

You have heard that it was said, "Love your neighbor and hate your enemies." But I say to you, love your enemies. Pray for those who hurt you. If you do this, you will be true children of your Father in heaven. He causes the sun to rise on good people and on evil people, and he sends rain to those who do right and to those who do wrong. If you love only the people who love you, you will get no reward. Even the tax collectors do that. And if you are nice only to your friends, you are no better than other people. Even those who don't know God are nice to their friends. So you must be perfect, just as your Father in heaven is perfect.

THOUGHT

By loving our enemies we put differences aside and choose to work towards God's perfection. There will be times when we love people who don't love us back, and that's actually amazing, because we get to show the world the way God loves. You get to carry with you the undying and all-inclusive love of God for everyone - especially those who aren't easy to love.

ACTION

How can you show love to your enemy today?

DAY 03
GIVING TO THE NEEDY

MATTHEW 6:1-4 NLV

Be sure you do not do good things in front of others just to be seen by them. If you do, you have no reward from your Father in heaven. When you give to the poor, do not be as those who pretend to be someone they are not. They blow a horn in the places of worship and in the streets so people may respect them. For sure, I tell you, they have all the reward they are going to get. When you give, do not let your left hand know what your right hand gives. Your giving should be in secret. Then your Father who sees in secret will reward you.

THOUGHT

When helping those in need, we should operate in humility, not expecting praise or reward for our actions, because God will reward us in His perfect timing. However, it can be reward enough just seeing how much of a change you make to the world around you by doing God's work and spreading His love. Go around doing good just for the sake of it - God loves a cheerful giver!

ACTION

Take time today to help another person and keep it a secret between you and God.

DAY 04
PRAYER

MATTHEW 6:5-14 NIV

But when you pray, go into your room, close the door and pray to your Father, who is unseen. Then your Father, who sees what is done in secret, will reward you. This, then, is how you should pray: "Our Father in heaven, hallowed be your name, your kingdom come, your will be done, on earth as it is in heaven. Give us today our daily bread. And forgive us our debts, as we also have forgiven our debtors. And lead us not into temptation, but deliver us from the evil one." For if you forgive other people when they sin against you, your heavenly Father will also forgive you.

THOUGHT

The length of your prayers doesn't matter. God will always cherish the time you spend with Him because while you pray, you speak to Him and get to know Him more. Prayer is such an essential part of our growing relationship with God that the Word encourages us to pray constantly (1 Thessalonians 5:17). You can speak to God about absolutely anything, but if you don't know where to start, this Scripture gives us the perfect guidelines. Go to God in private, honour Him, thank Him and talk to Him about what you need.

ACTION

Try to pray the Lord's prayer from the Scripture above in your own words.

DAY 05

FASTING

MATTHEW 6:16-18 NCV

When you fast, don't put on a sad face like the hypocrites. They make their faces look sad to show people they are fasting. I tell you the truth, those hypocrites already have their full reward. So when you fast, comb your hair and wash your face. Then people will not know that you are fasting, but your Father, whom you cannot see, will see you. Your Father sees what is done in secret, and he will reward you.

THOUGHT

Fasting is something we do personally for God, of our own accord. The goal of our actions and sacrifice is to seek Him alone! Fasting is a powerful tool for breakthrough and healing; God will honour and reward you for your sacrifice in secret. So next time you fast, take this passage into consideration. Take the time to enjoy the intimacy you can experience with God at this time.

ACTION

If it is safe for you to do so, try to fast food for a period of time (maybe a day) this week and spend time in prayer with God. If you are unable to give up food, try to fast something else like social media.

DAY 06

TREASURES IN HEAVEN

MATTHEW 6:19-24 NCV

Don't store treasures for yourselves here on earth where moths and rust will destroy them and thieves can break in and steal them. But store your treasures in heaven where they cannot be destroyed by moths or rust and where thieves cannot break in and steal them. Your heart will be where your treasure is. The eye is a light for the body. If your eyes are good, your whole body will be full of light. But if your eyes are evil, your whole body will be full of darkness. And if the only light you have is really darkness, then you have the worst darkness. No one can serve two masters. The person will hate one master and love the other, or will follow one master and refuse to follow the other. You cannot serve both God and worldly riches.

THOUGHT

You cannot serve both God and worldly riches. You cannot take money or possessions or any kind of wealth to heaven with you. Nothing on this earth is comparable with the value of what God has for us in heaven. Living a life with a mindset in which God is your utmost priority will be the most rewarding thing you can ever do. The only things we'll have with us in heaven are the people in our lives who follow Jesus.

ACTION

What can you do today to serve God?

DAY 07
DO NOT WORRY

MATTHEW 6:25-34 ESV

Therefore I tell you, do not be anxious about your life, what you will eat or what you will drink, nor about your body, what you will put on. Is not life more than food, and the body more than clothing? Look at the birds of the air: they neither sow nor reap nor gather into barns, and yet your heavenly Father feeds them. Are you not of more value than they? And which of you by being anxious can add a single hour to his span of life? And why are you anxious about clothing? Consider the lilies of the field, how they grow: they neither toil nor spin, yet I tell you, even Solomon in all his glory was not arrayed like one of these. But if God so clothes the grass of the field, which today is alive and tomorrow is thrown into the oven, will he not much more clothe you, O you of little faith? Therefore do not be anxious, saying, "What shall we eat?" or "What shall we drink?" or "What shall we wear?" For the Gentiles seek after all these things, and your heavenly Father knows that you need them all. But seek first the kingdom of God and his righteousness, and all these things will be added to you. Therefore do not be anxious about tomorrow, for tomorrow will be anxious for itself. Sufficient for the day is its own trouble.

THOUGHT

You can have full trust in God as He is the creator and author of your life.. He wouldn't put you through obstacles you cannot cope with as He has knows what is, what was and what is to come. Worrying is like a rocking horse - it gives you something to do but gets you nowhere. It is a great relief to know that God didn't design us to worry but instead to live in His peace.

ACTION

How has God helped you overcome your over-thinking?

DAY 01
JUDGING OTHERS

MATTHEW 7:1-6 TPT

"Refuse to be a critic full of bias toward others, and judgment will not be passed on you. For you'll be judged by the same standard that you've used to judge others. The measurement you use on them will be used on you. Why would you focus on the flaw in someone else's life and yet fail to notice the glaring flaws of your own? How could you say to your friend, 'Let me show you where you're wrong,' when you're guilty of even more? You're being hypercritical and a hypocrite! First acknowledge your own 'blind spots' and deal with them, and then you'll be capable of dealing with the 'blind spot' of your friend. Who would hang earrings on a dog's ear or throw pearls in front of wild pigs? They'll only trample them under their feet and then turn around and tear you to pieces!"

THOUGHT

Jesus is just as practical as He is spiritual. We can see from this Scripture that Jesus understands what it is to be human, and how judgement can so easily block our vision. He knows that we will tend to want to pick on the bits of sin in other people's lives before we clear out our own. God wants us to have 'clear vision' in order to fully see Him and the world He has put us in.

ACTION

Ask God if there is any 'blind spot' in your eye currently and what it would look like to remove it.

DAY 02
ASK, SEEK, KNOCK

MATTHEW 7:7-12 NIV

Ask and it will be given to you; seek and you will find; knock and the door will be opened to you. For everyone who asks receives; the one who seeks finds; and to the one who knocks, the door will be opened. Which of you, if your son asks for bread, will give him a stone? Or if he asks for a fish, will give him a snake? If you, then, though you are evil, know how to give good gifts to your children, how much more will your Father in heaven give good gifts to those who ask him! So in everything, do to others what you would have them do to you, for this sums up the Law and the Prophets.

THOUGHT

In Scripture, Jesus tells us how we can find what we're looking for and receive what we ask for. The blessings God has for us are absolutely abundant! The Bible says that He owns the cattle on a thousand hills, that He stores up resource and blessings in heaven - His goodness will never run out! No one can own more than God does and He wants to bless His children who ask Him! Have the courage to ask, seek and knock - continue to seek the blessings of God.

ACTION

If there is something you are in need of? Pray and ask God for what you need.

DAY 03
THE NARROW & WIDE GATES

MATTHEW 7:13-14 NIV

Enter through the narrow gate. For wide is the gate and broad is the road that leads to destruction, and many enter through it. But small is the gate and narrow the road that leads to life, and only a few find it.

THOUGHT

We have a choice of which path to follow. Pursuing God in the short term can be difficult at times and seem like the unpopular choice, and that is exactly what it is. The 'narrow road' of following God is what brings us to the fullness of life in the long run! The wide gate and broad road is the road of life without God - it may seem easy and popular in the short term but we know that it ultimately leads to destruction in the end. Let us persevere through difficulty to live a life with God! It is always better than life without Him.

ACTION

Ask God for strength today to continue to follow Him on the narrow road to life.

DAY 04
TRUE & FALSE PROPHETS

MATTHEW 7:15-20 NCV

"Be careful of false prophets. They come to you looking gentle like sheep, but they are really dangerous like wolves. You will know these people by what they do. Grapes don't come from thornbushes, and figs don't come from thorny weeds. In the same way, every good tree produces good fruit, but a bad tree produces bad fruit. A good tree cannot produce bad fruit, and a bad tree cannot produce good fruit. Every tree that does not produce good fruit is cut down and thrown into the fire. In the same way, you will know these false prophets by what they do."

THOUGHT

When Jesus is in our hearts we can see Him outworked in our lives. If someone's life is displaying what is 'good' fruit - love, joy, peace, patience, kindness, goodness, faithfulness, gentleness and self-control - we can know they are being fed by the ultimate good source. Similarly we can also see that when people are producing the opposite of these fruit, that their source is from the enemy. Jesus here gives us a fool-proof system for knowing who is His and who is not. We can look at what fruit is being produced in our heart and in the hearts of those we surround ourselves with.

ACTION

Think of the people who are the biggest influences in your life. What sort of fruit do you see from their life?

DAY 05

TRUE & FALSE DISCIPLES

MATTHEW 7:21-23 NIV

"Not everyone who says to me, 'Lord, Lord,' will enter the kingdom of heaven, but only the one who does the will of my Father who is in heaven. Many will say to me on that day, 'Lord, Lord, did we not prophesy in your name and in your name drive out demons and in your name perform many miracles?' then I will tell them plainly, 'I never knew you. Away from me, you evildoers!'"

THOUGHT

This is maybe one of the hardest passages in the Bible to process. We are called to do God's will, not our own. This teaches us that our faith isn't only in claiming we know God and doing what we want in His name, but it is being active in asking God what His will is for us and living in a way that fulfils it. We know that when we confess with our mouth and believe in our hearts that Jesus is Lord and that He was raised from the dead, we are saved (Romans 10:9). This passage is not negating our salvation but challenging the way in which we live it out. Knowing Jesus and operating out of a relationship with Him is the most important thing we can do.

ACTION

Spend time today meeting with God, talking with Him and learning about His will.

DAY 06

WISE & FOOLISH BUILDERS

MATTHEW 7:24-27 TPT

Everyone who hears my teaching and applies it to his life can be compared to a wise man who built his house on an unshakable foundation. When the rains fell and the flood came, with fierce winds beating upon his house, it stood firm because of its strong foundation. But everyone who hears my teaching and does not apply it to his life can be compared to a foolish man who built his house on sand. When it rained and rained and the flood came, with wind and waves beating upon his house, it collapsed and was swept away.

THOUGHT

We know that troubles are going to come in our lives. Things will try to beat us down and break us. But we also know that we have a God who offers us His strong foundation so that these hard times don't destroy us. The Word of God is intended to be lived out, not just heard. It is where our strength comes from. When we are obedient to His Word through our actions, our foundation is built on our rock which is God.

ACTION

What can you do to be a wise builder today that will help you in the storms of the future?

DAY 07

THE COST OF FOLLOWING JESUS

MATTHEW 8:18-22 ESV

Now when Jesus saw a crowd around him, he gave orders to go over to the other side. And a scribe came up and said to him, "Teacher, I will follow you wherever you go." And Jesus said to him, "Foxes have holes, and birds of the air have nests, but the Son of Man has nowhere to lay his head." Another of the disciples said to him, "Lord, let me first go and bury my father." And Jesus said to him, "Follow me, and leave the dead to bury their own dead."

THOUGHT

Being a disciple of God is a serious commitment as He is not confined to one location and can call us anywhere. Making a personal decision to follow Him says that we are willing to follow Him no matter the cost. This is why we see people travelling all over the world to third world countries, across borders and overseas to follow the call of God. They have seen and understood that God needs them in places that they might not call 'home'. What we can rest assured in as followers of Christ is that we find our true home in the house of God.

ACTION

What does 'home' mean for you? How can you find this is Jesus?

MODULE 08
HEROES OF FAITH

Would you believe me if I told you that an adulterer, a cheater, a drunk, a murderer, a gossiper, a worrier, a doubter, someone struggling with anger issues, someone dealing with mental health issues and someone with a speech problem are the people who are listed as the "heroes" throughout the bible? Probably not, but that's exactly who they are! They were typical, ordinary, everyday humans like you and I. What made their lives so extraordinary, that thousands of years later we are still reading and talking about them, weren't any super powers or magic potions. They struggled in areas of their lives identical to what we struggle with today. What made these "Heroes" so heroic was a simple (and in some cases tiny) thing called FAITH.

When we read the bible, we read the stories of different men and women, who throughout the most difficult circumstances and conditions, would put their trust in God and see how a life with Him would turn their world upside down. They trusted God in the "you're going to have a baby at the age of 100" kind of craziness, and believed in the miracle working power of God even past death (hello Lazarus). They had the faith to go God's paths even when they led them into the wilderness instead of the promised land, or into hiding instead of the throne. They trusted God in the persecution and in the prison walls, that there was purpose in every step of the journey, and saw it through to completion. They have been the forerunner of our faith and are role models for us today.

Over the next three weeks, we want to take a closer look at some of these heroes and learn from their lives how we can tap into the faith inside of ourselves in order to move mountains.

WEEK 26 | HEROES OF FAITH

DAY 01
ABEL

HEBREWS 11:1-4 (BELOW) & GENESIS 4:1-16 NIV

Now faith is confidence in what we hope for and assurance about what we do not see. This is what the ancients were commended for. By faith we understand that the universe was formed at God's command, so that what is seen was not made out of what is visible. By faith Abel brought God a better offering than Cain did. By faith he was commended as righteous, when God spoke well of his offerings. And by faith Abel still speaks, even though he is dead.

THOUGHT

God looks at the heart not the offering (Jeremiah 17:10, 2 Corinthians 9:7) and we know that Abel, from the place of a pure heart, brought before God his most excellent offering. We should humbly live for the praise of God, not for our own praise or to lift ourselves high. Abel had faith that giving his best to God was the best option, that putting God first is the most excellent choice - and he was right!

ACTION

How can you keep your life pure? (Hint: Psalm 119:9)

DAY 02

ENOCH

HEBREWS 11:5-6 (BELOW) & GENESIS 5:21-24 NIV

By faith Enoch was taken from this life, so that he did not experience death: "He could not be found, because God had taken him away." For before he was taken, he was commended as one who pleased God. And without faith it is impossible to please God, because anyone who comes to him must believe that he exists and that he rewards those who earnestly seek him.

THOUGHT

If we're to please God we must firstly believe that He exists! Secondly, we must believe that those who seek Him will be rewarded (at the appointed time) because He is a God of abundance. The faith of these Old Testament heroes was effective in gaining them a relationship with God because of the future death and resurrection of Jesus. God had a plan and He knew it would come about. We know today that because of the sacrifice Jesus made on the cross we are also able to experience everlasting life in heaven. But because of his faith, Enoch was taken straight from this life to everlasting life!

ACTION

Think about the best reward you've ever been given for your actions, and celebrate because God's reward for you is infinitely greater!

DAY 03

NOAH

HEBREWS 11:7 (BELOW) & GENESIS 6:1 – 9:17 NIV

By faith Noah, when warned about things not yet seen, in holy fear built an ark to save his family. By his faith he condemned the world and became heir of the righteousness that is in keeping with faith.

THOUGHT

We all need to be more like Noah. He had the confidence that God would be good to him and his family no matter what. Even as a mighty and dangerous storm approached, Noah stood in the confidence of God. While Noah was on the boat for more than a year during the flood, he trusted God and waited on Him for the go ahead to return to 'normal' life. While the promise was still unseen, Noah believed that God would come through just as He always had.

ACTION

Hebrews 11 talks about faith in the unseen. What makes it difficult for you to believe in the goodness of God when things are difficult? How can you be more like Noah in this situation?

DAY 04

ABRAHAM PT. 1

HEBREWS 11:8-10 (BELOW), GENESIS 12:1-9 & GENESIS 17:1-8

By faith Abraham, when called to go to a place he would later receive as his inheritance, obeyed and went, even though he did not know where he was going. By faith he made his home in the promised land like a stranger in a foreign country; he lived in tents, as did Isaac and Jacob, who were heirs with him of the same promise. For he was looking forward to the city with foundations, whose architect and builder is God.

THOUGHT

Abraham didn't know where his obedience would take him, yet he followed the voice of God through the unknown into the promised land. We have the assurance today that our promised land is heaven and know that is what we are moving towards. Let's live lives of obedience to God, just as Abraham did, looking forward to the place where the 'architect and builder is God'. Abraham's life is an example we should follow.

ACTION

What is the current uncharted territory in your life that God is calling you into?

DAY 05

ABRAHAM PT. 2

HEBREWS 11:17-19 (BELOW) & GENESIS 22:1-19

By faith Abraham, when God tested him, offered Isaac as a sacrifice. He who had embraced the promises was about to sacrifice his one and only son, even though God had said to him, "It is through Isaac that your offspring will be reckoned." Abraham reasoned that God could even raise the dead, and so in a manner of speaking he did receive Isaac back from death.

THOUGHT

We may not always understand the process that God takes us through, but in having faith we must give to God what we treasure the most. God is always faithful. Abraham is an example to us of how valuable our relationship with God is. It may seem extreme to trust in God so much that you would give even your own children over to Him, but in all we do, we must know that God is faithful. When we have the assurance of what God's will is in what He is asking us to do, let nothing stand in the way of that.

ACTION

What do you think it says to the people around you when you give something up because you want to obey God?

DAY 06

SARAH

HEBREWS 11:11-12 (BELOW), GENESIS 18:1-15 & GENESIS 21:1-8

And by faith even Sarah, who was past childbearing age, was enabled to bear children because she considered him faithful who had made the promise. And so from this one man, and he as good as dead, came descendants as numerous as the stars in the sky and as countless as the sand on the seashore.

THOUGHT

Do you think God is faithful and good in all that He does? Sarah had faith for what was unseen and seemed impossible. This situation is very applicable to our lives because while Sarah found the idea of bearing children so ridiculous that she laughed at the promise (Genesis 18:12), she knew that God - who made the promise - was faithful. God can call out promises in our lives that can seem straight up ridiculous but we just need to rest assured that He who promised is faithful to fulfill that promise.

ACTION

Take time to think and reflect on the faithfulness of God and what that means for your future.

DAY 07

WHAT FAITH LOOKS LIKE

HEBREWS 11:13-16 NIV

All these people were still living by faith when they died. They did not receive the things promised; they only saw them and welcomed them from a distance, admitting that they were foreigners and strangers on earth. People who say such things show that they are looking for a country of their own. If they had been thinking of the country they had left, they would have had opportunity to return. Instead, they were longing for a better country - a heavenly one. Therefore God is not ashamed to be called their God, for he has prepared a city for them.

THOUGHT

Faith is having confidence in what God has promised but may not yet be seen. We look upwards and have confidence that heaven awaits. All of the people we have looked at this week lived lives of faith are examples of what solid assurance in God looks like. These people placed their hope in God even before they saw or knew the promise to come. We have the blessing of knowing our eternal promise because of Jesus, so let's live lives that are honouring to that.

ACTION

How does the thought of being with God in heaven forever make you feel, and how does that affect the way you live your day to day life?

DAY 01

ISAAC

HEBREWS 11:20 (BELOW) & GENESIS 27:1-40

By faith Isaac blessed Jacob and Esau in regard to their future.

THOUGHT

There are times in life when things don't happen the way we intend them to. Isaac's intention was to bless Esau as he was the first born. When he was deceived by Jacob he had a decision to make: was he going to get angry and try and fix it in his own ability? Or was he going to trust God with what was ahead for both of his sons, even if it wasn't his original plan? Isaac chose to trust God beyond his circumstances. When things don't happen the way we planned them, instead of getting frustrated, we should try to make our first response to turn to God and trust Him with what comes next. He works all things together for good (Romans 8:28).

ACTION

What is your response when things don't happen the way you have planned?

DAY 02

JACOB

HEBREWS 11:21 (BELOW) & GENESIS 48:1-22

By faith Jacob, when he was dying, blessed each of Joseph's sons, and worshiped as he leaned on the top of his staff.

THOUGHT

Our words have power. They have the ability to create and impact those around us. When Jacob blessed Joseph's sons, he did so in partnership and relationship with God. When we partner with God and listen to what He wants to say in and through us, we open up our lives to the 'more' that God has for us. Even at the very end of Jacob's life, God had more for him. Jacob's blessing was not going to end with his life but continue on. God wanted him to be a part of speaking life and promise over the next generation. By being available and willing to partner with God to use our voice to speak encouragement and purpose over others, there is no end to what God will do in and through our lives.

ACTION

Take some time today and ask God if He has a word of encouragement for someone around you.

DAY 03

JOSEPH

HEBREWS 11:22 NIV

By faith Joseph, when his end was near, spoke about the exodus of the Israelites from Egypt and gave instructions concerning the burial of his bones.

GENESIS 50:22-25 NIV

Joseph stayed in Egypt, along with all his father's family… Joseph said to his brothers, "I am about to die. But God will surely come to your aid and take you up out of this land to the land he promised on oath to Abraham, Isaac and Jacob." And Joseph made the Israelites swear an oath and said, "God will surely come to your aid, and then you must carry my bones up from this place."

THOUGHT

Throughout Joseph's life he stayed faithful to God no matter what his circumstances looked like. Despite everything that happened in his past, through his belief and trust in God, Jacob's relationship with his family was restored and he was able to become a source of encouragement to them. Even at the end of his life, Joseph spoke in faith and prophesied over their future. We too can encourage those around us. The words we speak are powerful and have the ability to affect the atmosphere around us.

ACTION

Think about moments in your life when you have needed to speak out in faith. What happened?

DAY 04

MOSES

HEBREWS 11:13-16 NIV

By faith Moses' parents hid him for three months after he was born, because they saw he was no ordinary child, and they were not afraid of the king's edict.

NUMBERS 12:3-8 NIV

(Now Moses was a very humble man, more humble than anyone else on the face of the earth.) At once the Lord said to Moses, Aaron and Miriam, "Come out to the tent of meeting, all three of you." So the three of them went out. Then the Lord came down in a pillar of cloud; he stood at the entrance to the tent and summoned Aaron and Miriam. When the two of them stepped forward, he said, "Listen to my words: "When there is a prophet among you, I, the Lord, reveal myself to them in visions, I speak to them in dreams. But this is not true of my servant Moses; he is faithful in all my house. With him I speak face to face, clearly and not in riddles; he sees the form of the Lord. Why then were you not afraid to speak against my servant Moses?"

DAY 04

THOUGHT

From the very beginning of Moses' life, God had a purpose and plan for him. Like many of us, Moses made some wrong decisions along the way, but despite it all he came to the understanding that God's plan was bigger than any mistake he could ever make. This resulted in him having a relationship with God which not only changed his life but the lives of millions of Isralites. Moses overcame fear, and with humility and faithfulness to God's promise, paved the way for generations to come. Like Moses, God has a purpose and plan for our lives. So be intentional and spend time in His presence, listening out for His voice. If we only knew the full plans God had for our lives, we'd be amazed!

ACTION

Can you think of moments when you have spent purposeful time with God? Did He reveal something to you?

DAY 05

RAHAB

HEBREWS 11:31 (BELOW) & JOSHUA 2:1-24 & 6:21-25

By faith the prostitute Rahab, because she welcomed the spies, was not killed with those who were disobedient.

THOUGHT

Rahab showed us how a simple act of obedience and faith in God has a significant impact on our lives and the lives of those around us. By welcoming God's people into her home, despite the risk to her own life, she not only saved her life but her family's also. Rahab didn't allow fear to get in the way of the kindness she freely gave toward God's people, and in turn played an important part in the plan God had for humanity. Don't underestimate the power of kindness. Through faith in God our actions, big or small, are significant and can have an impact far greater than we can imagine.

ACTION

Take time to reflect on ways you have and can continue to honour your fellow believers.

DAY 06

DEBORAH

HEBREWS 11:32 (BELOW) & JUDGES 4:1-5:31

And what more shall I say? I do not have time to tell about Gideon, Barak, Samson and Jephthah, about David and Samuel and the prophets.

THOUGHT

Both Deborah and Barak showed great faith in God when they risked everything by walking into battle based purely on the promise of victory God had given them. They had such trust in who God was and what He had promised them that they were able to take action and follow His instruction, even before being able to see the miracle that was ahead. Sometimes God gives us promises that we can be afraid to pursue because of how impossible they may seem. Our God is the God of the impossible and doesn't break His promises. Sometimes all it takes is for us to take a risk and step out in faith towards what seems impossible so we are able to walk into the miracle He has for us.

ACTION

Has there been a time when you have seen God do something that seemed impossible? What did that look like?

DAY 07

GIDEON

HEBREWS 11:32 (BELOW) & JUDGES 6:1-8:33

And what more shall I say? I do not have time to tell about Gideon, Barak, Samson and Jephthah, about David and Samuel and the prophets.

THOUGHT

Through the story of Gideon we see how there can be times when God asks us to do things that don't always make sense to us. When God told Gideon to keep reducing the amount of men in his army, it would have been easy for him to have questioned God and not followed His instructions. Through the eyes of the world, having less men to fight would have decreased the chance of victory, not increased it, but God does not work as the world does, and Gideon knew that. Gideon was able to trust God and follow Him into the promise, even if he didn't understand everything God was doing. If there is something we know God is doing in our lives that doesn't make sense, we can try looking at it through His eyes and not the world's. Trusting God in the confusion can be hard sometimes, but He is always faithful to His promises.

ACTION

Can you think of an area where you are finding it hard to trust God completely? Why do you think this is?

DAY 01

JEPHTHAH

HEBREWS 11:32 (BELOW) & JUDGES 10:6 -12:8

And what more shall I say? I do not have time to tell about Gideon, Barak, Samson and Jephthah, about David and Samuel and the prophets.

THOUGHT

In Jepthah's story we see someone who was not defined by his ancestry (his mother was a prostitute) but by his God. Jepthah's family even pushed him away and denied him of his inheritance until it came to the point that they needed his leadership. In everything he did, Jepthah honoured his commitment to God and understood his place as a child of God, not defined by his family. An oath to God cost Jepthah the life of his only child, yet he continued to serve God faithfully. We know that we are adopted into God's family and so we can live a life free from the definitions of success from our natural families.

ACTION

Jepthah's family could have held him back but instead God elevated him. Are there areas in your life that you need to align yourself with what God says about you rather than what your family says?

DAY 02

SAMSON

HEBREWS 11:32 (BELOW) & JUDGES 13:1-16:31

And what more shall I say? I do not have time to tell about Gideon, Barak, Samson and Jephthah, about David and Samuel and the prophets.

THOUGHT

Samson's life had God-purpose from the start. He was born to his mother out of her barrenness and used his strength for God his whole life. Even though Samson messed up to the point of God leaving him (Judges 16:20), he still fulfilled his purpose and honoured God - even in his death. Samson knew his purpose, he knew what God had called him to do and what that would cost him. In our lives we may step away from God because of the temptations of this world. But we can rest in the knowledge that just like Samson, it is never too late to rely on God and fulfill all He called us to do.

ACTION

Is there a negative situation happening in your life? Dedicate it to God and watch what He can do through it.

DAY 03

SAMUEL

HEBREWS 11:32 & 1 SAMUEL 1:1 – 25:1
& 1 SAMUEL 3:10 NIV (BELOW)

The Lord came and stood there, calling as at the other times, "Samuel! Samuel!" Then Samuel said, " Speak, for your servant is listening."

THOUGHT

"Speak Lord, for your servant is listening". These words defined the way Samuel lived out his life. Samuel did so much in his lifetime in association with the royalty in Israel. He anointed kings and rebuked them. Samuel held so much power in Israel but what he did was always for the glory of God and in line with God's voice, never to elevate himself. We can rest in the knowledge that no matter how wise we may be, God's wisdom is always better. Samuel could have relied on his own strength (just as Saul did, which didn't end well) but instead he relied fully on God. He boldly spoke up for God when those around him weren't listening to God's voice.

ACTION

Think about a decision you need to make, and ask God for His guidance. Move forward in accordance to what God says (through words, impressions and senses, tested to be in line with God's Word).

DAY 04

DAVID

HEBREWS 11:32 & 1 SAMUEL 16:1 (BELOW)
& 2 SAMUEL & 1 KINGS 2:11

The Lord said to Samuel, "How long will you mourn for Saul, since I have rejected him as king over Israel? Fill your horn with oil and be on your way; I am sending you to Jesse of Bethlehem. I have chosen one of his sons to be king."

THOUGHT

David's story is seen from beginning to end in the Bible - from being chosen at a young age, defeating giants through the will of God, becoming king, being gracious with Saul - the man out to kill him, sinning, mourning, all the way to fining redemption. David was a man of humility, honour & respect for God, yet he was still brought down by his sinful, human nature. David was potentially the greatest king Israel ever had and was known as a man after God's own heart. It is amazing that God chose to use David in the lineage of Jesus knowing he would fail. We can follow David's example of seeking after God's own heart and knowing that even through our failures we cannot negate God's plans.

ACTION

Take a look at David's life and thank God that no matter where you come from or how you mess up, you can still be part of His plan

DANIEL

DANIEL 1:1 – 12:13 & DANIEL 3:17–18 NIV (BELOW)

If we are thrown into the blazing furnace, the God we serve is able to deliver us from it, and he will deliver us from Your Majesty's hand. But even if he does not, we want you to know, Your Majesty, that we will not serve your gods or worship the image of gold you have set up.

THOUGHT

Daniel stood for God against his culture all of his life. Daniel even risked death multiple times, certain that God would come through and save him. Knowing that God's power and love stood FAR above everything else never failed him. From blazing furnaces to a lion's den God protected Daniel and honoured him for his faithfulness. Standing for God, honouring Him and continuing to believe in Him may be totally against what the world around us says to do but God can and will blow our minds with His faithfulness.

ACTION

Has there been a time in your life that you have had to stand against your culture in order to stand for God? What did that look like?

THROW OFF RESISTANCE & SIN – PERSEVERE

HEBREWS 12:1 NIV

Therefore, since we are surrounded by such a great cloud of witnesses, let us throw off everything that hinders and the sin that so easily entangles. And let us run with perseverance the race marked out for us.

THOUGHT

Take 'this great cloud of witnesses' as the heroes of the faith we have been reading about. Use them as inspiration and assurance that throwing off the unnecessary stuff and running towards our salvation is the best thing to do. Live life according to the example of these people, but most importantly by the example of Jesus with everything! And in this race - keep on going, persevere! Noah was 600 years old when he got on the ark, God is faithful through all of our lives.

ACTION

What can you see in your life is holding you back & entangling you? Ask God what it would look like to throw that off.

DAY 07

JESUS THE ULTIMATE EXAMPLE

HEBREWS 12:2-3 NIV

Fixing our eyes on Jesus, the pioneer and perfecter of faith. For the joy set before him he endured the cross, scorning its shame, and sat down at the right hand of the throne of God. Consider him who endured such opposition from sinners, so that you will not grow weary and lose heart.

THOUGHT

Of all the heroes of our faith, Jesus is the greatest. In every single part of what He did an example was set to us for how our lives should be lived. We can look to Jesus as our inspiration for endurance, faith, joy & a life completely surrendered to God's will. Jesus experienced all of the emotions and temptations that we do today. He knows what it is to be human and to live a life in surrender to God - we can run to Him in any and every situation.

ACTION

Can you name some of Jesus' character attributes that you would want to have more of in your life?

MODULE 09
JESUS' MISSION

"Operation Overlord" was the initial codename for the Battle of Normandy, where the Allied forces launched the successful invasion of German-occupied Western Europe during World War II, on the 6th of June 1944.
The success of that mission would be the beginning of the end to the terror.

Every mission has a codename. There are many famous examples to be found in history. Jesus left this earth with a mission for us, that we follow His way and this mission's code word is plain and simple: GO.
In Matthew 28:18-19 it says "All authority in heaven and on earth has been given to me. Therefore GO...". It seems so simple yet we often do the opposite of what Jesus said. Instead of us "going" to the people, we do everything so that people "come" to us. The success of Jesus' mission truly depends on our "GOING". History has many examples of victories, breakthroughs, and success stories because people started to "go" and do something about it. It's time to GO, out of your comfort zone, into the darkness, the terror, the unknown, the evil (basically into enemy land, behind enemy lines) and invade the darkness with Jesus.

Let's take the next few weeks to look at what Jesus instructs us to go and do, and use the time to ask ourselves the question: The mission is clear, will you GO?

WEEK 29 | MAKING DISCIPLES

DAY 01
NOT TO BE SERVED, BUT TO SERVE

MARK 10:42-45 NCV

Jesus called them together and said, "The other nations have rulers. You know that those rulers love to show their power over the people, and their important leaders love to use all their authority. But it should not be that way among you. Whoever wants to become great among you must serve the rest of you like a servant. Whoever wants to become the first among you must serve all of you like a slave. In the same way, the Son of Man did not come to be served. He came to serve others and to give his life as a ransom for many people."

THOUGHT

Jesus does not have a problem with authority itself, authority is fine, but how authority is used is what Jesus is concerned with. No matter what position we are in, the job is to serve others! He is our ultimate example in how we lead and work with others - as it says in the scripture; He did not come to be served but to serve others. Let's examine the way we lead people (whether you believe you are a leader or not) and ensure that we are serving them while we serve Jesus.

ACTION

In what way can you switch from leading or managing someone to serving them as Jesus did?

DAY 02

ONLY DO WHAT I SEE THE FATHER GOD DOING

JOHN 5:19-20 NIV

Jesus gave them this answer: "Very truly I tell you, the Son can do nothing by himself; he can do only what he sees his Father doing, because whatever the Father does the Son also does. For the Father loves the Son and shows him all he does. Yes, and he will show him even greater works than these, so that you will be amazed."

THOUGHT

Jesus' answer here was in response to the Jewish leaders being unhappy with Him claiming equality with God. Jesus' answer in other words is: everything I do reflects the nature of God. In the same way we should live our lives so that our actions point others towards the nature of God. Jesus lived fully in accordance to the instructions of God and did not operate outside His will, just as we should live our lives in alignment with God.

ACTION

In what way can you copy the actions of Jesus in your life today?

DAY 03

LIFE IN ITS FULLNESS

JOHN 10:10 TPT

A thief has only one thing in mind—he wants to steal, slaughter, and destroy. But I have come to give you everything in abundance, more than you expect—life in its fullness until you overflow!

THOUGHT

The world has its own version of 'life to the full' which in reality is just a bunch of smoke and mirrors that ultimately lead to a dead end. This is the enemy's plan - to steal kill & destroy us & our fruitfulness. The life that Jesus brings is eternal! It lasts forever! As we live in the knowledge of life eternal and life in abundance through Jesus, we can become an example of this to everyone around us. It brings peace to know that God has chosen to give us life that is full in all the right ways!

ACTION

What areas in your life is the enemy stealing, killing and destroying? Ask Jesus to enter these areas and bring them to fullness.

DAY 04

LEAVING THE OLD LIFE TO FOLLOW JESUS

LUKE 5:1–11 NIV

… When he had finished speaking, he said to Simon, "Put out into deep water, and let down the nets for a catch." Simon answered, "Master, we've worked hard all night and haven't caught anything. But because you say so, I will let down the nets." When they had done so, they caught such a large number of fish that their nets began to break. So they signaled their partners in the other boat to come and help them, and they came and filled both boats so full that they began to sink. When Simon Peter saw this, he fell at Jesus' knees and said, "Go away from me, Lord; I am a sinful man!" … Then Jesus said to Simon, "Don't be afraid; from now on you will fish for people." So they pulled their boats up on shore, left everything and followed him.

THOUGHT

How great is Jesus! Simon had been working all night and caught nothing. But as soon as he partners with Jesus, he receives a catch that even his boat can't contain! Following Jesus is never easy but it is exciting. It's filled with moments like these - moments where we've been trying with all our strength to achieve something on our own and then all of a sudden Jesus partners with us and we've got more blessings that we can count!

ACTION

Are there any old ways you'd like to give up to Jesus in order to follow him?

DAY 05

BEING DISCIPLES

JOHN 15:8-16 (NLT)

"When you produce much fruit, you are my true disciples. This brings great glory to my Father. I have loved you even as the Father has loved me. Remain in my love. When you obey my commandments, you remain in my love, just as I obey my Father's commandments and remain in his love. I have told you these things so that you will be filled with my joy. Yes, your joy will overflow! This is my commandment: Love each other in the same way I have loved you. There is no greater love than to lay down one's life for one's friends. You are my friends if you do what I command. I no longer call you slaves, because a master doesn't confide in his slaves. Now you are my friends, since I have told you everything the Father told me. You didn't choose me. I chose you. I appointed you to go and produce lasting fruit, so that the Father will give you whatever you ask for, using my name."

THOUGHT

To be a disciple of Jesus means to act as He would, in love. Whatever situation you're in, whatever circumstance life finds you in, ask: what would Jesus do? We can see from this scripture that following Jesus looks like this: remaining with Him, keeping His commands, being filled with joy, loving one another & bearing fruit. A life with Jesus is one in abundance - He does not want you to live a boring life but one that will fulfill you & fulfill God's will.

ACTION

Take time to reflect on what being God's disciple has looked like in your life.

DAY 06

MAKING DISCIPLES

MATTHEW 28:16-20 NIV

Then the eleven disciples left for Galilee, going to the mountain where Jesus had told them to go. When they saw him, they worshiped him—but some of them doubted! Jesus came and told his disciples, "I have been given all authority in heaven and on earth. Therefore, go and make disciples of all the nations, baptizing them in the name of the Father and the Son and the Holy Spirit. Teach these new disciples to obey all the commands I have given you. And be sure of this: I am with you always, even to the end of the age.

THOUGHT

Before Jesus tells the disciples what to do, He intentionally says 'I have been given all authority in heaven and on earth' Therefore we don't have to be afraid about what Jesus tells us to do because we have the authority to act it out. This is the great commission - the call and purpose of every Christ follower, to go and make disciples! We are called to reach people, to baptize them & to teach them what Jesus commands. He also attaches a promise to this call, that He will be with us always - to the very end of the age! We can live in the knowledge that we do not have to do this alone because Jesus is with us.

ACTION

What way can you practically live out the great commission today?

DAY 07

MINISTERING TO THOSE IN NEED

LUKE 4:18-19 NIV

"The Spirit of the Lord is on me, because he has anointed me to proclaim good news to the poor. He has sent me to proclaim freedom for the prisoners and recovery of sight for the blind, to set the oppressed free, to proclaim the year of the Lord's favor."

THOUGHT

It is important for us to recognise what being a disciple of Jesus represents. All of these things are only able to be done in partnership with God; proclaiming good news to the poor, bringing freedom to prisoners, recovering the sight of the blind and setting the oppressed free. The very start of this verse writes that 'The Spirit of the Lord is on me', this means that we can do all of these things through the Spirit of God - for He is with us! His promises never fail and as His hands and feet on this Earth, we need to continue to outwork His justice.

ACTION

How would knowing you have the Spirit of God on you allow you to be able to walk out God's will in more confidence?

DAY 01

THEY FOLLOWED HIM

MATTHEW 9:9 NIV

As Jesus was walking along He saw a man named Matthew sitting at his tax collector's booth. "Follow me and be my disciple," Jesus said to him. So Matthew got up and followed him.

THOUGHT

In Jesus's time being a tax collector gave much social power, prestige and wealth, Matthew sacrificed all this just to follow Jesus. Let's be encouraged to forget any fears or judgement from friends and keep the simple focus of just following Him!

ACTION

If you were to simplify your life or thoughts, what could you leave behind to help yourself focus on following Jesus?

DAY 02

FAILING

MATTHEW 17:14-18 TPT

They came to where a large crowd had gathered to wait for Jesus. A man came and knelt before him and said, "Lord, please show your tender mercy toward my son. He has a demon who afflicts him. He has epilepsy, and he suffers horribly from seizures. He often falls into the cooking fire or into the river. I brought him to your followers, but they weren't able to heal him." Jesus replied, "Where is your faith? Can't you see how wayward and wrong this generation is? How much longer do I stay with you and put up with your doubts? Bring your son to me." Then Jesus rebuked the demon and it came out of him and the boy was instantly healed!

THOUGHT

We only fail if we choose to give up, the rest of our mistakes are just part of learning. We are always going to be growing and learning more in our relationship with Jesus. Here we see the disciples who did amazing miracles, started the church and changed the world, but in their early days they had to learn by mistakes just like us!

ACTION

What area of your life would you like to grow or learn more in your faith?

DAY 03

LEARNING

MATTHEW 17:19-21 TPT

Later the disciples came to him privately and asked, "Why couldn't we cast out the demon?" He told them, "It was because of your lack of faith. I promise you, if you have faith inside of you no bigger than the size of a small mustard seed, you can say to this mountain, 'Move away from here and go over there,' and you will see it move! There is nothing you couldn't do! But this kind of demon is cast out only through prayer and fasting."

THOUGHT

Here we see the disciples truly wanting to learn and grow by asking questions, Jesus wants us to do this also, really seeking His answers and not relying on our own understanding. Jesus then gave the disciples more than what they asked, an incredible promise to us all. When we get stuck, a great habit is to step back from the situation and start asking Jesus questions.

ACTION

It's good to take the time and privately reflect on your day and ask Jesus questions about whatever's on your mind? He wants you to ask! He wants to give you the answers but you have to ask first.

DAY 04

CHANGING

ACTS 5:12-16 NIV

Through the work of the apostles, many God-signs were set up among the people, many wonderful things done. They all met regularly and in remarkable harmony on the Temple porch named after Solomon. But even though people admired them a lot, outsiders were wary about joining them. On the other hand, those who put their trust in the Master were added right and left, men and women both. They even carried the sick out into the streets and laid them on stretchers and bedrolls, hoping they would be touched by Peter's shadow when he walked by. They came from the villages surrounding Jerusalem, throngs of them, bringing the sick and bedeviled. And they all were healed.

THOUGHT

A few days ago we were reading about the disciples not having enough faith, what a change there has been! We can see such a big difference in who the disciples are now so different that the change was worth changing their description to apostles. They're now doing the things Jesus did in the gospels; healing, preaching & leading. Jesus calls us to be the same, to persevere in learning and growing so we make the dramatic change and become like him!

ACTION

What does it look like for you to step into the authority and power Jesus gives like the apostles did?

DAY 05

PRAYER

LUKE 11:1-4 NLT

Once Jesus was in a certain place praying. As he finished, one of his disciples came to him and said, "Lord, teach us to pray, just as John taught his disciples." Jesus said, "This is how you should pray: Father, may your name be kept holy. May your Kingdom come soon. Give us each day the food we need, And forgive us our sins, As we forgive those who sin against us, And don't let us yield to temptation"

ACTS 1:14 NIV

[The apostles] all met together and were constantly united in prayer, along with Mary, mother of Jesus, several other women, and the brothers of Jesus.

THOUGHT

Some may think prayer is quite boring, often this is because we always focus on what we want from God. However in the scripture, the disciples main prayers were prayers directed to God not themselves. We can challenge ourselves with the way we pray; is it the way Jesus says we should? How much do we pray? It's simply having a conversation with God, it's how we develop our relationship with him, so the more we pray the stronger our relationship will be.

ACTION

For the next seven days can you commit first thing as you get up to pray the prayer in Luke 11:1-4, then spend a few minutes reflecting on it.

DAY 06

PRACTICE WHAT JESUS TAUGHT THEM

ACTS 2:43 NIV

Everyone was filled with awe at the many signs and wonders performed by the apostles.

THOUGHT

Here we see the end result of the apostles and ultimately our work for God; people to be filled with awe at the work done in and for Jesus' name. When the apostles simply did what Jesus taught them to do the entire world's belief changed. We have the same power within us this very day, so let's use it! It'll change the world.

ACTION

The apostles learnt together, who can you practice with in growing and using the power of God?

DAY 07

JUST LIKE JESUS THEY WERE FOCUSED ON OTHERS

ACTS 3:1-10 NLT

Peter and John went to the Temple one afternoon to take part in the three o'clock prayer service. As they approached the Temple, a man lame from birth was being carried in. Each day he was put beside the Temple gate, the one called the Beautiful Gate, so he could beg from the people going into the Temple. When he saw Peter and John about to enter, he asked them for some money. Peter and John looked at him intently, and Peter said, "Look at us!" The lame man looked at them eagerly, expecting some money. But Peter said, "I don't have any silver or gold for you. But I'll give you what I have. In the name of Jesus Christ the Nazarene, get up and walk!" Then Peter took the lame man by the right hand and helped him up. And as he did, the man's feet and ankles were instantly healed and strengthened. He jumped up, stood on his feet, and began to walk! Then, walking, leaping, and praising God, he went into the Temple with them. All the people saw him walking and heard him praising God. When they realized he was the lame beggar they had seen so often at the Beautiful Gate, they were absolutely astounded!

THOUGHT

Being a follower of Jesus - that's what it's all about! This passage gives us an image of what that really looks like. Simple compassion, simple obedience, simple giving and a SUPERNATURAL result! So follow him wherever he leads you, whatever the situation, FOLLOW HIM. Jesus had such a heart for the unpopular, the sick, the less fortunate. We are called to be like him in all things, including in our actions towards others.

ACTION

Can you be willing to stop your day to show love to the less fortunate? Perhaps a homeless person, even if it is just a conversation or prayer?

DAY 01
A LIFE FOR JESUS & A NEW MIND

ROMANS 12:1-3 NIV

Therefore, I urge you, brothers and sisters, in view of God's mercy, to offer your bodies as a living sacrifice, holy and pleasing to God—this is your true and proper worship. Do not conform to the pattern of this world, but be transformed by the renewing of your mind. Then you will be able to test and approve what God's will is—his good, pleasing and perfect will. For by the grace given me I say to every one of you: Do not think of yourself more highly than you ought, but rather think of yourself with sober judgment, in accordance with the faith God has distributed to each of you.

THOUGHT

This passage of scripture urges us to not conform to the way the world functions but to remain in Christ! In His good, pleasing and perfect will. This action alone requires an active mind and strong discipline in order to recentre and realign ourselves to this command. We can take this and apply it to our lives.. Self-discipline is key, also what we feed into our minds!

ACTION

How can you 'renew your mind' today?

DAY 02
WORK WITH OTHERS FOR THE GREATER GOOD

ROMANS 12:4-5 TPT

In the human body there are many parts and organs, each with a unique function. And so it is in the body of Christ. For though we are many, we've all been mingled into one body in Christ. This means that we are all vitally joined to one another, with each contributing to the others.

THOUGHT

In our everyday life we are constantly surrounded by people. Whether that is in family, school, college or work there are different strengths that we offer into those environments. However, alongside this individual strength there must be a oneness and unity because we are all one body. As the saying goes; there is no 'I' in 'TEAM'.

ACTION

Are there any relationships you have where your unity and togetherness makes you a better you? Take a few minutes to thank a couple of those people today.

DAY 03

IDENTIFY YOUR GOD GIVEN GIFT & USE IT

ROMANS 12:6-8 NLT

In his grace, God has given us different gifts for doing certain things well. So if God has given you the ability to prophesy, speak out with as much faith as God has given you. If your gift is serving others, serve them well. If you are a teacher, teach well. If your gift is to encourage others, be encouraging. If it is giving, give generously. If God has given you leadership ability, take the responsibility seriously. And if you have a gift for showing kindness to others, do it gladly.

THOUGHT

We need to be diligent in identifying what our gifts are! Ask the Holy Spirit and pray. When we think about what we do with ease that others may find hard this can be an indicator. When we pray about this God will give us answers - we can value the gifts He has given us and use them. The only way to master something is with practice, so go for it!

ACTION

Identify what gifts God has given you, and ask God for an opportunity to use that gift today

DAY 04

LOVE & POWER

ROMANS 12:9-13 NIV

Love must be sincere. Hate what is evil; cling to what is good. Be devoted to one another in love. Honor one another above yourselves. Never be lacking in zeal, but keep your spiritual fervor, serving the Lord. Be joyful in hope, patient in affliction, faithful in prayer. Share with the Lord's people who are in need. Practice hospitality.

THOUGHT

Let's be mindful to practically use love in our words and actions everyday - it can be hard at times when our emotions get in the way but like this scripture says; cling to what is good! Cling to Jesus and His word. When we do this & have the Word of God at the forefront of our lives - all of our actions can be filtered through Him rather than our emotions.

ACTION

Which of the suggested actions sticks out as you read this, How can you put it into practice today?

DAY 05
A DIFFERENT APPROACH

ROMANS 12:16 TPT

Live happily together in a spirit of harmony, and be as mindful of another's worth as you are your own. Don't live with a lofty mind-set, thinking you are too important to serve others, but be willing to do menial tasks and identify with those who are humble minded. Don't be smug or even think for a moment that you know it all.

THOUGHT

Much of our world today lives in chaos. We need to hold the harmony and the grace that the world lacks by stepping down from ourselves and putting others before us. Pride down, ego down. Love all people regardless of their status with the same love God gave us. He is our perfect example.

ACTION

Is there someone you don't feel like associating with? What could you do to show them love today?

DAY 06
JUDGEMENT BELONGS TO GOD, NOT US

ROMANS 12:17-20 NIV

Do not repay anyone evil for evil. Be careful to do what is right in the eyes of everyone. If it is possible, as far as it depends on you, live at peace with everyone. Do not take revenge, my dear friends, but leave room for God's wrath, for it is written: "It is mine to avenge; I will repay," says the Lord. On the contrary: "If your enemy is hungry, feed him; if he is thirsty, give him something to drink. In doing this, you will heap burning coals on his head.

THOUGHT

We are often quick to make judgements and form opinions and dish them out as we fancy. However as this scripture clearly says, judgement is not something for us to make - it belongs to God. The responsibilities that belong to us are to remain in a place of love and peace with each other.

ACTION

Do you have an enemy, how could you show them God's goodness through an action today?

DAY 07

YOUR LIFE'S WORK

ROMANS 12:21 NIV

Do not be overcome by evil, but overcome evil with good.

THOUGHT

As humans we are naturally born into a sinful flesh, naturally tempted by the enemy. However, through Jesus, the power of that is broken. This is not just for us to be a good person and avoid evil, but the power Jesus gives us is to overcome and destroy the evil in our worlds.

ACTION

Where have you had victory over evil, who could you share that with that it would encourage to also overcome?

MODULE 10
CHURCH

"The Church is not a religious community of worshippers of Christ but is Christ himself who has taken form among people." *mic drop*

The Church can mean many things to different people. There are different expressions of Church, different styles, different denominations with different theologies. For a lot of people, church is their first contact to God and their first image of who Jesus is. Regardless of how church is outworked in the different denominations and in different cultures all over the world, all have one thing in common: people gathering together because of one name, the name of Jesus. The Church is not just a building, a temple, or an ancient religious place, but it is found wherever there are people who gather together with a love for Jesus and a heart to see others reached with the gospel. The Church is God's tool to reach humanity, a place for every person from every imaginable background, and a place that exists to love God and love people. If you are a follower of Christ, that makes YOU the Church, and you are called and qualified to play your part in building the Church to be all that God has designed it to be.

We want to take a closer look, in this next chapter, at what the purpose of the Church is, and what the bible tells us about it - to understand what it means when it calls us "the bride of Christ" and to fully understand what role we can play in God's Church.

WEEK 32 | VALUE OF GOD'S HOUSE

DAY 01
JESUS STAYS IN THE TEMPLE

LUKE 2:41-49 ESV

Now his parents went to Jerusalem every year at the Feast of the Passover. And when he was twelve years old, they went up according to custom. And when the feast was ended, as they were returning, the boy Jesus stayed behind in Jerusalem. His parents did not know it, but supposing him to be in the group they went a day's journey, but then they began to search for him among their relatives and acquaintances, and when they did not find him, they returned to Jerusalem, searching for him. After three days they found him in the temple, sitting among the teachers, listening to them and asking them questions. And all who heard him were amazed at his understanding and his answers. And when his parents saw him, they were astonished. And his mother said to him, "Son, why have you treated us so? Behold, your father and I have been searching for you in great distress." And he said to them, "Why were you looking for me? Did you not know that I must be in my Father's house?"

THOUGHT

As God's children, we belong in His house! More than that, His house becomes like a 2nd home to us, it's a spiritual home where we can learn, grow and walk through life with a Spiritual family. The Christian faith should never be a solo-journey, it's meant to be walked together within a community. Don't miss out on it!

ACTION

If Jesus had to be in His Father's house, there was clearly a need Jesus had for it. List 5 things that you gain from being in your church.

DAY 02

JESUS, HEAD OF THE CHURCH

EPHESIANS 1:17–23 NIV

I keep asking that the God of our Lord Jesus Christ, the glorious Father, may give you the Spirit of wisdom and revelation, so that you may know him better. I pray that the eyes of your heart may be enlightened in order that you may know the hope to which he has called you, the riches of his glorious inheritance in his holy people, and his incomparably great power for us who believe. That power is the same as the mighty strength he exerted when he raised Christ from the dead and seated him at his right hand in the heavenly realms, far above all rule and authority, power and dominion, and every name that is invoked, not only in the present age but also in the one to come. And God placed all things under his feet and appointed him to be head over everything for the church, which is his body, the fullness of him who fills everything in every way.

THOUGHT

Knowing God is amazing! This scripture is such an encouragement about the hope, power and inheritance we have from our heavenly Father through Jesus and the Spirit. It captures so many of the amazing truths available to us through those relationships.

ACTION

Jesus is the head of the Church, we are his body. He lives in us with His fullness; the power that raised Christ from the dead is in us! Can you grasp that? Read the verses a couple of times and highlight the things that stick out to you.

DAY 03

JESUS PROMISES TO BUILD HIS CHURCH & SHARE HIS AUTHORITY

MATTHEW 16:18–19 NLV

"And I tell you that you are Peter. On this rock I will build My church. The powers of hell will not be able to have power over My church. I will give you the keys of the holy nation of heaven. Whatever you do not allow on earth will not have been allowed in heaven. Whatever you allow on earth will have been allowed in heaven."

THOUGHT

Jesus has been given all authority in heaven and on earth. He shares his authority with us so we can glorify Him. God wants to use us to build His kingdom and His commitment is to give us the power to do that! What God began building through Peter & the early Church has not stopped, but is to be continued through us every day.

ACTION

You have the keys to the Kingdom of heaven, what could you use them to unlock in your church?

DAY 04
YOU ARE THE TEMPLE

1 CORINTHIANS 6:19-20 NIV

Do you not know that your bodies are temples of the Holy Spirit, who is in you, whom you have received from God? You are not your own; you were bought at a price. Therefore honour God with your bodies.

THOUGHT

God paid the highest price so we could be His. Our bodies are fearfully and wonderfully made in His image. He didn't just create us in order for us to be alone, but for us to share ourselves with Him. That's how close He wants to be with us and How much He values us. In addition to this He wants to work through us to be present & active on the Earth!

ACTION

From the body you have, how can you honour God? For example using your muscles to set up kids church or your voice in worship.

DAY 05
UNITED AS ONE BODY

1 CORINTHIANS 12:12-14 NLV

Our own body has many parts. When all these many parts are put together, they are only one body. The body of Christ is like this. It is the same way with us. Jews or those who are not Jews, men who are owned by someone or men who are free to do what they want to do, have all been baptized into the one body by the same Holy Spirit. We have all received the one Spirit. The body is not one part, but many parts.

THOUGHT

Just as in a human body every part is needed, every Christian contributes in a unique way to the church. Everybody is equally important, regardless of human status or different gifts and talents. We are co-workers, not competitors when it comes to building God's Kingdom.

ACTION

Is there anywhere in church that I compete with people I should be co working with?

DAY 06

THE BRIDE OF CHRIST

2 CORINTHIANS 11:2 NIV

(Paul writes to the church) I am jealous for you with a godly jealousy. I promised you to one husband, to Christ, so that I might present you as a pure virgin to him.

THOUGHT

Jesus calls the church His bride. That's the kind of intimate, loving relationship He wants to have with us! We belong to Him and He belongs to us, He is jealous of the other things that we sometimes put before Him in our lives. Purity in this sense is choosing to make Jesus first in everything, not giving ourselves first to other things in this world.

ACTION

How can you remain pure and ready for Jesus?

DAY 07

OUR ETERNAL HOME

JOHN 14:1-4 NCV

Jesus said, "Don't let your hearts be troubled. Trust in God, and trust in me. There are many rooms in my Father's house; I would not tell you this if it were not true. I am going there to prepare a place for you. After I go and prepare a place for you, I will come back and take you to be with me so that you may be where I am. You know the way to the place where I am going."

THOUGHT

One day, we will be with God forever. What a glorious place this will be! Jesus prepares a room there especially for each one of us! We have an eternal home - a forever home that will never have disunity. While we are on Earth, let's not allow our hearts to be troubled, but trust in God that His eternal life is ready for us.

ACTION

Take a few moments to reflect on the verse. Allow God's peace to fill your heart, because He has your eternal salvation assured.

DAY 01

SAVED IN GROUPS

ACTS 2:36-41 NIV

Therefore let all Israel be assured of this: God has made this Jesus, whom you crucified, both Lord and Messiah. When the people heard this they were cut to the heart and said to Peter and the other apostles, "Brothers, what shall we do?" Peter replied, "Repent and be baptised, every one of you, in the name of Jesus Christ for the forgiveness of your sins. And you will receive the gift of the holy spirit. The promise is for you and your children and for all who are far off - for all whom the Lord our God will call" With many other words he warned them; and he pleaded with them, "Save yourselves from this corrupt generation." Those who accepted his message were baptised, and about three thousand were added to their number that day.

THOUGHT

The foundations of the first church were built upon a spiritual family. They all saw each other as brothers and sisters. Life can be harder when we feel alone, like the only one following Jesus. We find strength in the people around us to convict and guide us to be closer to Jesus.

ACTION

What if it wasn't just you saved, but your friends as well! Today, is there somebody who doesn't know Jesus that you could you share your story of finding Jesus?

DAY 02

APOSTLES' TEACHING

ACTS 2:42 NIV

They devoted themselves to the Apostles' teaching and to fellowship, to the breaking of the bread and to prayer.

THOUGHT

When we devote time to studying how the Apostles grew the first church we can see the key principles that are important. Our devotion to knowing and following Bible teaching is a key part of what will grow the church in depth and numbers. It is the blueprint which we can follow to build and share God's Kingdom.

ACTION

Is there a friend or friends in church that you can take time to talk about the Bible with?

DAY 03

FELLOWSHIP & BREAKING BREAD

ACTS 2:42 NIV

They devoted themselves to the Apostles' teaching and to fellowship, to the breaking of the bread and to prayer.

THOUGHT

A church divided cannot grow, fellowship is doing life with other people in church. We grow fellowship through consistent communion and remembrance of what Jesus did. This brings strength & community to our group of believers so we might build the church just as it was in the beginning.

ACTION

Through prayer take a few moments to name some specific things you can thank Jesus for doing in you.

DAY 04

PRAYER

ACTS 2:42 NIV

They devoted themselves to the Apostles' teaching and to fellowship, to the breaking of the bread and to prayer.

THOUGHT

We can never pray too much! Regular communication with God is key to building up our spirit and life. Both private prayer & prayer with our church family is so important. When the early Church prayed they were speaking to God, seeking His wisdom and honouring Him for who He is. We have the mandate to do the same today.

ACTION

If Jesus was sitting in front of you now what would you talk to Him about? Start to pray today with this as a scenario in your mind.

DAY 05
PRAYERS ANSWERED WITH POWER

ACTS 2:43 NIV

Everyone was filled with awe at the many wonders and signs performed by the Apostles.

THOUGHT

When there is a group of people devoted to the three things we have just covered, bible teaching, remembering Jesus and prayer, we will start to see God move in ways that are mind-blowing! This is the true adventure of following Jesus.

ACTION

There is power in agreement. Who could you get together with to be pray into situations and start to see God do these amazing things?

DAY 06
SELFLESSLY SHARED

ACTS 2:44-45 NIV

All the believers were together and had everything in common. They sold property and possessions to give to anyone who had need.

THOUGHT

When we are devoted to God together, a commitment is created between one another to share within a community of generosity so that no one has to go without. The early church is a beautiful example of this, they literally shared ALL of their possessions so that no one within their community was in need. What would our churches look like today if we have this same spirit?

ACTION

Giving isn't about the value of the item but about the value it adds to someone else. Is there anything you have that could be given or shared to help someone else?

DAY 07

GOD ADDED TO THEM DAILY

ACTS 2:46-47 NIV

Every day they continued to meet together in the temple courts. They broke bread in their homes and ate together with glad and sincere hearts, praising God and enjoying the favour of all the people. And the Lord added to their number daily those who were being saved.

THOUGHT

Giving isn't just about money or time: your heartfelt words of encouragement, a smile or a simple act of kindness can make all the difference and give God glory. This verse shows us that the first church began a tradition of thanksgiving and prayer and set a perfect example of how our churches should look today. Not only that but they had a culture of always inviting people to be a part of their lives. Their community, invitation & faith in God is what grew their numbers daily.

ACTION

In what way can you work to bring the early church culture into your church today?

MODULE 11
RELATIONSHIPS

The dictionary describes relationships as, *"The way in which two or more people or things are connected, or the state of being connected or the way in which two or more people or groups regard and behave towards each other."*

Through the Internet and especially social media we have an amazing opportunity to be connected and to be "friends" with pretty much anyone on this planet. The issue with that is, that it can be quite tough to have a real relationship. Especially since there are so many different views on relationships, how they have to look like and what's important about them.

The question that comes up is "when is a relationship a real one?" The relationship to my family or my best friends, is that a real relationship? Is a real relationship only possible if I date someone or get married to them? Do I have to know everything about someone (no secrets, no lies) in order to have a real relationship to them?

Real relationship is about acknowledging what the other person has to say. Real relationship is about accepting the other person with all their faults and failures. Real relationship is the commitment to walk alongside someone, encourage, help, strengthen and correct them when they need it, in order that the best that God has put inside of them comes out. That's why it needs love on top of commitment for a relationship to work.

Over the next 2 weeks we will have a look at good and healthy relationships and how to be a good friend.

WEEK 34 | DEEP SPIRITUAL FRIENDSHIPS

DAY 01
BE A FRIEND OF JESUS

JOHN 15:9-17 NLT

"I have loved you even as the Father has loved me. Remain in my love. When you obey my commandments, you remain in my love, just as I obey my Father's love. I have told you these things so that you will be filled with my joy. Yes, your joy will overflow! This is my commandment: Love each other in the same way I have loved you. There is no greater love than to lay down one's life for one's friends. You are my friends if you do what I command. I no longer call you slaves, because a master doesn't confide in his slaves. Now you are my friends, since I have told you everything the Father told me. You didn't choose me. I chose you. I appointed you to go and produce lasting fruit, so that the Father will give you whatever you ask for, using my name. This is my command: Love each other."

THOUGHT

It's through receiving Jesus' love and outworking it in our lives that we are able to inherit so many of the good things that God has for us. In addition to this, living out the Love of Jesus is often the best explanation to other people of who Jesus is. He longs to be our friend, so that He knows us and we know Him & His heart.

ACTION

What is a new way you could receive and share the love of Jesus today?

DAY 02

VALUES FOR FRIENDSHIP

PHILIPPIANS 2:1-4 NLT

Is there any encouragement from belonging to Christ? Any comfort from his love? Any fellowship together in the Spirit? Are your hearts tender and compassionate? Then make me truly happy by agreeing wholeheartedly with each other, loving one another, and working together with one mind and purpose. Don't be selfish; don't try to impress others. Be humble, thinking of others as better than yourselves. Don't look out only for your own interests, but take an interest in others, too.

THOUGHT

Within our spiritual family, we should find comfort and safety. It is our responsibility to work together as one to further the kingdom. Division makes us weak, but together we have more of His strength! Looking at this scripture we have a perfect outline for how to make Godly friendships work - agree, love one another and work together for the same purpose.

ACTION

It's so easy to be selfish and neglect others, take a minute to think of some of your friends in church and how you can look out for what is good for them.

DAY 03

FRIENDS ALWAYS LOVE

PROVERBS 17:17 NLT

A friend is always loyal, and a brother is born to help in time of need.

THOUGHT

If friendship is about loyalty and helping each other, then why waste time on friendships built on other things? If we want successful relationships then we need to build them on the basis of loyalty, both to one another and to God. As children of God we have also been designed to help one another in times of need. Let's be there for, and stick by each other!

ACTION

What friendships can you identify in your life that show good loyalty?

DAY 04
PAUL & TIMOTHY

1 TIMOTHY 1:1-2 NLT

This letter is from Paul, an apostle of Christ Jesus, appointed by the command of God our Saviour and Christ Jesus, who gives us hope. I am writing to Timothy, my true son in the faith. May God the Father and Christ Jesus our Lord give you grace, mercy, and peace.

THOUGHT

Within a healthy friendship, the base should always be about faith and building each other up. Great friends love and encourage each other. Paul & Timothy worked together in establishing the early church. Their friendship is one that is an example to us of not just a healthy friendship - but also a fruitful one.

ACTION

Who do you believe God has put around you to be family through faith?

DAY 05
PROPHECY & ENCOURAGEMENT

1 TIMOTHY 1:18-19 NLT

Timothy, my son, here are my instructions for you, based on the prophetic words spoken over you earlier. May they help you fight well in the Lord's battles. Cling to your faith in Christ, and keep your conscience clear. For some people have deliberately violated their consciences; as a result, their faith has been shipwrecked.

THOUGHT

Sometimes we may feel like it is not our place to give instructions to our friends, as if it would be hypocritical or not our place. But the Word clearly tells us that we are called to guide and build each other up through this kind of Bible based encouragement. Just as Paul encouraged Timothy to remember what was spoken over him previously and remain strong in that, so can we encourage our friends.

ACTION

Who in your life could you ask for biblical guidance and instruction from?

DAY 06

CONSTANT ENCOURAGEMENT

1 TIMOTHY 4:12-16 NLT

Don't let anyone think less of you because you are young. Be an example to all believers in what you say, in the way you live, in your love, your faith, and your purity. Until I get there, focus on reading the Scriptures to the church, encouraging the believers, and teaching them. Do not neglect the spiritual gift you received through the prophecy spoken over you when the elders of the church laid their hands on you. Give your complete attention to these matters. Throw yourself into your tasks so that everyone will see your progress. Keep a close watch on how you live and on your teaching. Stay true to what is right for the sake of your own salvation and the salvation of those who hear you.

THOUGHT

Timothy was a great man of God! From the scripture we can also see that Timothy is a young man and Paul's encouragement is not to let that affect him. We might not always have confidence from experience, but the example of the way we live always comes before our achievements. In our lives we can both be Timothy, receiving encouragement and Paul - giving encouragement out to others. Either way we should aim to live our lives as an encouragement to others.

ACTION

In what areas of your life are you a great example to those around you?

DAY 07

GENUINE, DEEP RELATIONSHIPS

2 TIMOTHY 1:1-8 NLT

This letter is from Paul, chosen by the will of God to be an apostle of Christ Jesus. I have been sent out to tell others about the life he has promised through faith in Christ Jesus. I am writing to Timothy, my dear son. May God the Father and Christ Jesus our Lord give you grace, mercy and peace. Timothy, I thank God for you - the God I serve with a clear conscience, just as my ancestors did. Night and day I constantly remember you in my prayers. I long to see you again, for I remember your tears as we parted. And I will be filled with joy when we are together again. I remember your genuine faith, for you share the faith that first filled your grandmother Lois and your mother, Eunice. And I know that same faith continues strong in you. This is why I remind you to fan into flames the spiritual gift God gave you when I laid my hands on you. For God has not given us a spirit of fear and timidity, but of power, and self-discipline. So never be ashamed to tell others about our Lord. And don't be ashamed of me, either, even though I'm in prison for him. With the strength God gives you, be ready to suffer with me for the sake of the Good News.

DAY 07

THOUGHT

Even whilst in a place of pain, Paul prioritised his friendship with and encouragement to Timothy. Relationships have highs and lows, but Paul and Timothy show that despite the challenges we face, we can always encourage each other to remain rooted in Jesus and pursuing His purpose despite the obstacles we face.

ACTION

Who manages to help ignite your faith and spiritual gifts, maybe write a message to let that person know what they mean to you today.

DAY 01
BAD COMPANY CORRUPTS

1 CORINTHIANS 15:33-34 NIV

Do not be misled: "Bad company corrupts good character." Come back to your senses as you ought, and stop sinning; for there are some who are ignorant of God—I say this to your shame.

THOUGHT

This scripture is Paul urging people to base their relationships in Christ - not people. We need to let ourselves be this straight to the point; don't mess about with bad company! Relationship with God is the top priority - it is where all of our other relationships should stem from.

ACTION

Having a look at your friendships; is there someone that is a companion for compromise in your life?

DAY 02
WHO NOT TO JOIN

2 CORINTHIANS 6:14 - 7:1 MSG

Don't become partners with those who reject God. How can you make a partnership out of right and wrong? That's not partnership; that's war. Is light best friends with dark? Does Christ go strolling with the Devil? Do trust and mistrust hold hands? Who would think of setting up pagan idols in God's holy Temple? But that is exactly what we are, each of us a temple in whom God lives. God himself put it this way: "I'll live in them, move into them; I'll be their God and they'll be my people. So leave the corruption and compromise; leave it for good," says God. "Don't link up with those who will pollute you. I want you all for myself. I'll be a Father to you; you'll be sons and daughters to me."

THOUGHT

God created us to be temples of Him - uncontaminated by darkness. In this passage we don't find condemnation for partnering with darkness but freedom by choosing instead to partner with Christ. We shouldn't hold ourselves in the bondage that comes from joining with those who are not in Christ but instead experience the freedom of equal relationships!

ACTION

What is one area today where we can let God live and move in us to partner with Him?

DAY 03
AVOID FOOLS

PROVERBS 14:7–17 NKJV

Go from the presence of a foolish man, When you do not perceive in him the lips of knowledge. The wisdom of the prudent is to understand his way, But the folly of fools is deceit. Fools mock at sin, But among the upright there is favor. The heart knows its own bitterness, And a stranger does not share its joy. The house of the wicked will be overthrown, But the tent of the upright will flourish. There is a way that seems right to a man, But its end is the way of death. Even in laughter the heart may sorrow, And the end of mirth may be grief. The backslider in heart will be filled with his own ways, But a good man will be satisfied from above. The simple believes every word, But the prudent considers well his steps. A wise man fears and departs from evil, But a fool rages and is self-confident. A quick-tempered man acts foolishly, And a man of wicked intentions is hated.

THOUGHT

Fools aren't just class clowns, they are people whose actions and mentalities are damaging to themselves and those around them. Today, try to leave their presence and be with those who are wise in Christ.

ACTION

Is there anything you believe that troubles you? Does it line up with the Bible?

DAY 04
HOW TO BE BLESSED

PSALMS 1:1–3 NIV

Blessed is the one who does not walk in step with the wicked or stand in the way that sinners take or sit in the company of mockers, but whose delight is in the law of the Lord, and who meditates on his law day and night. That person is like a tree planted by streams of water, which yields its fruit in season and whose leaf does not wither—whatever they do prospers.

THOUGHT

The way to blessing and fulfillment is through spending time in relationship with God. Surround yourself with people who encourage this relationship with God and help guide you towards Him always.

ACTION

Where in your life do you need refreshment from God?

DAY 05

PEOPLE TO DO LIFE WITH YOU ARE VITAL

ECCLESIASTES 4:9–12 NIV

Two are better than one, because they have a good return for their labour: If either of them falls down, one can help the other up. But pity anyone who falls and has no one to help them up. Also, if two lie down together, they will keep warm. But how can one keep warm alone? Though one may be overpowered, two can defend themselves. A cord of three strands is not quickly broken.

THOUGHT

Do you have a tendency to try to face life alone? God designed us to do life together. All through the Bible people face and overcome so much together: battles, challenges, travel, imprisonment and release, giving us examples of God-relationships in almost every context.

ACTION

Can you name at least one godly friend who you do or will do life with in this season?

DAY 06

TOUGH LOVE IS TRUE LOVE

PROVERBS 27:5–6 TPT

It's better to be corrected openly if it stems from hidden love. You can trust a friend who wounds you with his honesty, but your enemy's pretended flattery comes from insincerity.

THOUGHT

A sign of a good relationship is one in which correction can be made. God designed us to help each other become closer models of Christ's life. Get some friends and be the friend that corrects in love to build up.

ACTION

Can you identify people in your life who are 'friends' and 'enemies' according to the definition of the verse above? Ask God to guide you in who to trust to help you.

DAY 07
NEXT LEVEL LOVE FOR OTHERS

LUKE 6:32-36 NIV

"If you love those who love you, what credit is that to you? Even sinners love those who love them. And if you do good to those who are good to you, what credit is that to you? Even sinners do that. And if you lend to those from whom you expect repayment, what credit is that to you? Even sinners lend to sinners, expecting to be repaid in full. But love your enemies, do good to them, and lend to them without expecting to get anything back. Then your reward will be great, and you will be children of the Most High, because he is kind to the ungrateful and wicked. Be merciful, just as your Father is merciful.

THOUGHT

The main goal of all our relationships should be to love others as God loves them, regardless of what we get in return. Our lives should be focussed on God and others - to love God above all and love others as yourself.

ACTION

Take some time to pray. Ask God for His love in your life to be so great that you are free to love others without needing to be loved in return.

MODULE 12

FAMILY

It's the 3rd of August 1992. Everybody awaits the shot to open the semi finals of the 400m men sprint. Everybody's eyes are focused on eight men. One of the sprinters is British athlete Derek Redmond, who is currently at the peak of his career and one of the favourite contestants to win the gold medal. Only one more race to go through to the final. One more race to make his dream come true: to win an Olympic medal.

On your marks, get set, BANG.

Redmond starts well, running around the first bend and on to the first straight, looking strong. Suddenly he hears it. A snap, about 250 metres from the finish. It's his hamstring. He goes down and buries his head in his hands, looks up and witnesses how the other sprinters are finishing the race. It's in that moment that he knows, that was it. His dream of winning an Olympic medal: gone. All the years of training and preparing, here is where it ends in the most crucial and painful way. But Derek isn't finished yet. Stretcher bearers make their way over to him, but Redmond is determined, he wants to finish this race. He continues hobbling along the track towards the finishing line, his face covered in tears, and in that moment he feels someone approach from behind. Someone that has been supporting him all along, right there when he had his first races. Someone that stood there on the sidelines in the pouring rain, when he went through his amateur competitions. Someone that cheered him on all his life, that supported him in every step and someone that would be there for him, in the most difficult moment of his career. It was Jim Redmond, his father who barged past security and onto the track to get to his son. Jim picked up Derek and completed the end of the race together with his son. The '92 400m semi final becomes one of the most memorable moments in the history of the Olympics.

Family are the people who carry you when you feel like you can no longer walk. Family are the people that love you at your best and your worst. Family is the place where you can be you and where you are home. Family is a safe place for you to express how you feel and to express your giftings. This is what God designed the family to be and what we are entitled to be part of. Regardless of whether this is your experience of family, or whether yours may be the complete opposite, over the next few weeks we want to look at the spiritual family that we all belong to when we become a follower of Christ, that carries this culture; and we want to look at how God intended our natural family to be.

WEEK 36 | FAMILY

DAY 01

HONOUR OVER ARROGANCE

EPHESIANS 6:1-3 NIV

'Children, obey your parents in the Lord, for this is right. "Honour your father and mother" – which is the first commandment with a promise – "so that it may go well with you and that you may enjoy long life on the earth".

THOUGHT

If you choose to follow God's instructions, it leads to a happy, fulfilled life. Family is our training ground and doing the right thing, isn't always easy. Developing a habit of honour to others reaps a reward of respect.

ACTION

If honour and obedience leads to blessing, how can you improve putting this into practise in your own family?

DAY 02

TRUST OVER TANTRUMS

MATTHEW 7: 1–2 NIV

'Do not judge, or you too will be judged. For in the same way you judge others, you will be judged, and with the measure you use, it will be measured to you.'

THOUGHT

Act in a way that you would like to be treated yourself. Life is better with positivity and encouragement surrounding us, celebrating our victories and successes with those around us. Often it's more important to trust your parents than it is to understand or even agree with them.

ACTION

Sometimes our own naivety can make it easier to point the finger others than the mirror at ourselves, how can we be more gracious in the way we see our family members today.

DAY 03

OTHERS VALUE OVER OUR VICTORY

PHILIPPIANS 2: 3–4 NIV

'Do nothing out of selfish ambition or vain conceit. Rather, in humility value others above yourselves, not looking to your own interests but each of you to the interests of the others.'

THOUGHT

No one can make it to the top on their own. Great successes usually rely on the part played by many. Helping each other raises everyone, and you will be swept up with the general momentum. Value your parents and all they have done for you, think about that before you think about yourself in family situations and it will help.

ACTION

Do something today where you are generous or kind to another family member, with no agenda but wanting to do your best for them.

DAY 04

TRUTH OVER TURMOIL

JAMES 3:17 NIV

'But the wisdom from above is first of all pure. It is also peace loving, gentle at all times, and willing to yield to others. It is full of mercy and the fruit of good deeds. It shows no favouritism and is always sincere.'

THOUGHT

If you feel like your family life is in turmoil, relook at whom you are following. Are you being ruled by what culture says is wise, what your friends see as cool, or are you looking to a pure God who is sincere in his counsel.

ACTION

Is there a family situation where you need to park an argument and instead ask questions and listen until you find a place of understanding or agreement?

DAY 05

ANSWERS OVER ANGER

EPHESIANS 4:26 NLT

'And "don't sin by letting anger control you." Don't let the sun go down while you are still angry'

THOUGHT

God is asking for every part of us, not just the parts we find easy to release. He wants to refine us fully. Anger leads to a life of bitterness, so why not place your anger in His hands & instead allow the Holy Spirit to renew you with his peace. Is there someone in your family you need to apologize to, then do it quickly, don't let bad things become bigger than they need to be.

ACTION

Take a moment to pray: Close your eyes and ask the Holy Spirit if there is anyone in your family you need to forgive. If someone comes to mind simply pray "Jesus I choose to forgive [Name]"

(Don't worry if this is difficult, forgiveness is a choice, not a feeling.)

DAY 06

WE ARE CHOSEN AS GOD'S FAMILY

EPHESIANS 1:3-5 NLT

'All praise to God, the Father of our Lord Jesus Christ, who has blessed us with every spiritual blessing in the heavenly realms because we are united with Christ. Even before he made the world, God loved us and chose us in Christ to be holy and without fault in his eyes. God decided in advance to adopt us into his own family by bringing us to himself through Jesus Christ. This is what he wanted to do, and it gave him great pleasure.'

THOUGHT

God loved us before he even made the world, so practise building a habit of daily giving God praise in all you do. The vastness of his love is amazing but YOU have to choose to believe it to feel part of His family. God never changes His mind, so it's you who has to make your mind up to follow!

ACTION

We are without fault through Jesus, but do you still fault find in yourself?

DAY 07

YOU HAVE A PLACE IN GOD'S PEOPLE

1 PETER 2:9-10 NLT

"But you are not like that, for you are a chosen people. You are royal priests, a holy nation, God's very own possession. As a result, you can show others the goodness of God, for he called you out of the darkness into his wonderful light. Once you had no identity as a people; now you are God's people. Once you received no mercy; now you have received God's mercy."

THOUGHT

Once you understand your true identity in God, you will feel free to wholeheartedly be yourself, able to approach each day shining your light to others & therefore reaping God's goodness for yourself.

ACTION

Do you keep who you really are in darkness, or are you proud of your identity in Jesus letting it shine like wonderful light?

MODULE 13

SEX & SEXUALITY

Let's talk about sex, baby.

Madonna once described sex as "the handshake of the 21st century". In our society, sex is everywhere: it's in 99% of the films we watch; it's splattered all over social media; it's Netflix and chill; everybody's singing about how to have sex, about not getting enough sex, about all their different kinds of sex; the Internet is advertising sex, selling sex, filming sex; thousands of books are describing how to have sex, what's "good" sex and how to experiment in your sex... it's an absolute overload of sex. Yet with all this information, explanation and examination of sex in our society, we're all left confused asking ourselves, what actually is sex? Is it something quick and casual? Is it something to do with someone I love? Is it dirty and perverse? Is it a way to express my sexuality? Is it just to satisfy my physical needs? Can I have it with anyone and everyone? Is less, more or am I missing out?

We have completely lost sight of the boundaries of sex and what it was created for so much so that we have no understanding of the impact of sex on a persons body, mind, soul and spirit. Unfortunately, the global church has either been silent about a healthy and godly sexuality or branded it is sin. The truth is, we have all been created as sexual beings, and God has a plan and purpose in that. So sex isn't wrong and it isn't the problem - how we perceive it, is. So we want to look at this very relevant topic over the next few weeks and find out why God created sex, how he intended us to enjoy it, and what impact it has on our lives.

WEEK 37 | GOD'S PLAN FOR BLESSING

DAY 01

BLESSING FLOWS FROM GOD TO MAN

GENESIS 2:7 NIV

Then the Lord God formed a man from the dust of the ground and breathed into his nostrils the breath of life, and the man became a living being.

THOUGHT

God formed man and breathed into him life! To know that we are intentionally made as an individual by God's hands and given life by His breath is a wonderful thing! God formed us perfectly and we should be proud of who He has uniquely designed us to be.

ACTION

What does it mean to you to know you were formed and breathed into life by God?

DAY 02

BLESSING FLOWS FROM MAN TO WOMAN

GENESIS 2:21–22 NIV

So the Lord God caused the man to fall into a deep sleep; and while he was sleeping, he took one of the man's ribs and then closed up the place with flesh. Then the Lord God made a woman from the rib he had taken out of man, and brought her to the man.

THOUGHT

Despite having everything he needed to survive, God knew man needed a partner to help him to thrive. God created woman, a suitable partner, a companion to be joined with so that man could thrive, not just survive, throughout his days on Earth.

ACTION

How does this scripture help us understand what to look for in finding our life companion?

DAY 03

BLESSING FLOWS FROM WOMAN TO CHILDREN

GENESIS 4:1 NIV

*Adam made love to his wife Eve, and she became pregnant and gave birth to Cain. She said,
'With the help of the Lord I have brought forth a man.'*

THOUGHT

The introduction of sex in the Bible follows the union of man and woman blessed by God. Eve understood that God's hand was on this relationship and the fruit of the union was new life. This helps create a clear picture of God's plan for sex and humanity. United in marriage man and woman come together to produce new life.

ACTION

From reading this scripture, what do you think God's plan is for sex and humanity?

DAY 04

BLESSING FLOWS FROM CHILDREN TO GENERATIONS

GENESIS 9:1 NIV

Then God blessed Noah and his sons saying to them, 'Be fruitful and increase in number and fill the earth.'

THOUGHT

God has a specific design and plan for man and woman which is recognised in this scripture. We have read during this week that God created man to be unified with woman, to have children, and, as we read in day 4, to be fruitful and increase in number. His best is for one generation to pass their blessing to the next generation.

ACTION

Think of someone in an older generation that has blessed you. How can you repeat that for others younger than you?

DAY 05

BLESSING FLOWS FROM GENERATIONS TO NATIONS

GENESIS 12:1–2 NIV

The Lord had said to Abram, 'Go from your country, your people and your father's household to the land I will show you. 'I will make you into a great nation, and I will bless you; I will make your name great, and you will be a blessing.'

THOUGHT

Despite his mistakes Abram had proved faithful in building his family God's way. Through his family, and the blessing they built, a wider community grew until it became the start of a great nation.

ACTION

What does following God's plan in love and obedience look like for you in the area of sex?

DAY 06

BLESSINGS OF MARRIAGE

PROVERBS 18:22 NIV

He who finds a wife finds what is good and receives favour from the Lord.

THOUGHT

We can spend our time worrying over the big questions of who do I marry? With sex, what is ok when? But God's answer to these questions is so wonderfully simple- He created us for union, Holy matrimony (marriage) and to be fruitful. He desires to bless us with this: God doesn't hold back His best for us.

ACTION

God has made promises of favour and blessings of marriage. What commitments are wise to make to God in your pursuit of relationships and love?

DAY 07

BLESSINGS OF A GREAT WOMAN

PROVERBS 31:10-12 AND 30-31 NIV

A wife of noble character who can find? She is worth far more than rubies. Her husband has full confidence in her and lacks nothing of value. She brings him good, not harm, all the days of her life. Charm is deceptive, and beauty is fleeting; but a woman who fears the Lord is to be praised. Honor her for all that her hands have done, and let her works bring her praise at the city gate.

THOUGHT

The character you carry matters. The Bible is clear in the value of good character in a marriage but this is great guidance in developing relationships throughout life. When you bring noble character you bring confidence, life and lasting value!

ACTION

Do you have the maturity to measure your compatibility with a potential partner beyond physical attraction? How does this proverb help you shape what you look for in a partner?

DAY 01

AVOID BEING PLAYED

PROVERBS 5:1–6 NIV

My son, pay attention to my wisdom, turn your ear to my words of insight, that you may maintain discretion and your lips may preserve knowledge. For the lips of the adulterous woman drip honey, and her speech is smoother than oil; but in the end she is bitter as gall, sharp as a double-edged sword. Her feet go down to death; her steps lead straight to the grave. She gives no thought to the way of life; her paths wander aimlessly, but she does not know it.

THOUGHT

Sex, outside the framework God permits, can look appealing on the surface but do not be deceived! Solomon, the man who wrote this scripture, was a man who had 300 wives and 700 mistresses. He found that pursuing a sexual relationship outside of God's parameters wasn't fulfilling at all. Solomons relationships, in the end, led to his demise.

ACTION

What bible verse could you memorise to help you withstand sexual temptation?

DAY 02

AVOID THE STEPS TO SIN

PROVERBS 5:7–14 NIV

Now then, my sons, listen to me; do not turn aside from what I say. Keep to a path far from her, do not go near the door of her house, lest you lose your honor to others and your dignity to one who is cruel, lest strangers feast on your wealth and your toil enrich the house of another. At the end of your life you will groan, when your flesh and body are spent. You will say, "How I hated discipline! How my heart spurned correction! I would not obey my teachers or turn my ear to my instructors. And I was soon in serious trouble in the assembly of God's people."

THOUGHT

Boundaries. Even with more wisdom than anyone to ever walk this earth, it took Solomon a while to realise God's boundaries were for his benefit. Do what's necessary to build them, maintain them and develop them. They are for your benefit.

ACTION

What boundaries can you create to prevent you from falling into sexual sin? Who can help you stay accountable to these boundaries?

DAY 03

GOD SEES YOUR PRIVATE CHOICES

PROVERBS 5:18-23 NIV

May your fountain be blessed and may you rejoice in the wife of your youth. A loving doe, a graceful deer—may her breasts satisfy you always, may you ever be intoxicated with her love. Why, my son, be intoxicated with another man's wife? Why embrace the bosom of a wayward woman? For your ways are in full view of the Lord, and he examines all your paths. The evil deeds of the wicked ensnare them; the cords of their sins hold them fast. For lack of discipline they will die, led astray by their own great folly.

THOUGHT

Sex is precious, an incredible act of oneness between a husband and wife, no one else. Don't trade this for cheap thrills. It won't be long before you realise you've sold yourself short. Love yourself and understand the value God has placed on your life and the union He has destined for you.

ACTION

Is there anyone you're currently lusting after? If so, how can you repent of this and walk in what God wants for you?

DAY 04

WISDOM STEERS YOU AWAY FROM SIN

PROVERBS 7:1-5 NIV

My son, keep my words and store up my commands within you. Keep my commands and you will live; guard my teachings as the apple of your eye. Bind them on your fingers; write them on the tablet of your heart. Say to wisdom, "You are my sister," and to insight, "You are my relative." They will keep you from the adulterous woman, from the wayward woman with her seductive words.

THOUGHT

The apple of the eye is the pupil, aka, the source of sight. We're urged here to let God's word be like our pupils, shaping what we see, our source of sight on how we view sex. Keep God's word at the core of you, protect your sight at all costs!

ACTION

What's currently informing your view on sexuality? Is it culture, the media, friends or the Bible? How is what's informing your view on sexuality impacting your sexual choices?

DAY 05

YOU MAY BE YOUNG, BUT YOU DON'T HAVE TO BE FOOLISH

PROVERBS 7:6-13 NIV

At the window of my house I looked down through the lattice. I saw among the simple, I noticed among the young men, a youth who had no sense. He was going down the street near her corner, walking along in the direction of her house at twilight, as the day was fading, as the dark of night set in. Then out came a woman to meet him, dressed like a prostitute and with crafty intent. (She is unruly and defiant, her feet never stay at home; now in the street, now in the squares, at every corner she lurks.) She took hold of him and kissed him.

THOUGHT

Solomon sees the mistake of this young person unfolding before his very eyes. Solomon had been in the same situation many times and knew where it would lead. So much wisdom can be found in older, experienced people that can prevent calamity in our lives if we just watch, listen and learn.

ACTION

Who's 25+ and trustworthy, you can go to and talk with to help inform your sexual choices?

DAY 06

DON'T GIVE IN TO OTHER PEOPLE'S PERSUASION

PROVERBS 7:14-27 NIV

"Today I fulfilled my vows, and I have food from my fellowship offering at home. So I came out to meet you; I looked for you and have found you! I have covered my bed with colored linens from Egypt. I have perfumed my bed with myrrh, aloes and cinnamon. Come, let's drink deeply of love till morning; let's enjoy ourselves with love! My husband is not at home; he has gone on a long journey. He took his purse filled with money and will not be home till full moon." With persuasive words she led him astray; she seduced him with her smooth talk. All at once he followed her like an ox going to the slaughter, like a deer stepping into a noose till an arrow pierces his liver, like a bird darting into a snare, little knowing it will cost him his life. Now then, my sons, listen to me; pay attention to what I say. Do not let your heart turn to her ways or stray into her paths. Many are the victims she has brought down; her slain are a mighty throng. Her house is a highway to the grave leading down to the chambers of death.

THOUGHT

There's power in persuasion! Two people don't just stumble into sex, there's a build-up. So learn to spot the signs, the signs of seduction. They're probably not spraying their bed in cinnamon but are their actions opposing God's word?

ACTION

Is there anyone currently leading you astray? How can you stand against the tide of peer pressure and choose purity?

DAY 07

JUST BECAUSE YOU CAN, DOESN'T MEAN YOU SHOULD

1 CORINTHIANS 6:12-20 NIV

"I have the right to do anything," you say—but not everything is beneficial. "I have the right to do anything"—but I will not be mastered by anything. You say, "Food for the stomach and the stomach for food, and God will destroy them both." The body, however, is not meant for sexual immorality but for the Lord, and the Lord for the body. By his power God raised the Lord from the dead, and he will raise us also. Do you not know that your bodies are members of Christ himself? Shall I then take the members of Christ and unite them with a prostitute? Never! Do you not know that he who unites himself with a prostitute is one with her in body? For it is said, "The two will become one flesh." But whoever is united with the Lord is one with him in spirit. Flee from sexual immorality. All other sins a person commits are outside the body, but whoever sins sexually, sins against their own body. Do you not know that your bodies are temples of the Holy Spirit, who is in you, whom you have received from God? You are not your own; you were bought at a price. Therefore honor God with your bodies.

THOUGHT

Sex is the ultimate act of oneness, therefore it requires the protection of marriage. Scripture calls us to become one spiritually, emotionally, socially, financially, AND THEN, we're to marry and become one physically. This order protects us from hurt.

ACTION

Is there any sexual immorality, sex, masturbation, porn, sexting, for example, in your life you need to flee from? Who do you know who's walking in sexual purity that you can walk your Christian journey alongside?

DAY 01
SINGLE IS GOOD

1 CORINTHIANS 7:32-35 NIV

I would like you to be free from concern. An unmarried man is concerned about the Lord's affairs—how he can please the Lord. But a married man is concerned about the affairs of this world—how he can please his wife— and his interests are divided. An unmarried woman or virgin is concerned about the Lord's affairs: Her aim is to be devoted to the Lord in both body and spirit. But a married woman is concerned about the affairs of this world—how she can please her husband. I am saying this for your own good, not to restrict you, but that you may live in a right way in undivided devotion to the Lord.

THOUGHT

Singleness is not second class! The great Paul the apostle was a single man and was used powerfully for God. God still has a purpose for you whether you are in a relationship or remaining single. In your young teenage years, remain single as long as you can, enjoy life, have fun, get some great friends, explore, work hard. Opportunities will come your way to have a significant relationship but don't rush into it. Waiting before dating develops great character within you and often a serious relationship too early can cause a lot of confusion and temptation. Become the best you that you can be.

ACTION

What life long habits can you build now to clear your mind from distractions and look to please God?

DAY 02
SINGLE IS BETTER

1 CORINTHIANS 7:36-38 NIV

If anyone is worried that he might not be acting honorably toward the virgin he is engaged to, and if his passions are too strong and he feels he ought to marry, he should do as he wants. He is not sinning. They should get married. But the man who has settled the matter in his own mind, who is under no compulsion but has control over his own will, and who has made up his mind not to marry the virgin—this man also does the right thing. So then, he who marries the virgin does right, but he who does not marry her does better.

THOUGHT

Paul remained single so that he could remain solely focused and undistracted from the mission that God has called him to. Marriage is great but Paul is trying to help people understand that the priority of life is to serve God. However best you can do that, do it! For Paul it was singleness, for others it's marriage. God is happy with both - He just desires you to serve Him wholeheartedly.

ACTION

Do you realise being single is great? If you are single, consider some of the benefits and thank God for the season you are in.

DAY 03
SEX HAS A CONTEXT

1 CORINTHIANS 7:1-3 NIV

Now for the matters you wrote about: "It is good for a man not to have sexual relations with a woman." But since sexual immorality is occurring, each man should have sexual relations with his own wife, and each woman with her own husband. The husband should fulfill his marital duty to his wife, and likewise the wife to her husband.

THOUGHT

What God had ordained for good, humanity was using for bad. Sex was never created for self satisfaction, it was created for the closest form of unity between a man and a woman. When we distort what God created for the purpose of intimacy, we never truly experience the fullness of that creation.

ACTION

When you are not in a place of temptation you have the clarity to make a decision. Why not make a commit to yourself to follow the bible's instructions and save sex until marriage today.

DAY 04
MARRIAGE IS THE CORRECT CONTEXT FOR SEX

1 CORINTHIANS 7:8-9 NIV

Now to the unmarried and the widows I say: It is good for them to stay unmarried, as I do. But if they cannot control themselves, they should marry, for it is better to marry than to burn with passion.

THOUGHT

Sex is a gift from God to be enjoyed within marriage! Sex is too powerful and too beautiful for it not to be shared in the context of a deep love and commitment between husband and wife. The covenant (deep level of agreement and togetherness) between a husband and wife is one of the deepest forms of unity and passion you will ever find. When sex is used outside of the context of marriage, you share deeply intimate moments with somebody who hasn't agreed to share their life with you through good and bad.

ACTION

Once sexual passion is ignited it is not easy to control. What practical things can you do to not awaken this passion before the right time?

DAY 05
1 CANNOT BE DIVIDED TO MAKE 2

1 CORINTHIANS 7:10–11 NIV

To the married I give this command (not I, but the Lord): A wife must not separate from her husband. But if she does, she must remain unmarried or else be reconciled to her husband. And a husband must not divorce his wife.

THOUGHT

Divorce hurts everybody involved. It's so sad to see husband and wife divorce and disconnect their unity. Love shared between a family is the most precious thing in life. We should never judge people who are going through separation or divorce but should pray for them. If you or a friend have parents who are divorced or going through a difficult time, the best thing to do is find a youth leader and talk about how you are feeling. Process those feelings with prayer, the Bible, worship and encouragement.

ACTION

Choosing who you are going to marry isn't just about finding the right person, but more about you being the right person. You have to be ready to commit for life. Store this thought away for when the time is right.

DAY 06
VIRGINITY IS A PRIZED GIFT

1 CORINTHIANS 7:25–28 NIV

Now about virgins: I have no command from the Lord, but I give a judgment as one who by the Lord's mercy is trustworthy. Because of the present crisis, I think that it is good for a man to remain as he is. Are you pledged to a woman? Do not seek to be released. Are you free from such a commitment? Do not look for a wife. But if you do marry, you have not sinned; and if a virgin marries, she has not sinned. But those who marry will face many troubles in this life, and I want to spare you this.

THOUGHT

This was written as advice at the time, but is still relevant today. In relationships people can look for someone else to complete them or add something to their life that they don't have. They put a married partner in the position to meet needs that you should only ever look to God for. Marriage doesn't fix these problems and, like anything we add to our lives, it can add complications and problems of its own.

ACTION

What can you do to grow yourself, and healthy habits, now so you are ready when you do meet the right person?

DAY 07

MARRIAGE COMMITMENT

EPHESIANS 5:21-33 NIV

Submit to one another out of reverence for Christ. Wives, submit yourselves to your own husbands as you do to the Lord. For the husband is the head of the wife as Christ is the head of the church, his body, of which he is the Savior. Now as the church submits to Christ, so also wives should submit to their husbands in everything. Husbands, love your wives, just as Christ loved the church and gave himself up for her to make her holy, cleansing her by the washing with water through the word, and to present her to himself as a radiant church, without stain or wrinkle or any other blemish, but holy and blameless. In this same way, husbands ought to love their wives as their own bodies. He who loves his wife loves himself. After all, no one ever hated their own body, but they feed and care for their body, just as Christ does the church— for we are members of his body. "For this reason a man will leave his father and mother and be united to his wife, and the two will become one flesh." This is a profound mystery—but I am talking about Christ and the church. However, each one of you also must love his wife as he loves himself, and the wife must respect her husband.

THOUGHT

Divorce hurts everybody involved. It's so sad to see husband and wife divorce and disconnect their unity. Love shared between a family is the most precious thing in life. We should never judge people who are going through separation or divorce but should pray for them. If you or a friend have parents who are divorced or going through a difficult time, the best thing to do is find a youth leader and talk about how you are feeling. Process those feelings with prayer, the Bible, worship and encouragement.

ACTION

Choosing who you are going to marry isn't just about finding the right person, but more about you being the right person. You have to be ready to commit for life. Store this thought away for when the time is right.

MODULE 14

CHANGING WITH GOD'S HELP

Everyone does it, every year on the 31st of December: New Year's resolutions....

We tell ourselves, "This year will be the year...

...I'm gonna work out three times a week, so I finally get the body I always dreamt about (those summer bod goals and what not).

...I'm gonna lose five pounds, so I can finally fit into the pair of jeans again, that has been sitting in my wardrobe for the last 4 years (too real)"

...I'm gonna eat healthier, so no more fast food, no more sugar (sugars from fruits included), no more unhealthy or artificial trans fats, no more white bread, no more fried, grilled or broiled food, no more pastries, pizza, sweets, cookies, cakes, chips, crisps or other snacks, no more ice cream, processed meat and cheese (ah what the heck, I mean all kinds of processed foods), no more refined grains, no more alcohol and no more coffee". So you'll basically live off cotton balls and water. Good luck with that one!

We set our resolutions and goals only to find ourselves almost every year on the 31st of December at the same spot again, in the same situation, making the same resolutions.

The pressure to change, adapt and keep up to date with everything that is happening around us is enormous, or soon you'll be #retro, #oldschool, #vintage (and not in the hipster cool kind of way). We live in a society that constantly advertises changes. Everybody around us seems to change. Every week there is a new trend, a new challenge, a new update or a new technology that revolutionizes and changes our world. But how about our personal life? The life that nobody sees, that is well hidden from the public. The life that only you and God know about. The part of you that you fight against, that you want to change, but can't seem to change. We want to change, but instead we find ourselves in a constant circle of failure - regret - new try - failure - regret - new try.

Here comes the good news. Change is possible, but in order to really change, it requires the help of God. He created and designed you and knows exactly what you need and what you are missing. These next three weeks will be a guideline of how change is possible, with the help of God and look at creating lasting change instead of quick fixes. Open up your heart and let the Holy Spirit show you where you need to let him in!

DAY 01

TEMPTATION & TESTING

1 CORINTHIANS 10:13 TPT

We all experience times of testing, which is normal for every human being. But God will be faithful to you. He will screen and filter the severity, nature, and timing of every test or trial you face so that you can bear it. And each test is an opportunity to trust him more, for along with every trial God has provided for you a way of escape that will bring you out of it victoriously.

THOUGHT

Every single person faces some tests and trials. As Christians we have someone on our side, helping us and strengthening us. This translation says God will provide a way for us to escape! Not to run away or hide. God's way of us escaping is when we withdraw and spend time with him. To escape means to break free from confinement and control. It is God's desire that nothing confine or control us, that we find freedom from walking through life and doing life in close relationship with Him.

ACTION

Why don't you put some worship music on right now and spend a moment reminding your soul that He is with you. If there is an area in your life you think is testing your faith, how can you see a way to escape it?

DAY 02

TEMPTATION HAPPENS TO EVERYONE

1 CORINTHIANS 10:13 NLV

You have never been tempted to sin in any different way than other people. God is faithful. He will not allow you to be tempted more than you can take. But when you are tempted, He will make a way for you to keep from falling into sin.

THOUGHT

So often when we are facing a trial we assume it's a punishment or a consequence for something we have done. While occasionally that may be the case, more often than not, it's not that. In times of confusion we question God. 'Why has this happened? Why have you allowed this to happen?' The bible says all GOOD things come from Him, but God wants an authentic relationship with us and is ok with us asking tough and painful questions. He loves you and wants you to stick around so you can see answers unfold. One of the things 'trials' provides us with is an opportunity to trust God. It's easy to trust someone when things are great, but when things are rocky it can be so confusing, that is the test of our faith. If God remains faithful to us when we are rocky, how much more special is our relationship when we can cling to him when life is full of uncertainties.

ACTION

When you can't see the hand of God in your life, we go back to trusting His heart. When you can't hear the whisper of Gods voice in your life, trust in His promises - there are hundreds to choose from through the Bible. Why not take a few moments to find one of them and think about the difference that promise makes to your outlook, even if you haven't fully seen that promise fulfilled yet!

DAY 03
JACOB WRESTLED TO BECOME BLESSED

GENESIS 32:24-30 NIV

So Jacob was left alone, and a man wrestled with him till daybreak. When the man saw that he could not overpower him, he touched the socket of Jacob's hip so that his hip was wrenched as he wrestled with the man. Then the man said, "Let me go, for it is daybreak." But Jacob replied, "I will not let you go unless you bless me." The man asked him, "What is your name?" "Jacob," he answered. Then the man said, "Your name will no longer be Jacob, but Israel, because you have struggled with God and with humans and have overcome." Jacob said, "Please tell me your name." But he replied, "Why do you ask my name?" Then he blessed him there. So Jacob called the place Peniel, saying, "It is because I saw God face to face, and yet my life was spared."

THOUGHT

This is a strange but powerful story. Jacobs name meant deceived and from a young age that's what he was. But being a deceiver means you can never truly rest. In the dark times of our life and soul if we wrestle with God. We often begin with being honest, vulnerable, frustrated, even angry with Him. What Jacob got right in this story was to refuse to leave the wrestle with God until he had received a blessing from Him. When things are challenging don't quit your wrestle with God in the early stages! Only be willing to let go once you know God has touched you and you are forever changed.

ACTION

Think about an area you're wrestling or even trying to manipulate your way through. Take time to pray and involve God to shape your thoughts about what's going on.

DAY 04

MOSES HEARS GOD & QUESTIONS HIM

EXODUS 3:1–12 NIV

… There the angel of the Lord appeared to him in flames of fire from within a bush. Moses saw that though the bush was on fire it did not burn up. So Moses thought, "I will go over and see this strange sight—why the bush does not burn up." When the Lord saw that he had gone over to look, God called to him from within the bush, "Moses! Moses!" And Moses said, "Here I am." "Do not come any closer," God said. "Take off your sandals, for the place where you are standing is holy ground." Then he said, "I am the God of your father, the God of Abraham, the God of Isaac and the God of Jacob." At this, Moses hid his face, because he was afraid to look at God. The Lord said, "… Now the cry of the Israelites has reached me, and I have seen the way the Egyptians are oppressing them. So now, go. I am sending you to Pharaoh to bring my people the Israelites out of Egypt." But Moses said to God, "Who am I that I should go to Pharaoh and bring the Israelites out of Egypt?" And God said, "I will be with you. And this will be the sign to you that it is I who have sent you: When you have brought the people out of Egypt, you will worship God on this mountain."

THOUGHT

When Moses realised it was God speaking to him he immediately covered his face because, as the passage said, Moses was afraid. The truth is Moses had spent 40 years avoiding God because he was so embarrassed and ashamed of an event that happened that saw Moses kill an Egyptian. Pretty intense stuff. But God, in his love and mercy, though knowing exactly what had happened, didn't come to remind Moses of his past mistakes but came to remind Moses of a desire for good things to happen to his people, and how that reflected God's own heart.

The enemy would love to keep us immobile by reminding us of all our mess ups and lack of skills. God does the opposite and reminds Moses 'I will be with you'. Allow your faith in Almighty God to always be bigger than your fear. Fear is a liar that wants to come and steal your future from you. Faith calls you to greater adventures with God. Moses still felt fear as he returned back to Egypt, but it was overridden by the faith he had in God. If God's desire was to work with Moses and restore him, of course God has the same desire for you and I.

ACTION

Why not think about an area that you're currently operating more out of fear than faith, maybe an area where you are hiding from God. Spend some time praying ask God for boldness and courage.

DAY 05

MOSES DOUBTS GOD, GOD MIRACULOUSLY HELPS HIM

EXODUS 4:1-9 NIV

Moses answered, "What if they do not believe me or listen to me and say, 'The Lord did not appear to you'?" Then the Lord said to him, "What is that in your hand?" "A staff," he replied. The Lord said, "Throw it on the ground." Moses threw it on the ground and it became a snake, and he ran from it. Then the Lord said to him, "Reach out your hand and take it by the tail." So Moses reached out and took hold of the snake and it turned back into a staff in his hand. "This," said the Lord, "is so that they may believe that the Lord, the God of their fathers—the God of Abraham, the God of Isaac and the God of Jacob—has appeared to you." Then the Lord said, "Put your hand inside your cloak." So Moses put his hand into his cloak, and when he took it out, the skin was leprous[a]—it had become as white as snow. "Now put it back into your cloak," he said. So Moses put his hand back into his cloak, and when he took it out, it was restored, like the rest of his flesh. Then the Lord said, "If they do not believe you or pay attention to the first sign, they may believe the second. But if they do not believe these two signs or listen to you, take some water from the Nile and pour it on the dry ground. The water you take from the river will become blood on the ground."

THOUGHT

This is a crazy story! Imagine this happening now! It would be on the news headlines all around the world, the best magician or trick the world has ever seen! But Moses was not a magician and nor was this a trick. This was God kindly giving Moses evidence that He really was with him.

I'm not suggesting that today you should throw your pencil case, bag or coat on the floor in the hope it will turn into a snake, but I do believe that God is kind enough to still give us evidence that He is with us. I think about this every time I see a rainbow - a sign that God will always keep his promises.

Maybe in your doubt or fear you feel like you would like a physical sign God is with you. Maybe you are the only Christian in your family or group of friends and you feel like everyone is questioning you. I believe that the sign of the staff , cloak and hand was actually more about helping Moses believe God was with him rather than proving it to anyone else.

ACTION

One of the signs God gives us is the gift of the Holy Spirit. Put some worship on and ask God out loud for this gift, Begin to worship Him out loud, not just in your heart. It's ok for you to ask God for a sign. Don't be afraid to ask.

DAY 06

MOSES DOESN'T THINK HE CAN DO IT, GOD IS FRUSTRATED, BUT STILL HELPS HIM WITH A FRIEND

EXODUS 4:10-17 NIV

Moses said to the Lord, "Pardon your servant, Lord. I have never been eloquent, neither in the past nor since you have spoken to your servant. I am slow of speech and tongue." The Lord said to him, "Who gave human beings their mouths? Who makes them deaf or mute? Who gives them sight or makes them blind? Is it not I, the Lord? Now go; I will help you speak and will teach you what to say." But Moses said, "Pardon your servant, Lord. Please send someone else." Then the Lord's anger burned against Moses and he said, "What about your brother, Aaron the Levite? I know he can speak well. He is already on his way to meet you, and he will be glad to see you. You shall speak to him and put words in his mouth; I will help both of you speak and will teach you what to do. He will speak to the people for you, and it will be as if he were your mouth and as if you were God to him. But take this staff in your hand so you can perform the signs with it."

THOUGHT

Have you ever seen a friend struggle with something that you know they can do but they won't even try because they think it's too hard? Have you ever seen your friends do something that you'd love to have a go at but rule yourself out because you're 'not as able, not as funny, not as gifted' or something else we make up - as them?

Moses had so many doubts in his own ability he forgot about God's ability. Let's be careful we don't become so consumed with our lack or insecurity that we forget God's power and provision. As frustrated as God was, He worked with Moses and allowed Aaron to be his helper. God isn't against us having helpers on earth at all! But He wants us to see He is the all powerful, all mighty one who will ALWAYS provide what we need.

ACTION

Spend some time thinking are there areas where you're looking more for human help than God's help? God uses and works through people to help us so let's spend some time thanking God for the people He placed in our lives that are helping us.

DAY 07

I DO BELIEVE, HELP ME OVERCOME MY UNBELIEF

MARK 9:20-24 NIV

So they brought him. When the spirit saw Jesus, it immediately threw the boy into a convulsion. He fell to the ground and rolled around, foaming at the mouth. Jesus asked the boy's father, 'How long has he been like this?' 'From childhood,' he answered. 'It has often thrown him into fire or water to kill him. But if you can do anything, take pity on us and help us.' "'If you can"?' said Jesus. 'Everything is possible for one who believes.' Immediately the boy's father exclaimed, 'I do believe; help me overcome my unbelief!'

THOUGHT

This is a story of a loving father bringing his sick son to Jesus and asking if he could heal him. The last line the father says is 'I do believe ; help me to overcome my unbelief!'

I think we have all said something similar. It might be 'I do want to believe I just have so many questions' or 'I believe some stuff but don't understand it all' or 'I know that it says in the Bible that God has good plans for me, but I can't see any of that in my life right now'.

A big part of our faith is trust and honesty. If I was to meet a total stranger I wouldn't trust them to perform open heart surgery. I would have to know that they were fully qualified and had done the operation I needed before for me to trust them with my life. Seems obvious doesn't it? In the same way, the longer we walk with God and do life with Him, we become more honest with Him so that there is a true and authentic relationship that grows. As we know God more we trust him more.

ACTION

Jesus was so pleased that despite any 'doubts or unbelief' the father knew to bring the sick child to him. What area can you bring to Jesus to talk about today where you need His help with doubts and unbelief?

DAY 01

BETRAYING JESUS

MATTHEW 26:14-16 NIV

Then one of the Twelve—the one called Judas Iscariot—went to the chief priests and asked, "What are you willing to give me if I deliver him over to you?" So they counted out for him thirty pieces of silver. From then on Judas watched for an opportunity to hand him over.

THOUGHT

Judas was one of Jesus' disciples, he was a close friend, Judas had spent the recent years travelling and listening to Jesus teaching. He had had his life changed by following Jesus , yet when Judas was presented a lucrative offer, he chose to betray Jesus. We might not think we have much in common with this scenario but if we boil it down, Judas chose to do something that would benefit himself rather than doing what he knew was true and right. We can all face opportunities to choose things that will feel good to us in the moment but long term we will ultimately regret them and sometimes not be able to retrace oursteps. We will all face temptation.

Often if we prepare for certain temptations and decide ahead of time, when opportunities arise we find that with God's help we are able to withstand temptation and remain true to our beliefs and build a life based on truth and convictions not feelings and temptation.

ACTION

Think of some scenarios you know you will be tempted in. Write them down and then write how you would like to respond being led by the Spirit not the flesh.

DAY 02
JESUS IS ONLY EVER ONE PRAYER AWAY

MATTHEW 27:1- 4 NIV

Early in the morning, all the chief priests and the elders of the people made their plans how to have Jesus executed. So they bound him, led him away and handed him over to Pilate the governor. When Judas, who had betrayed him, saw that Jesus was condemned, he was seized with remorse and returned the thirty pieces of silver to the chief priests and the elders. "I have sinned," he said, "for I have betrayed innocent blood." "What is that to us?" they replied. "That's your responsibility."

THOUGHT

Judas realised that he had made a bad choice, he knew he had done the wrong thing. That's the thing with decisions based on flesh - so often in an instant we feel the regret. There was nothing he could physically do to take back what he had done, yet he incredible grace Jesus offers means that this didn't have to be the end for Judas. Yes he felt regret and we imagine huge remorse, but if Judas had repented - which means to turn from his ways, for forgiveness he could have received Grace and Mercy. Shame and guilt will make you not feel you can approach Jesus again, this is called condemnation it will always take you further away from Jesus Love and forgiveness. If we feel the conviction of the Holy Spirit, we can still feel regret and remorse but it makes us run to the loving heart of God, and ask for forgiveness. There we receive grace and mercy and a fresh start.

ACTION

Is there an area where you feel shame and don't want to talk to God about this. Realise today he loves you so much, bring to him what you are ashamed and embarrassed about and begin to talk to him, you'll be amazed the grace you will receive.

DAY 03
DISOWNING JESUS

GENESIS 32:24-30 NIV

Now Peter was sitting out in the courtyard, and a servant girl came to him. "You also were with Jesus of Galilee," she said. But he denied it before them all. "I don't know what you're talking about," he said. Then he went out to the gateway, where another servant girl saw him and said to the people there, "This fellow was with Jesus of Nazareth." He denied it again, with an oath: "I don't know the man!" After a little while, those standing there went up to Peter and said, "Surely you are one of them; your accent gives you away." Then he began to call down curses, and he swore to them, "I don't know the man!" Immediately a rooster crowed. Then Peter remembered the word Jesus had spoken: "Before the rooster crows, you will disown me three times." And he went outside and wept bitterly.

DAY 03

THOUGHT

Peter, in a time of pressure chose to deny he knew Jesus. He felt outnumbered by everyone else's opinion and in fear for what people would think and even do to him. He caved to the pressures of the opinions of those around him and chose to disown Jesus and who he knew Jesus was. So many times it feels easier to just go along with the flow of what everyone else is saying / doing / believing even if we know this to be wrong, unhelpful and not what we believe. Jesus had previously told Peter this would happen - something Peter strongly disagreed. Jesus knew Peter would disown him, yet Jesus still loved Peter, included him and had great plans for his life.

ACTION

Spend some time thanking Jesus for sticking with you even if you waver (we all have) and have given into external pressure rather than pursuing God's will for our lives.

DAY 04

SECOND CHANCES

JOHN 21:15-19 NIV

When they had finished eating, Jesus said to Simon Peter, "Simon son of John, do you love me more than these?" "Yes, Lord," he said, "you know that I love you." Jesus said, "Feed my lambs." Again Jesus said, "Simon son of John, do you love me?" He answered, "Yes, Lord, you know that I love you." Jesus said, "Take care of my sheep." The third time he said to him, "Simon son of John, do you love me?" Peter was hurt because Jesus asked him the third time, "Do you love me?" He said, "Lord, you know all things; you know that I love you." Jesus said, "Feed my sheep. Very truly I tell you, when you were younger you dressed yourself and went where you wanted; but when you are old you will stretch out your hands, and someone else will dress you and lead you where you do not want to go." Jesus said this to indicate the kind of death by which Peter would glorify God. Then he said to him, "Follow me!"

THOUGHT

Peter was given the opportunity to make things right with Jesus after disowning him in yesterday's reading. This shows that despite what we do, Jesus wants to be in relationship with us and will always give us that option. We need to choose to turn to him. We might not have found ourselves denying Jesus like Peter did, maybe it's more subtle in our lives - we keep our faith only for certain settings or with certain friends. God wants to be included in every area of your life, the areas we are proud of and doing well in, and the areas we feel are hard or maybe embarrassing. But he will wait to be invited by you.

ACTION

Where in your life have you not included Jesus, or maybe you used to but now you have stopped. Spend some time identifying why, and ask Jesus to forgive you and invite him to be involved once more.

DAY 05

JESUS DOESN'T TAKE OUR LIVES, IT'S OUR CHOICE TO GIVE THEM

MATTHEW 19:16-30 NIV

Just then a man came up to Jesus and asked, "Teacher, what good thing must I do to get eternal life?" "Why do you ask me about what is good?" Jesus replied. "There is only One who is good. If you want to enter life, keep the commandments." "Which ones?" he inquired. Jesus replied, "'You shall not murder, you shall not commit adultery, you shall not steal, you shall not give false testimony, honor your father and mother,' and 'love your neighbor as yourself.'" "All these I have kept," the young man said. "What do I still lack?" Jesus answered, "If you want to be perfect, go, sell your possessions and give to the poor, and you will have treasure in heaven. Then come, follow me. When the young man heard this, he went away sad, because he had great wealth. Then Jesus said to his disciples, "Truly I tell you, it is hard for someone who is rich to enter the kingdom of heaven. Again I tell you, it is easier for a camel to go through the eye of a needle than for someone who is rich to enter the kingdom of God." When the disciples heard this, they were greatly astonished and asked, "Who then can be saved?" Jesus looked at them and said, "With man this is impossible, but with God all things are possible." Peter answered him, "We have left everything to follow you! What then will there be for us?" Jesus said to them, "Truly I tell you, at the renewal of all things, when the Son of Man sits on his glorious throne, you who have followed me will also sit on twelve thrones, judging the twelve tribes of Israel. And everyone who has left houses or brothers or sisters or father or mother or wife or children or fields for my sake will receive a hundred times as much and will inherit eternal life. But many who are first will be last, and many who are last will be first.

THOUGHT

The rich young ruler's wealth was more important to him than following Jesus. He likened the riches of this world to the riches we receive from our relationship with Jesus. Truth is, there is no way the two can be compared. Jesus has never said following him will be easy or without sacrifice, but whatever we sacrifice because of following him, he will repay us with more incredible riches than we can ever imagine.

ACTION

Spend some time writing down and thanking God for everything we gain by living our life in relationship with Him. Whenever things are hard, re-read your list to gain heaven's perspective.

DAY 06

THERE ARE TWO RESPONSES TO ANY SITUATION

LUKE 23:39-43 NIV

One of the criminals who hung there hurled insults at him: "Aren't you the Messiah? Save yourself and us!" But the other criminal rebuked him. "Don't you fear God," he said, "since you are under the same sentence? We are punished justly, for we are getting what our deeds deserve. But this man has done nothing wrong." Then he said, "Jesus, remember me when you come into your kingdom." Jesus answered him, "Truly I tell you, today you will be with me in paradise."

THOUGHT

What an amazing account of Jesus' final moments on earth - still offering love, hope and inclusion to people - even criminals, who the world had condemned. What's also amazing is the thief on the cross knew who Jesus was. Maybe he had thought his life choices had been too terrible to ever come close to Jesus, maybe he had never had forgiveness explained to him. But Jesus knew all his past, and still said He loved him, forgave him and prepared a place for him in paradise. It doesn't matter what you have done, it is never too late to start a relationship with Jesus!

ACTION

Are there people in your world that need an opportunity to accept Jesus as their saviour? Spend some time today praying for them.

DAY 07

RECOGNIZING GOD WITH THANKFULNESS

LUKE 17:11-19 NIV

Now on his way to Jerusalem, Jesus traveled along the border between Samaria and Galilee. As he was going into a village, ten men who had leprosy met him. They stood at a distance and called out in a loud voice, "Jesus, Master, have pity on us!" When he saw them, he said, "Go, show yourselves to the priests." And as they went, they were cleansed. One of them, when he saw he was healed, came back, praising God in a loud voice. He threw himself at Jesus' feet and thanked him—and he was a Samaritan. Jesus asked, "Were not all ten cleansed? Where are the other nine? Has no one returned to give praise to God except this foreigner?" Then he said to him, "Rise and go; your faith has made you well."

THOUGHT

The leper's lives had been changed by Jesus' goodness and kindness, but only one came to give praise and be thankful. Do we truly understand the significance of what God has done for us? One of the most powerful ways to live our lives - is to live a life of gratitude. We can be so consumed with what we 'don't have' or feel we 'lack' that we forget to be thankful for what we truly have in life. Both physically and more importantly spiritually. If every day we can begin to consciously be more thankful, it's amazing how we will begin to see the blessings and provisions of God all around us.

ACTION

Spend some time each day thanking God for your salvation and for all he has provided for you here on earth. Maybe it will surprise your just how good God is to us.

DAY 01

GETTING YOUR OWN WAY CAN MEAN IT'S NOT GOD'S WAY

JAMES 4:1-10 MSG

"Where do you think all these appalling wars and quarrels come from? Do you think they just happen? Think again. They come about because you want your own way, and fight for it deep inside yourselves. You lust for what you don't have and are willing to kill to get it. You want what isn't yours and will risk violence to get your hands on it. You wouldn't think of just asking God for it, would you? And why not? Because you know you'd be asking for what you have no right to. You're spoiled children, each wanting your own way. You're cheating on God. If all you want is your own way, flirting with the world every chance you get, you end up enemies of God and His way. And do you suppose God doesn't care? The proverb has it that "He's a fiercely jealous lover." And what He gives in love is far better than anything else you'll find. It's common knowledge that "God goes against the willful proud; God gives grace to the willing humble." So let God work His will in you. Yell a loud no to the Devil and watch him scamper. Say a quiet yes to God and He'll be there in no time. Quit dabbling in sin. Purify your inner life. Quit playing the field. Hit bottom, and cry your eyes out. The fun and games are over. Get serious, really serious. Get down on your knees before the Master; it's the only way you'll get on your feet."

THOUGHT

This is a pretty hard hitting Scripture! But if we zoom out we realise the world's wars and conflict are still so accurately described in this Scripture. If we zoom in on our own lives, if we are really honest, it can be true of our lives too. We can often wonder if our desires for success or blessing, favour and opportunity are therefore 'wrong' to pray for. God absolutely wants to bless us and give us those things - but it's ok to ask Him where the motive and desire comes from. God desires us to live a life of freedom and when our motives are out of kilter it's often, if not always, based on an underlying fear. Praying 'give me more money' can reveal an underlying belief that 'only if I am wealthy will I feel secure'. 'Give me more friends' shows up that insecurity of 'if I'm popular then I'll be safe'. Living a life of holiness and devotion to God is a choice. It may not be easy at times but it is so worth it. Pray prayers out of faith not fear, and if you're confused ask God to help you and reveal to you how to live freer in this area.

ACTION

Don't be afraid to ask God to bless you but begin to ask God to help you dream how you could use your blessings to bless others.

DAY 02

GREAT FORGIVENESS CREATES GREAT LOVE

LUKE 7:44-48 NKJV

Then he turned towards the woman and said to Simon, 'Do you see this woman? I came into your house. You did not give me any water for my feet, but she wet my feet with her tears and wiped them with her hair. You did not give me a kiss, but this woman, from the time I entered, has not stopped kissing my feet. You did not put oil on my head, but she has poured perfume on my feet. Therefore, I tell you, her many sins have been forgiven – as her great love has shown. But whoever has been forgiven little loves little.' Then Jesus said to her, 'Your sins are forgiven.'

THOUGHT

Jesus bridges the gap between God the Father and mankind. The woman in the story saw that Jesus loved her for who she was and forgave her. We don't know, but maybe this was the first time she had received this kind of acceptance and love. Jesus loves you and offers you the same forgiveness. It can be easy for us to think 'well, I wasn't a really terrible person before I asked Jesus into my heart' and that may very well be true! But however 'good' we are none of us are perfect and all of us need saving. We couldn't pay the debt of sin; we couldn't receive salvation and have security that heaven is our eternal home without a Waymaker. We cannot compare our 'good' with the perfection of Jesus. When we realise that, the gratitude for all Jesus went through for us is far easier to see and no matter how long you have known Jesus, minutes or years, that revelation can blow your mind again and again.

ACTION

What is significant about the woman's actions compared to those around her?

DAY 03

WE FORGIVE OTHERS BECAUSE GOD FORGAVE US

MATTHEW 18:21-35 NKJV

... 'Therefore, the kingdom of heaven is like a king who wanted to settle accounts with his servants. As he began the settlement, a man who owed him ten thousand bags of gold was brought to him. Since he was not able to pay, the master ordered that he and his wife and his children and all that he had be sold to repay the debt. At this the servant fell on his knees before him. "Be patient with me," he begged, "and I will pay back everything." The servant's master took pity on him, cancelled the debt and let him go. 'But when that servant went out, he found one of his fellow servants who owed him a hundred silver coins. He grabbed him and began to choke him. "Pay back what you owe me!" he demanded. 'His fellow servant fell to his knees and begged him, "Be patient with me, and I will pay it back." 'But he refused. Instead, he went off and had the man thrown into prison until he could pay the debt. When the other servants saw what had happened, they were outraged and went and told their master everything that had happened. 'Then the master called the servant in. "You wicked servant," he said, "I cancelled all that debt of yours because you begged me to. Shouldn't you have had mercy on your fellow servant just as I had on you?" In anger his master handed him over to the jailers to be tortured, until he should pay back all he owed...

THOUGHT

Most of the time forgiving is hard to do but freedom comes when you do forgive. It is a choice not a feeling. Feeling angry, disappointed, let down - these are all emotions we can experience that lead us to struggle to forgive. Forgiveness is not justifying other people's actions or deeds towards you - it is choosing to say 'I forgive you. I do not want what you have done to have more power over me than the love and power of Jesus'. He is the great Redeemer and He will fight for you. The truth is that Jesus has forgiven us of so much - that is why His love and power is able to be at work in our lives to help us forgive.

ACTION

Think about how the forgiveness of Jesus has offered you a different way of living. Are there people in your life you are struggling to extend forgiveness to? Spend some time asking God to help you in this area and pray for those you need to forgive.

DAY 04

FATHER GOD ALWAYS FORGIVES SIN (YOUNGER SON) & ALWAYS REWARDS RIGHTEOUSNESS (OLDER SON)

LUKE 15:11-32 NIV

Jesus continued: 'There was a man who had two sons. The younger one said to his father, "Father, give me my share of the estate." So he divided his property between them. 'Not long after that, the younger son got together all he had, set off for a distant country and there squandered his wealth in wild living. After he had spent everything, there was a severe famine in that whole country, and he began to be in need… So he got up and went to his father. But while he was still a long way off, his father saw him and was filled with compassion for him; he ran to his son, threw his arms round him and kissed him. The son said to him, "Father, I have sinned against heaven and against you. I am no longer worthy to be called your son." But the father said to his servants, "Quick! Bring the best robe and put it on him. Put a ring on his finger and sandals on his feet. Bring the fattened calf and kill it. Let's have a feast and celebrate. For this son of mine was dead and is alive again; he was lost and is found." So they began to celebrate. Meanwhile, the elder son was in the field. When he came near the house, he heard music and dancing. So he called one of the servants and asked him what was going on. "Your brother has come," he replied, "and your father has killed the fattened calf because he has him back safe and sound." The elder brother became angry and refused to go in. So his father went out and pleaded with him. But he answered his father, "Look! All these years I've been slaving for you and never disobeyed your orders. Yet you never gave me even a young goat so I could celebrate with my friends. But when this son of yours who has squandered your property with prostitutes comes home, you kill the fattened calf for him!" "My son," the father said, "you are always with me, and everything I have is yours. But we had to celebrate and be glad, because this brother of yours was dead and is alive again; he was lost and is found."'

THOUGHT

In the time and culture this passage was based, it would have been seen as shameful for a father to run, having to hold his garment up to his knees - but this father's love for his son was greater. When his son returned home the father was so full of joy that he ran to meet him, threw a party and lavished gifts on him. The brother who hadn't left was confused but what he failed to understand was the anguish his father had experienced and had lost sight that he too was a son. When we think about a lost child returning home we far greater understand the reaction of the father.

ACTION

Which son can you relate to? Wild living but empty, or living a life of duty? Whichever you relate to, you are a child of God and He wants nothing more than to be with you and you with Him. How does this truth change how you relate to 'the other brother'?

DAY 05

SIN MAKES YOU IT'S SLAVE

JOHN 8:34 NIV

Jesus replied, 'Very truly I tell you, everyone who sins is a slave to sin.

THOUGHT

Jesus shares these words as His desire is not for us to be powerless and obedient to sin, and be far away from Him, but to walk in His freedom. Every action has a consequence. As we sin we are choosing a way to live far less than the life God has for us. We are being caught up and bound by the consequences of our sinful actions whereas God wants us to be free and living in peace that comes from living 'the Jesus way'.

ACTION

A slave ('doulos' in greek - meaning 'slave, servant, attendant') is a person who serves the will of their master. What do you think the characteristics of being a slave to sin are?

DAY 06

JESUS RELEASES US FROM SIN'S SLAVERY

JOHN 8:36 NIV

So if the Son sets you free, you will be free indeed.

THOUGHT

Jesus died to set you free. He loves you so much. When we ask Him to set us free He is listening - so why don't you talk to Him? When we ask Jesus to be Lord and Saviour of our lives we instantly receive freedom from the consequences of sin, which is separation from God, and we now have an open relationship with God. But there are many other areas where outworking our freedom may be less 'instant'. There are things we will need to work through or understand. Jesus wants to accompany you on that journey too. Every day is an opportunity for us to ask and receive greater levels of freedom in Christ. It's like He has opened the gates to a vast and incredible world but He wants to guide and accompany you as you explore this new landscape.

ACTION

How does the 'Son' (Jesus) set you free?

DAY 07

FREEDOM IS PURCHASED THROUGH FOLLOWING JESUS & PURPOSED THROUGH OBEDIENCE TO THE BIBLE

JOHN 8:31-32 NIV

To the Jews who had believed him, Jesus said, 'If you hold to my teaching, you are really my disciples. Then you will know the truth, and the truth will set you free.'

THOUGHT

Often when you see the word 'FREE' on an advert there is always a catch. Jesus' offer is simple: believe, belong and be set free. Holding to His teachings doesn't mean we won't ever make a mistake, or ever choose our own way, but it is a heart's desire and decision that you have made, and with God's help He will help you live His way. When we have 'wandered away' and done things our own way, we can once again ask today for forgiveness and receive a fresh start to live in His way, experience His truth and once again receive His life.

ACTION

What is Jesus saying when He says 'The truth will set you free'? Who is the truth?

MODULE 15
HOLISTIC HEALTH

To live a healthy life we need to be healthy in our mind, body and spirit. We are created with these three components and need to look after them equally. A healthy body is probably the most talked about topic in our society right now. There are literally thousands of different fitness plans, diet plans, apps and fitness studios to help us keep in shape and look after our bodies. For our spirits, the world offers hundreds of different programs and retreats to get in touch with your spirituality, and not that we are recommending any of them, but it shows that there is an emphasis on keeping your spirit healthy and uplifted. So what about our mind? Check this out:

"A recent index of 301 diseases found mental health problems to be one of the MAIN causes of the overall disease burden worldwide… [In the UK] NEARLY HALF (43.4%) of adults think that they have had a diagnosable mental health condition at some point in their life (35.2% of men and 51.2% of women). A fifth of men (19.5%) and a third of women (33.7%) have had diagnoses confirmed by professionals. In 2014, 19.7% of people in the UK aged 16 and older showed symptoms of anxiety or depression – a 1.5% increase from 2013...
The World Health Organization (WHO) estimates that between 35% and 50% of people with severe mental health problems in developed countries, and 76 – 85% in developing countries, receive NO TREATMENT." (*Mental Health Foundation. (2016). Fundamental Facts About Mental Health 2016. Mental Health Foundation: London.)

When we read these stats and numbers, we can see that mental health state of our society is not healthy; and it is not a minor, insignificant issue. It's an epidemic across the world, that often because of, "not talking about it", "not taking it seriously", "sort yourself out" and "it's just something in your head" kind of attitude, doesn't really get the attention it deserves and needs. The stigma attached to mental health problems has caused people who struggle to feel ashamed and often unable to voice what they are going through. If these stats are anything to go by, it shows us that:
1. YOU ARE NOT THE ONLY ONE. Many more people than you may think are battling fights in the mind. It happens to a lot of people and is nothing you should feel ashamed of.
2. YOU ARE NOT ALONE. If this particular chapter speaks directly into your current situation, please talk to someone about it. There is nothing wrong with getting help for something you are struggling with. If you had a problem on any other part of your body, you would get help for it at the doctors. The mind is no different and shouldn't be treated any differently. Talk to your parents, a family member, your youth pastor/leader, a teacher or check www.childline.org.uk (number: 0800 1111) or www.samaritans.org (number: 116 123) and let people help you on your journey.

We want to spend the next two weeks and have a look at holistic health as it's such a key issue in our society, how to cultivate a healthy mind and how we can deal with depression, emotions and anxiety. You are important, and you matter.

DAY 01

GOD HELPS WITH TRANSFORMATION

ROMANS 12:1-2 NIV

Therefore, I urge you, brothers and sisters, in view of God's mercy, to offer your bodies as a living sacrifice, holy and pleasing to God—this is your true and proper worship. Do not conform to the pattern of this world, but be transformed by the renewing of your mind. Then you will be able to test and approve what God's will is—his good, pleasing and perfect will.

THOUGHT

When this passage talks about not conforming to the patterns of this world, that can sound daunting, hard work and that we are constantly going to stand out like a sore thumb. The truth of this passage is that, as we begin to think how Jesus thinks, our actions change and that leads to habits changing, and ultimately how you and I help transform our neighbourhoods, communities and countries! It all starts with renewing our minds; replacing how the world thinks, and therefore acts, with how God thinks and therefore our actions will also be different. It's a daily discipline and a Godly habit of asking yourself 'what would Jesus be thinking about this?' 'how would Jesus talk in this situation?' 'where can I respond like Jesus would rather than how I would like to?'.

ACTION

Think of something you will do today or this week that you may find a difficult situation. Ask God to help you renew your mind, to have the mind of Christ as you approach it and see how you will handle things differently as a result of involving God.

DAY 02

TAKE EVERY THOUGHT CAPTIVE

2 CORINTHIANS 10:5 NIV

"We demolish arguments and every pretension that sets itself up against the knowledge of God, and we take captive every thought to make it obedient to Christ."

THOUGHT

Your thoughts are seeds for actions, intentions and beliefs that you may think are only small now but they will grow into something powerful in your future. That's why it is so important that we develop the strength and discipline to regularly check the thoughts we have about ourselves, other people and the future to make sure they line up with what God says.

ACTION

Ask God if there are any lies you are believing about yourself, others or the future? Allow God to drop things into your heart. Ask God to help you find a truth about this instead. Every time that thought re-enters your mind replace it with God's truth. Keep doing this!!

DAY 03
CHOOSE WHAT YOUR MIND IS LOYAL TO

ROMANS 8:5-8 NIV

"Those who live according to the flesh have their minds set on what the flesh desires; but those who live in accordance with the Spirit have their minds set on what the Spirit desires. The mind governed by the flesh is death, but the mind governed by the Spirit is life and peace. The mind governed by the flesh is hostile to God; it does not submit to God's law, nor can it do so. Those who are in the realm of the flesh cannot please God."

THOUGHT

When we allow our lives to be lead by the spirit of God we always receive a fresh perspective. Things that might have been consuming us with worry or fear, the stress and strain actually begins to lift when we pray for the Spirit of God to help us. In the same way, our plans for our lives and our future may look daunting but as we involve the Holy Spirit and ask for His guidance we can often imagine a different future for our lives. We become more aware of His love and goodness, not just for us, but also how He plans to use and work with us to show this love and goodness to other people too. God's thoughts are simply so much better than ours, so let's involve Him in our thinking.

ACTION

Simply ask God today, and as many times as you can, to help you have your mind set on what the Spirit of God desires. Receive His peace and His perspective.

DAY 04
LIFE WITH PEACE IN OUR MINDS

ROMANS 8:6 NIV

….the mind governed by the Spirit is life and peace.

THOUGHT

This Scripture helps us to understand what has power and control in our mind. Is our mind full of life and peace? If not, we probably have areas of our mind that we need to take back. Like weeds overgrowing in a garden that were not planted, and are choking out the good things, it's good for us to identify and uproot those thoughts that do not build life and peace.

ACTION

Maybe there is a pattern of thought that takes life or peace from you. Ask yourself, 'where does this come from?'. Make a choice to replace it with something that comes from the Holy Spirit.

DAY 05

SUFFERING BUILDS US UP

ROMANS 5:1-5 NIV

"Therefore, since we have been justified through faith, we have peace with God through our Lord Jesus Christ, through whom we have gained access by faith into this grace in which we now stand. And we boast in the hope of the glory of God. Not only so, but we also glory in our sufferings, because we know that suffering produces perseverance; perseverance, character; and character, hope. And hope does not put us to shame, because God's love has been poured out into our hearts through the Holy Spirit, who has been given to us."

THOUGHT

When things are tough in our lives or don't go 'as planned' we can often find ourselves questioning 'why?', and even, 'where is God in our suffering?'. God is with you, whether our situations appear good or really tough. When we submit to God and involve Him we can be confident that He is able to work things out in the end. It might not be on our timescale, or with our preferred outcome, but He is a loving God. Our setbacks in life are so often an opportunity for God to set something up for our future.

ACTION

If there is something going on in your life right now that's causing you confusion, spend time speaking to God about it and asking for His perspective. Then spend some time thanking God that He is always able to make something beautiful come out of something tough.

DAY 06

SUFFERING LEADS TO GLORY

ROMANS 8:14-18 NIV

"For those who are led by the Spirit of God are the children of God. The Spirit you received does not make you slaves, so that you live in fear again; rather, the Spirit you received brought about your adoption to sonship. And by him we cry, "Abba, Father." The Spirit himself testifies with our spirit that we are God's children. Now if we are children, then we are heirs—heirs of God and co-heirs with Christ, if indeed we share in his sufferings in order that we may also share in his glory. I consider that our present sufferings are not worth comparing with the glory that will be revealed in us."

THOUGHT

There was an incredible change that happened when Jesus died for us. We became co-heirs with Christ because God by His Spirit adopted us into His family. It was always His desire, longing and passion that we would live in community with Him. As adopted sons and daughters we now can approach God the Father as His children. This is the prize: whatever suffering or hardship we go through in this life we are able to gain great strength and joy that our suffering is nothing in comparison to what we now have inherited as adopted co-heirs with Christ.

ACTION

If you think of yourself as a co-heir with Christ does this change how you approach challenges?

DAY 07

DIFFICULT TIMES GIVE YOU GOOD THINGS IN THE END

JAMES 1:2-4 NIV

"Consider it pure joy, my brothers and sisters, whenever you face trials of many kinds, let perseverance finish its work so that you may be mature and complete, not lacking anything."

THOUGHT

There are lessons in life we choose to learn because we can see the instant benefit to our lives. There are lessons that are taught to us, sometimes through situations or circumstances, that we wouldn't choose to learn. These are hard but if we take a deep breath and choose to ask God what he is teaching us, there is always something He is engineering in our lives that will benefit us. Whether it is trust, patience, love, kindness - these can be hard lessons but wonderful when we have them in our lives.

ACTION

Can you ask God today 'what are you teaching me that maybe I'm missing? Help me grasp it more today.'

DAY 01

WE HAVE HOPE EVEN IF LIFE IS TOUGH

LAMENTATIONS 3:21-27 NIV

Yet this I call to mind and therefore I have hope: Because of the Lord's great love we are not consumed, for his compassions never fail. They are new every morning; great is your faithfulness. I say to myself, "The Lord is my portion; therefore I will wait for him." The Lord is good to those whose hope is in him, to the one who seeks him; it is good to wait quietly for the salvation of the Lord. It is good for a man to bear the yoke while he is young.

THOUGHT

Being a Christian doesn't mean that life is all good. You will hit tough times and challenges in your internal and external world. The difference is you are not in it on your own; God is with you. Sometimes you just have to take it a day at a time and trust in who God is beyond your current circumstances. It has been said ' when you cant see the hand of God, trust the heart of God'. Keep your Hope alive and remind yourself of the promises of God.

ACTION

Find a promise of God from the scriptures (do a simple google search if you're stuck) Write it out and put it somewhere to remind yourself of it daily.

DAY 02

THERE'S A TIME & A PROCESS FOR EVERYTHING

ECCLESIASTES 3:1-8 NIV

There is a time for everything, and a season for every activity under the heavens: a time to be born and a time to die, a time to plant and a time to uproot, a time to kill and a time to heal, a time to tear down and a time to build, a time to weep and a time to laugh, a time to mourn and a time to dance, a time to scatter stones and a time to gather them, a time to embrace and a time to refrain from embracing, a time to search and a time to give up, a time to keep and a time to throw away, a time to tear and a time to mend, a time to be silent and a time to speak, a time to love and a time to hate, a time for war and a time for peace.

THOUGHT

Life has many different sides and seasons to it and we naturally want the good but the reality is there will also be a flip side - the bad times. The bible encourages us to identify and not ignore tough times but to understand it is 'a time' and not the final destination. This time will pass. God is there to walk with us through it all.

ACTION

What time or season are you in right now? What would it look like for God to walk through that with you?

DAY 03

WHAT TO DO WITH ANXIETY

PHILIPPIANS 4:6-7 NIV

Do not be anxious about anything, but in every situation, by prayer and petition, with thanksgiving, present your requests to God. And the peace of God, which transcends all understanding, will guard your hearts and your minds in Christ Jesus.

THOUGHT

Anxiety in this context relates to situations. A situation can affect your heart and mind, so focusing on the way you feel and think alone has the ability to build anxiety. This is why God asks you to get Him involved through prayer and petition by involving other people in prayer too. The structure of this prayer should be: thankfulness, requesting to God and receiving peace from God to guard your heart and mind.

ACTION

What situations do you require peace about? Find someone you can involve to pray with you about these things.

DAY 04

GOD UNDERSTANDS US IN EVERY WAY

PSALM 139:1-7 NIV

You have searched me, Lord, and you know me. You know when I sit and when I rise; you perceive my thoughts from afar. You discern my going out and my lying down; you are familiar with all my ways. Before a word is on my tongue you, Lord, know it completely. You hem me in behind and before, and you lay your hand upon me. Such knowledge is too wonderful for me, too lofty for me to attain. Where can I go from your Spirit? Where can I flee from your presence?

THOUGHT

Sometimes, our heads can feel like a big mess like we don't know where to start with sorting it all out. Today's truth shows that God knows us better than we know ourselves and he remains with us through it all. Sometimes it helps for us to start explaining our thoughts and feelings to God. Other times all we can simply say is ' God you know what's going on and I feel overwhelmed, I need Your help. His hand is resting on you - a hand that offers comfort, companionship, guidance and power.

ACTION

Because God knows us so well, what thoughts could we ask Him to help us with?

DAY 05

LONELINESS IS A LIE

PSALM 139:7–12 NIV

Where can I go from your Spirit? Where can I flee from your presence? If I go up to the heavens, you are there; if I make my bed in the depths, you are there. If I rise on the wings of the dawn, if I settle on the far side of the sea, even there your hand will guide me, your right hand will hold me fast. If I say, "Surely the darkness will hide me and the light become night around me," even the darkness will not be dark to you; the night will shine like the day, for darkness is as light to you.

THOUGHT

God is your constant companion, whether you see Him or not. Often we can feel lonely, maybe outnumbered or misunderstood. But loneliness implies there is no one who understands us and who is with us - and this is simply not true. God himself understands you, and He has sent His Spirit to accompany you so you are not alone EVER. Of course we can want and long for friends too, but when we grasp that God himself is with us, we stop looking for our friends to fill our lives in a way only God can.

ACTION

God is with you right now so why not speak to Him about where you are currently at?

DAY 06

BODY IMAGE (GOD MADE YOU WITH WONDER)

PSALM 139:13–18 NIV

For you created my inmost being; you knit me together in my mother's womb. I praise you because I am fearfully and wonderfully made; your works are wonderful, I know that full well. My frame was not hidden from you when I was made in the secret place, when I was woven together in the depths of the earth. Your eyes saw my unformed body; all the days ordained for me were written in your book before one of them came to be. How precious to me are your thoughts, God! How vast is the sum of them! Were I to count them, they would outnumber the grains of sand- when I awake, I am still with you.

THOUGHT

When it comes to our body image, culture offers us a value system based on human comparison. God sets a very different value system on your body. This is based on Him creating and forming you as a wonderful one off creation. A bespoke masterpiece. You are not the product of simply DNA coming together, but God was involved in your life and in forming you from the very start. When a baby is born the parents look in amazement at this miracle and how perfect their baby is. God looks at you like this too. You are fearfully and wonderfully made.

ACTION

Why not take 5 minutes now to ask God what His thoughts are about you?

DAY 07

VULNERABILITY WITH GOD GUIDES YOU

PSALM 139:23-24 NIV

Search me, God, and know my heart; test me and know my anxious thoughts. See if there is any offensive way in me, and lead me in the way everlasting.

THOUGHT

Because God knows and cares for us so well, it is wise to ask Him to help us with our heart and mind. When we involve God like this He is not going to uncover things He didn't know were there but He will help us understand where our thoughts or actions are not inline with what He (who made and formed us) says about us. From there we can then ask God to help us change and experience more of His freedom and love.

ACTION

Ask God if there is any offensive way in you. If there is, repent and ask God to lead you in His ways.

MODULE 16

SCHOOL LIFE

Romans 12:1-2 (MSG) tells us "So here's what I want you to do, God helping you: Take your EVERYDAY, ORDINARY life—your sleeping, eating, going-to-work (or to school *authors note), and walking-around life—and place it before God as an offering." Often we are all about the Sunday life - Sunday Funday, hashtag church vibes, hashtag rather be at church. Sunday to us is THE spiritual day of the week. That's when we get our input, where we are challenged and where we grow. We can encounter God in a powerful way and experience the transforming power of the cross... and then it's Monday again. By the time it's second period we can't even remember what the preach was about and the prayers we said and the decisions we wanted to deliberately implement in our lives that week. Our lives as a Christian were never meant to be lived once a week though.

Jesus wants to permeate every aspect of our lives, and if you are between the ages of 5-18, most of your life is spent in school. That may be the worst sentence you read in this devotional if school isn't really your thing! But instead of being discouraged, let's look at things in a different way: if Jesus wants to get involved in all areas of my life, and can make the ordinary in my life become extraordinary, than my school is my zone. It's full of my people that have the opportunity to be blown away by Jesus through me. It's my responsibility to own it and shape its culture. It's my opportunity to make a difference in my society.

It's your everyday life and a lot of the time it may just seem ordinary, but we want to use this next week to look at how you can impact your school and what Jesus wants to do in and through you. It just begins with simply letting God be involved in all areas of your life, every day of the week and expecting him to turn up wherever you are.

WEEK 45 | SCHOOL LIFE

DAY 01

DOING AS YOUR PARENTS ASK MATTERS TO GOD

COLOSSIANS 3:20 NLT

"Children, always obey your parents, for this pleases the Lord"

THOUGHT

When we accept Christ, we are immediately saved. But our ways of doing things don't immediately change - we have to make an effort to align ourselves with Jesus teachings - changing the way we think. This then leads to changing the way we act. It also includes accepting the wisdom of our parents, even if we don't initially agree. Whether they are parents, grandparents, foster parents - we obey them, as they guide us in good ways. This shows a level of humility and respect that God approves of.

ACTION

Is there a specific area you know you need to obey your parents in?

DAY 02

OBEYING PEOPLE WITH AUTHORITY OVER YOU MATTERS TO GOD

COLOSSIANS 3:22 MSG

Servants, do what you are told by your earthly masters. And don't just do the minimum that will get you by. Do your best.

THOUGHT

We have lots of different inputs in our lives but we need to recognise the voices of real authority. Authority has been often misunderstood and therefore resisted. Authority has been given to people over you for your benefit. If we work with this understanding, our work ethic increases too. So when the time comes we are given authority over people - we will treat people well knowing there is a responsibility we have for them.

ACTION

Who are the voices of authority in your life- Parents/ teachers/ youth leaders? Think of one way you can do your best for these people.

DAY 03

IMAGINE YOU ARE WORKING FOR GOD DIRECTLY

COLOSSIANS 3:23 NLT

Work willingly at whatever you do, as though you were working for the Lord rather than for people

THOUGHT

Let willingness be the attitude you approach everything with. More can be done with a light spirit and a giving heart because you know what you do is working to glorify the Lord! This is a challenge for us all because some 'tasks' are hard and unenjoyable! But when we work 'as if we are working for the Lord rather than for people' we will have a greater level of satisfaction knowing we did our best and God rewards that kind of attitude.

ACTION

What area of our daily lives can we approach with a better attitude so we can truly say 'I did my best for God in that?'

DAY 04

USE YOUR TALENT TO THE BEST OF YOUR ABILITY

MATTHEW 25:29 NLT

To those who use well what they are given, even more will be given, and they will have an abundance.

THOUGHT

God made you uniquely good at some things so embrace your talents. There is no need to be embarrassed because when you use the talents He gave you, you glorify Him. What opportunities have we been given that we are not really embracing? Often this is a great way of discovering gifts and talents God has blessed us with. Doing so will lead to opportunities and blessings that only come when we are diligent with our opportunities today.

ACTION

Think about all the things that you are naturally good at. What opportunities do you have right now to use them to the best of your ability?

DAY 05

WISDOM GAINED IS WORTH THE WORK

PROVERBS 4:5-8 NLT

Get wisdom; develop good judgment. Don't forget my words or turn away from them. Don't turn your back on wisdom, for she will protect you. Love her, and she will guard you. Getting wisdom is the wisest thing you can do! And whatever else you do, develop good judgment. If you prize wisdom, she will make you great. Embrace her, and she will honour you.

THOUGHT

"Getting wisdom is the wisest thing you can do!" But how do you get it ? You get it from knowing what God would do in that situation. Wisdom is not a cheats way to 'get to the next level faster'. It's an understanding of who God is and a filling of our lives with what the bible says so we can be like Him. Then mix that with a humility to require God's help, because God says if we lack wisdom we can ask Him for it and He will give it to us.

ACTION

Where do you need God's wisdom? Ask Him right now for His help.

DAY 06

SHINE JESUS IN YOUR SCHOOL

LUKE 8:16-18 NLT

No one lights a lamp and then covers it with a bowl or hides it under a bed. A lamp is placed on a stand, where its light can be seen by all who enter the house. For all that is secret will eventually be brought into the open, and everything that is concealed will be brought to light and made known to all. So pay attention to how you hear. To those who listen to my teaching, more understanding will be given. But for those who are not listening, even what they think they understand will be taken away from them.

THOUGHT

Shining Jesus in your school, home or college is an amazing opportunity we have. The truth is that just as a light helps people see in the darkness, your life and your relationship with Jesus can help others find their way to their salvation too. You do not have to have all the answers or be perfect. Your honest authentic relationship with Jesus is what needs to shine. Let's not allow our fear or insecurities make us hide the truth about having a relationship with Jesus and the difference it makes.

ACTION

How can you shine Jesus in your school, home or college? Next time someone has a problem why not offer to pray for them?

DAY 07

RISE UP & BE BOLD

MATTHEW 5:14-16 NLT

You are the light of the world—like a city on a hilltop that cannot be hidden. No one lights a lamp and then puts it under a basket. Instead, a lamp is placed on a stand, where it gives light to everyone in the house. In the same way, let your good deeds shine out for all to see, so that everyone will praise your heavenly Father.

THOUGHT

Sometimes it feels daunting to explain everything about our faith. But the bible says that people will notice our actions (or deeds) and our attitudes. This is truth so let's start 'shining our light' with these things. When people ask us about our actions and attitudes we can explain our faith to them and how its changed us from the inside out.

ACTION

Write down what you would say to someone about how Jesus has changed your life so you are ready when they ask you about your faith. It's good to be prepared and ask God for an opportunity to shine who He is.

FUTURE, CALLING, GIFTING

Future. Calling. Gifting. Three things that we all have and are entitled to because of the price Jesus paid.

You have a future. No matter what has happened in your past, you have a future. It says in the Word, that God has plans for your life, to give you a hope and a future (Jer 29:11) - that means he has thought about you and carefully designed a life for you no matter what happens! Sometimes life can feel overwhelming if we are riddled with shame about our past, or fear about the decisions we have to make, but it's important in the chaos of it all, to focus on the God of peace who has spoken your future out over you and has you covered.

You have a calling. No matter what your current circumstances may say, you are called. In life we go through different seasons, and some seasons can appear more 'fruitful' than others, leaving us questioning our calling. Can God really use me? Has he really got a call on my life? Is there space for me in his Kingdom? Is there any purpose to any of this? The answer is yes - God loves you, and he has chosen you for a specific purpose. You have a race to run, and the path will take you to places that you can't even imagine right now! So stick to the path and watch your calling unfold.

You have a gifting. No matter what anybody may have said about you, you are gifted. You have an amazing God Potential placed inside of you, from the moment you were formed and it is bursting to come out of you. You have individual giftings in your life, inside of you for an individual purpose. Don't become consumed with others giftings and allow them to make you feel smaller or less significant. Your gifting is just as powerful as anybody else's and can be used in a mighty way. So tap into what your passion is, and what you're good at and see how God can take it and reach new levels with you.

Let's use these next couple of weeks to discover what your future, calling and gifting look like both spiritually and practically, and listen to the Holy Spirit as he speaks to us about this topic.

DAY 01

GOD DESIGNED HUMANITY WITH A SECOND CHANCE (STORY OF ADAM & JESUS)

ROMANS 5:5-9 NIV

Nor can the gift of God be compared with the result of one man's sin: The judgment followed one sin and brought condemnation, but the gift followed many trespasses and brought justification. For if, by the trespass of the one man, death reigned through that one man, how much more will those who receive God's abundant provision of grace and of the gift of righteousness reign in life through the one man, Jesus Christ! Consequently, just as one trespass resulted in condemnation for all people, so also one righteous act resulted in justification and life for all people. For just as through the disobedience of the one man the many were made sinners, so also through the obedience of the one man the many will be made righteous.

THOUGHT

God always has a way to keep us in relationship with Himself. Humans are hardwired to make mistakes, sin and hide from God. However, in Jesus, God has a greater plan and power than humanity's faulty hardwiring. It's certainly something to thank God for that He didn't leave us to our own ways.

ACTION

As you understand more that Jesus is the only hope for humanity, spend some time thanking God for Jesus and what He has done.

DAY 02

JESUS FINDS YOUR BEST VERSION

JOHN 1:40-42 NIV

The first thing Andrew did was to find his brother Simon and tell him, "We have found the Messiah" (that is, the Christ). And he brought him to Jesus. Jesus looked at him and said, "You are Simon son of John. You will be called Cephas" (which, when translated, is Peter)."

THOUGHT

Jesus always gives us a chance to become a new and improved version of who we are. This is especially true in the moment we first choose to follow Him, resulting in the big life and identity change of salvation. He makes us new and sees us from the perspective of God's best in us and God's best for us.

ACTION

What do you think God's best in you and for you looks like at this time?

DAY 03

YOUR NEW IDENTITY GIVEN BY JESUS HAS ETERNAL PURPOSE & POWER

MATTHEW 16:17-19 NIV

Jesus replied, "Blessed are you, Simon son of Jonah, for this was not revealed to you by flesh and blood, but by my Father in heaven. And I tell you that you are Peter, and on this rock I will build my church, and the gates of Hades will not overcome it. I will give you the keys of the kingdom of heaven; whatever you bind on earth will be bound in heaven, and whatever you loose on earth will be loosed in heaven."

THOUGHT

Our new identity is in Christ, which means we become like Jesus. We have spiritual power and the opportunity to make an eternal impact on the world. God revealed who Jesus really was to Peter and Jesus backed it with the implications of that revelation.

ACTION

In a time of prayer ask God if there is anything He wants to reveal to you about who Jesus is.

DAY 04

GOD OFTEN CHOOSES THE WORST PEOPLE

ACTS 9:1-9 NIV

Meanwhile, Saul was still breathing out murderous threats against the Lord's disciples. He went to the high priest and asked him for letters to the synagogues in Damascus, so that if he found any there who belonged to the Way, whether men or women, he might take them as prisoners to Jerusalem. As he neared Damascus on his journey, suddenly a light from heaven flashed around him. He fell to the ground and heard a voice say to him, "Saul, Saul, why do you persecute me?" "Who are you, Lord?" Saul asked. "I am Jesus, whom you are persecuting," he replied. "Now get up and go into the city, and you will be told what you must do." The men traveling with Saul stood there speechless; they heard the sound but did not see anyone. Saul got up from the ground, but when he opened his eyes he could see nothing. So they led him by the hand into Damascus. For three days he was blind, and did not eat or drink anything.

THOUGHT

Stop for a moment, don't allow past or current sin dictate your future calling. Your shame and past mistakes do not decide what God has for you. God sees through the sin and into your heart, He believes in you and He has most definitely called worse people than you. You are called. You have a purpose.

ACTION

Spend some time in prayer with worship music on quietly. Ask God if there is anything He wants to open your eyes to.

DAY 05

GOD MAKES THE WORST PEOPLE HIS BEST PEOPLE

ACTS 9:10-15 NIV

In Damascus there was a disciple named Ananias. The Lord called to him in a vision, "Ananias!" "Yes, Lord," he answered. The Lord told him, "Go to the house of Judas on Straight Street and ask for a man from Tarsus named Saul, for he is praying. In a vision he has seen a man named Ananias come and place his hands on him to restore his sight." "Lord," Ananias answered, "I have heard many reports about this man and all the harm he has done to your holy people in Jerusalem. And he has come here with authority from the chief priests to arrest all who call on your name." But the Lord said to Ananias, "Go! This man is my chosen instrument to proclaim my name to the Gentiles and their kings and to the people of Israel."

THOUGHT

As a Christian, it can often be tempting to write people with a 'bad' lifestyle off from ever being saved, let alone used by God. Often there's people in our world who we would be afraid to share Jesus with because we think they may not appreciate it or worse turn on us for it. However it's not unusual for God to be at work in people's lives, deeper than their external appearances.

ACTION

Pray and ask God to bring anyone to your mind that you need to share the good news of Jesus with today. If someone comes to your mind then ask God what to say to them.

DAY 06

WE ARE LOVED & MADE NEW FOR GOOD THINGS

EPHESIANS 2:1-10 NIV

As for you, you were dead in your transgressions and sins, in which you used to live when you followed the ways of this world and of the ruler of the kingdom of the air, the spirit who is now at work in those who are disobedient. All of us also lived among them at one time, gratifying the cravings of our flesh and following its desires and thoughts. Like the rest, we were by nature deserving of wrath. But because of his great love for us, God, who is rich in mercy, made us alive with Christ even when we were dead in transgressions—it is by grace you have been saved. And God raised us up with Christ and seated us with him in the heavenly realms in Christ Jesus, in order that in the coming ages he might show the incomparable riches of his grace, expressed in his kindness to us in Christ Jesus. For it is by grace you have been saved, through faith—and this is not from yourselves, it is the gift of God— not by works, so that no one can boast. For we are God's handiwork, created in Christ Jesus to do good works, which God prepared in advance for us to do.

THOUGHT

We were never chosen by God because we were good, we were only ever saved because of God's goodness towards us, not our good works for Him. We became good when we accepted Jesus. At that point there was an everlasting deposit of Jesus made within us. This deposit is designed to flow out of us. That's where our goodness comes from.

ACTION

If there is a struggle to do good, maybe you've created a distance from the One who is goodness - Jesus. Take some time to pray and talk with Him. Draw close to Him.

DAY 07

WHO WE REALLY ARE IS FOUND IN GOD

ACTS 17:27-28 NIV

"God did this so that they would seek him and perhaps reach out for him and find him, though he is not far from any one of us. 'For in him we live and move and have our being.' As some of your own poets have said, 'We are his offspring.'"

THOUGHT

We love it when a friend messages us; it makes us happy when people invite us to join them in the things they love. God is wired the same. He is always close to us but when we involve or invite Him into our daily lives there's a special chemistry that builds. Like that click you have with a best friend. What an opportunity we have to live in that sort of connection with the Creator and sustainer of the entire world.

ACTION

How can you be more mindful to involve God in your daily life?

DAY 01

MAKE A PLAN, BUT ALLOW GOD TO ESTABLISH IT

PROVERBS 16:9 NIV

In their hearts humans plan their course, but the Lord establishes their steps.

THOUGHT

So many of us have good plans for our lives, and it's great to have a plan. But what do we do when the plan doesn't work out the way we thought? We do not need to be in fear. Lets involve God at every step of our plans, and then if things take a detour we can rest in the confidence that God establishes our steps, so a 'detour' in our eyes, always has a purpose in Gods.

ACTION

What plans do you have for your life? Spend some time praying and asking God how He wants to direct them.

DAY 02

BE HUMBLE & HUNGRY (FOR IT IS GOD'S WORD THAT GIVES DIRECTION)

DEUTERONOMY 8:1-3 NIV

Be careful to follow every command I am giving you today, so that you may live and increase and may enter and possess the land the Lord promised on oath to your ancestors. Remember how the Lord your God led you all the way in the wilderness these forty years, to humble and test you in order to know what was in your heart, whether or not you would keep his commands. He humbled you, causing you to hunger and then feeding you with manna, which neither you nor your ancestors had known, to teach you that man does not live on bread alone but on every word that comes from the mouth of the Lord.

THOUGHT

Thousands of years ago, God led many people out of captivity. But before they entered the 'promised land', they spent 40 years in the wilderness. This wasn't cruel of God. He was teaching them that HE will provide for, and sustain them. By giving God our trust and reading His Word, we will also be guided through hard times. He sustains us, and provides for us. Stay humble. Stay hungry. Trust Him.

ACTION

Can you think of anything that may be getting in the way of you being 'hungry' for God?

DAY 03

WE ALREADY HAVE EVERYTHING WE NEED & IT LASTS FOREVER

1 PETER 1:3-4 NIV

Praise be to the God and Father of our Lord Jesus Christ! In his great mercy he has given us new birth into a living hope through the resurrection of Jesus Christ from the dead, and into an inheritance that can never perish, spoil or fade. This inheritance is kept in heaven for you,

THOUGHT

We give praise to Jesus because, through His death, we have a brand new life! We have a living hope because He is alive and working in our lives. Sometimes it is good for us to reassess the things we 'want' and things we 'need'. This scripture tells us that everything we need, is found in the life of Jesus, a life he now shares with us - therefore everything we need has been made available to us. wow.

ACTION

What is the inheritance that we will receive in heaven?

DAY 04

LEARN TO OVERCOME

REVELATION 12:11 NIV

They triumphed over him by the blood of the Lamb and by the word of their testimony; they did not love their lives so much as to shrink from death

THOUGHT

Through Jesus we have the ability to overcome difficulties we may face. Testimonies are people's stories that they share to encourage and inspire others. It's a great thing we can do because it boosts each others faith when we are facing trials. Through holding on to promises of God, and by being encouraged by other peoples testimonies, it often given us the faith and ability to 'hold on' that we need.

ACTION

What testimony of your own could you share, and who could you share it with today?

DAY 05

HOW YOU LOSE YOUR INHERITANCE FROM GOD

LUKE 15:11-20 NIV

Jesus continued: "There was a man who had two sons. The younger one said to his father, 'Father, give me my share of the estate.' So he divided his property between them. Not long after that, the younger son got together all he had, set off for a distant country and there squandered his wealth in wild living. After he had spent everything, there was a severe famine in that whole country, and he began to be in need. So he went and hired himself out to a citizen of that country, who sent him to his fields to feed pigs… When he came to his senses, he said, 'How many of my father's hired servants have food to spare, and here I am starving to death! I will set out and go back to my father and say to him: Father, I have sinned against heaven and against you. I am no longer worthy to be called your son; make me like one of your hired servants.' So he got up and went to his father. But while he was still a long way off, his father saw him and was filled with compassion for him; he ran to his son, threw his arms around him and kissed him.

THOUGHT

Sometimes we can lose focus and go our own way. Even if you do find yourself away from God, there is always a place for you. We must repent (turn from our way of doing things, and ask for forgiveness) and return to father God. The truth is God loves us so much, that even when we 'wander away' He never takes his eyes off us and is looking for an opportunity to be reunited with us once again.

ACTION

Spend some time with some worship music on, thanking God for his boundless love towards you.

DAY 06

HOW YOU GAIN YOUR INHERITANCE FROM GOD

LUKE 15:25-31 NIV

Meanwhile, the older son was in the field. When he came near the house, he heard music and dancing. So he called one of the servants and asked him what was going on. 'Your brother has come,' he replied, 'and your father has killed the fattened calf because he has him back safe and sound.' The older brother became angry and refused to go in. So his father went out and pleaded with him. But he answered his father, 'Look! All these years I've been slaving for you and never disobeyed your orders. Yet you never gave me even a young goat so I could celebrate with my friends. But when this son of yours who has squandered your property with prostitutes comes home, you kill the fattened calf for him!' 'My son,' the father said, 'you are always with me, and everything I have is yours.

THOUGHT

This story reminds us that each person's journey is different. The 'prize' isn't the gifts we have of the presents we are given, the greatest 'prize' of it all is the relationship with the Father. The first son had lost sight of this. It's easy for us to do the same. We can want gifts from God rather than loving the giver. However the faithfulness of the older son is still rewarded when the father says 'everything I have is yours' it's both a reminder and a challenge - what do we have access to that we have got so used to we fail to be amazed by it anymore. Also, the inheritance that's waiting for us is so much greater than the present reality we see.

ACTION

Pray for those who are not in relationship with the Father, that they would return home.

DAY 07

RUN FOR THE PRIZE

1 CORINTHIANS 9:24-27 NIV

Do you not know that in a race all the runners run, but only one gets the prize? Run in such a way as to get the prize. Everyone who competes in the games goes into strict training. They do it to get a crown that will not last, but we do it to get a crown that will last forever. Therefore I do not run like someone running aimlessly; I do not fight like a boxer beating the air. No, I strike a blow to my body and make it my slave so that after I have preached to others, I myself will not be disqualified for the prize

THOUGHT

As followers of Jesus we live our lives differently. Live your life full of energy and determination. Run for that prize of eternal life! Your life is not pointless, but has purposes and promises all over it! Keep encouraging yourself, it is easy to get tired in a race, but when we set our eyes on the prize we find we can keep going with greater enthusiasm.

ACTION

When you are 'tired of running your race' what can you do to strengthen yourself? Who else can you involve to help you ?

DAY 01

ALL-DAY EVERYDAY

ROMANS 12:1-2 (MSG)

So here's what I want you to do, God helping you: Take your everyday, ordinary life—your sleeping, eating, going-to-work, and walking-around life—and place it before God as an offering. Embracing what God does for you is the best thing you can do for him. Don't become so well-adjusted to your culture that you fit into it without even thinking. Instead, fix your attention on God. You'll be changed from the inside out. Readily recognize what he wants from you, and quickly respond to it. Unlike the culture around you, always dragging you down to its level of immaturity, God brings the best out of you, develops well-formed maturity in you.

THOUGHT

God wants to use every dimension of our lives. We don't need to come perfect because He will prepare us, no matter our past. He will build us and bring the best out of us when we give our best to Him.

ACTION

What can you do to grow in maturity in your faith?

DAY 02

NO SOLO'S

ROMANS 12:3-5 (MSG)

For by the grace given me I say to every one of you: Do not think of yourself more highly than you ought, but rather think of yourself with sober judgment, in accordance with the faith God has distributed to each of you. For just as each of us has one body with many members, and these members do not all have the same function, so in Christ we, though many, form one body, and each member belongs to all the others.

THOUGHT

We are all unique, and display the beauty of God through our unique identity. We are not called by God to fit in, but we are called to fit together as we need each other to function fully. Our mission is to build a church family and stand strong in our faith together living in harmony.

ACTION

Who is it that you can celebrate today? Someone who makes a vital addition to your life. Why not thank God for them and let them know how they add a richness to your life.

DAY 03
FIND YOUR PART

ROMANS 12:6-8 (MSG)

If you preach, just preach God's Message, nothing else; if you help, just help, don't take over; if you teach, stick to your teaching; if you give encouraging guidance, be careful that you don't get bossy; if you're put in charge, don't manipulate; if you're called to give aid to people in distress, keep your eyes open and be quick to respond; if you work with the disadvantaged, don't let yourself get irritated with them or depressed by them. Keep a smile on your face.

THOUGHT

Using your God given gift is a lot of fun, it's often something we really enjoy. These verses encourage us to use these gifts, but to make sure our motivator isn't self fulfillment, but the benefit of others. So not just doing the right thing, but ensuring it's the right motives that shape our methods.

ACTION

What gift do I have and how can I help to keep my motive behind it pure?

DAY 04
SPIRITUAL IS ALSO PRACTICAL

ROMANS 12:9-13 (MSG)

Love from the center of who you are; don't fake it. Run for dear life from evil; hold on for dear life to good. Be good friends who love deeply; practice playing second fiddle. Don't burn out; keep yourselves fueled and aflame. Be alert servants of the Master, cheerfully expectant. Don't quit in hard times; pray all the harder. Help needy Christians; be inventive in hospitality.

THOUGHT

God is the source of love, so when we centre or lives on Him, then a genuine love will be at the centre of who we are. That genuine God given love helps us to put others first, being cheerful and sticking it out in tough times.

ACTION

Looking at the situations in your life at the moment is there one that you could approach in a more loving way?

DAY 05

DIFFERENT GIFTS, ALL FOR A COMMON GOOD

1 CORINTHIANS 12:4-7 (MSG)

God's various gifts are handed out everywhere; but they all originate in God's Spirit. God's various ministries are carried out everywhere; but they all originate in God's Spirit. God's various expressions of power are in action everywhere; but God himself is behind it all. Each person is given something to do that shows who God is: Everyone gets in on it, everyone benefits. All kinds of things are handed out by the Spirit, and to all kinds of people!

THOUGHT

You don't have to be a special Christian to receive his gifts. When you receive His Spirit you receive His gifts. Everything originates from him, God is behind everything, and gives His gifts to everyone, each having different gifts, but they should all work together to build the best outcome.

ACTION

Can you think of a gift God has given you and how that fits well with someone else's gift?

DAY 06

FIND YOUR GIFT(S)

1 CORINTHIANS 12:8-10 (MSG)

The variety is wonderful: wise counsel, clear understanding, simple trust, healing the sick, miraculous acts, proclamation, distinguishing between spirits, tongues, interpretation of tongues.

THOUGHT

Don't force your gift, we all have one, sometimes it just takes time to know which one is yours, pray about it but if you don't get a response don't be disheartened, you may already have it but have not realised yet.

ACTION

Which of these initially jumps out as relatable to you, when one does, go speak to your youth leader and ask them to help you develop it.

DAY 07
EVERY GIFT IS REQUIRED

1 CORINTHIANS 12:11-27 (NIV)

All these are the work of one and the same Spirit, and he distributes them to each one, just as he determines. Just as a body, though one, has many parts, but all its many parts form one body, so it is with Christ. For we were all baptized by one Spirit so as to form one body—whether Jews or Gentiles, slave or free—and we were all given the one Spirit to drink. Even so the body is not made up of one part but of many... God has put the body together, giving greater honor to the parts that lacked it, so that there should be no division in the body, but that its parts should have equal concern for each other. If one part suffers, every part suffers with it; if one part is honored, every part rejoices with it. Now you are the body of Christ, and each one of you is a part of it

THOUGHT

Everyone has a gift, no matter how big or small you may think. Yours is, it's a gift from God, and it is required to build his kingdom. You are a gift from God to this world, flourish and love on each other.

ACTION

What stands out to you about this passage?

DAY 01

SMALL BEGINNINGS

ZECHARIAH 4:10 NLT

"Do not despise these small beginnings, for the Lord rejoices to see the work begin,
to see the plumb line in Zerubbabel's hand."

THOUGHT

Small beginnings are a training ground. They set us on the proper course & prepare us for success. Don't be disheartened if a goal seems distant as someday it'll be reality - God's timing is perfect.

ACTION

How can you work on developing yourself for the future in the situation you are currently in?

DAY 02

GOD'S PLANS

JEREMIAH 29:11 NIV

"For I know the plans I have for you," declares the Lord, "plans to prosper you and not to harm you,
plans to give you hope and a future."

THOUGHT

It's easy to dismiss the power of this verse, as we hear it so much or at times it doesn't seem to fit. But when we trust God at His word, we can choose to use it as a declaration of faith and a beacon of hope. God has a plan regardless of the situations we are currently in, or the dreams with have that we haven't seen happen yet.

ACTION

How can you change your perspective, to view your situation through God's word and His plan?

DAY 03

SEEK GOD'S PLAN

JEREMIAH 29:12-13 NIV

Then you will call on me and come and pray to me, and I will listen to you.
You will seek me and find me when you seek me with all your heart.

THOUGHT

God sought us first, with the purpose for us to then seek Him. This is how His plans for our life will become evident. Any misconceptions and doubts we have will fade away when we seek God with our whole heart.

ACTION

Forgetting about the need to have a plan for the next step of your life, how can you refocus yourself on fully seeking God with all your heart?

DAY 04

GOOD WORKS PREPARED

EPHESIANS 2:10 NLT

For we are God's masterpiece. He has created us anew in Christ Jesus,
so we can do the good things he planned for us long ago.

THOUGHT

God has created us as a masterpiece, a beautiful one off work of art. So we can't imitate others, our masterpiece in nature comes when we display the unique beauty He has given to us individually. Part of painting that unique beauty is the good things that we do, which reflects the very nature of who God is.

ACTION

Consider what good things you love to do, that feel like a natural part of who you are. They are part of your masterpiece.

DAY 05

GREATEST IS THE LEAST

MATTHEW 23:10-12 NLT

And don't let anyone call you 'Teacher,' for you have only one teacher, the Messiah. The greatest among you must be a servant. But those who exalt themselves will be humbled, and those who humble themselves will be exalted.

THOUGHT

To be the greatest, we must lower ourselves to understand that what we have is from God. Therefore we should fulfill the responsibilities He gives us with the correct intentions and motives - to glorify Him rather than ourselves.

ACTION

What does it mean to be humble before God?

DAY 06

CALLING & ELECTION

2 PETER 1:10 NLT

So, dear brothers and sisters, work hard to prove that you really are among those God has called and chosen. Do these things, and you will never fall away.

THOUGHT

God elected and saved us for His purpose before we were even born! We simply have to accept & follow what He is calling us to do, in order to stay on track for Him and to prevent us from stumbling. It says 'work hard' so following Jesus is sometimes hard work.

ACTION

Is there an area of your walk with Jesus that you've stepped back from because it was hard work, if so how could you re engage with Jesus on it?

DAY 07

SUBMIT TO GOD

JAMES 4:6-10 NIV

But he gives us more grace. That is why Scripture says: "God opposes the proud but shows favor to the humble." Submit yourselves, then, to God. Resist the devil, and he will flee from you. Come near to God and he will come near to you. Wash your hands, you sinners, and purify your hearts, you double-minded. Grieve, mourn and wail. Change your laughter to mourning and your joy to gloom. Humble yourselves before the Lord, and he will lift you up.

THOUGHT

We can easily take advantage of God's grace and choose which of His teachings we follow. Yet to see all of God's plans for our lives, we have to submit to Him in ALL our ways, not just what we feel comfortable with!

ACTION

Are there any area of your life where you feel like you need lifting up? Why not humbly talk to God about it and ask for His help.

MODULE 18
THIS IS LIFE

"Aye, fight and you may die. Run and you'll live -- at least a while. And dying in your beds many years from now, would you be willing to trade all the days from this day to that for one chance, just one chance to come back here and tell our enemies that they may take our lives, but they'll never take... our freedom!
Every man dies, not every man really lives..."
- Quote from "Braveheart"s William Wallace just before entering the final battle.. intense and epic all at the same time.

A survey was carried out with people in their 80s and 90s asking the following 2 questions:
1. What are the greatest regrets you have in your life?
2. If you would have the chance to start all over again, what would you do differently? Surprisingly the top answers weren't "I would have worked more", or "I would have made more money", or "I would have tried to be more famous or known", but the following...

- I wish I'd CARED LESS about what other people thought.
- I wish I had told people how I TRULY FELT.
- I wish I had STOOD UP for myself more.
- I wish I had FOLLOWED MY PASSION in life.
- I wish I had worked LESS.
- I wish I had TRAVELLED more.
- I wish I'd taken BETTER CARE of myself.
- I wish I'd taken MORE risks.
- I wish I hadn't worried SO MUCH.
- I wish I would have APPRECIATED people more.
- I wish I'd spent more time with my FAMILY.
- I wish I hadn't taken myself SO SERIOUSLY.
- I wish I'd done more for OTHERS.
- I wish I'd LIVED MORE in the moment.

Your life (no matter how old you are now and however many years are ahead of you) is SHORT. We have anywhere up to around 100 years to leave a legacy on this earth. So the question is: "are you really living, or are you just existing?" The earlier you know and stop wasting time with things that are not really worth living for, the sooner you will see what life really is and what it means to be truly alive. We want to make every second of this life count.

We have reached the final theme and the last three weeks of our devotional "THIS IS LIFE". We will have a look at setting valuable priorities and the lifestyle it requires to live this life with Jesus. God has this life planned for you. You are called for this life. So go and live it to the fullness of the potential that God has placed inside of you. Live wild, live free, live creative and crazy, because this life is His gift for you.

DAY 01

DONE WITH SIN

1 JOHN 5:18 NIV

We know that everyone who has been born of God does not keep on sinning, but he who was born of God protects him, and the evil one does not touch him.

THOUGHT

Once we give our life to Jesus, the bible says we are born again, not physically, but in our Spirit. In this way we are called to be like God and through Him we have the power to defeat sin. Adding to that, we are born as one of God's kids, so He looks over us to protect us as any good father would.

ACTION

Is there an area of your life you need to ask God to protect you so you can leave sin behind?

DAY 02

DON'T HOLD BACK

ROMANS 12:1-2 MSG

So here's what I want you to do, God helping you: Take your everyday, ordinary life - your sleeping, eating, going-to-work, and walking-around life - and place it before God as an offering. Embracing what God does for you is the best thing you can do for him. Don't become so well-adjusted to your culture that you fit into it without even thinking. Instead, fix your attention on God. You'll be changed from the inside out. Readily recognize what He wants from you, and quickly respond to it. Unlike the culture around you, always dragging you down to its level of immaturity, God brings the best out of you, develops well-formed maturity in you.

THOUGHT

This is a reminder for us to check our lives, to make sure that we live the way God intended us to. God handmade each and everyone of us to be different. So why would we blend into the culture around us when we are meant to stand out? If God wanted us to fit in then He would have made us the same, but He didn't. Don't be afraid to stand out in faith!

ACTION

Think and see if there is one thing in your everyday life that is a distraction. What practical steps could you take to get past that so you can fix your attention on God?

DAY 03
LOVE JESUS FIRST

MATTHEW 10:37-39 MSG

If you prefer father or mother over me, you don't deserve me. If you prefer son or daughter over me, you don't deserve me. "If you don't go all the way with me, through thick and thin, you don't deserve me. If your first concern is to look after yourself, you'll never find yourself. But if you forget about yourself and look to me, you'll find both yourself and me.

THOUGHT

If someone puts on a shirt and get the top button wrong, as they button up the rest everything else is out of shape. What Jesus is saying is that the love between us and Him is the pure love that makes all other loving relationships possible, even our ability to love ourselves. If we fail to love Him first we'll soon find our lives, identities and relationships get out of shape.

ACTION

When you talk to Jesus your focus is a good indicator of your first love. Do you start the prayer conversation with thankfulness and praise or asking for your own needs? Try focusing on praying in a way that puts Jesus first.

DAY 04
WISDOM & UNDERSTANDING

JOB 28:28 MSG

Then he addressed the human race: 'Here it is! Fear-of-the-Lord - that's Wisdom, and Insight means shunning evil.'

THOUGHT

Look at Job's life. God allowed satan to gradually take away all the things that were important to him, but he never said anything bad about God, even when he had nothing. Job might not have understood the actions that God allowed, but he stuck by Him. Job showed wisdom as he kept on turning to God for direction. Sometimes wisdom and understanding doesn't always come hand in hand.

ACTION

What wisdom are you asking God to give you in this season of your life?

DAY 05
POOR MOTIVES

JAMES 4:1-6 MSG

Where do you think all these appalling wars and quarrels come from? Do you think they just happen? Think again. They come about because you want your own way, and fight for it deep inside yourselves. You lust for what you don't have and are willing to kill to get it. You want what isn't yours and will risk violence to get your hands on it. And why not? Because you know you'd be asking for what you have no right to. You're spoiled children, each wanting your own way. You're cheating on God. If all you want is your own way, flirting with the world every chance you get, you end up enemies of God and his way. And do you suppose God doesn't care? The proverb has it that "he's a fiercely jealous lover." And what he gives in love is far better than anything else you'll find. It's common knowledge that "God goes against the willful proud; God gives grace to the willing humble."

THOUGHT

We can make poor decisions in life by thinking about what we want instead of what we need. God has planned our lives for us and gives us what we need, when we need it. So why do we ignore His directions when all He does is gives us the best? Our hearts and motives really matter.

ACTION

Think about the things that you want. Is the motivation for this to benefit yourself or others?

DAY 06

PURE MOTIVES

JAMES 4:7-12 MSG

So let God work his will in you. Yell a loud no to the Devil and watch him scamper. Say a quiet yes to God and he'll be there in no time. Quit dabbling in sin. Purify your inner life. Quit playing the field. Hit bottom, and cry your eyes out. The fun and games are over. Get serious, really serious. Get down on your knees before the Master; it's the only way you'll get on your feet. Don't bad-mouth each other, friends. It's God's Word, his Message, his Royal Rule, that takes a beating in that kind of talk. You're supposed to be honoring the Message, not writing graffiti all over it. God is in charge of deciding human destiny. Who do you think you are to meddle in the destiny of others?

THOUGHT

Our voice holds the power to cast away the devil and bring forth an omnipotent, and all powerful God to help us do this. We need to line up our intentions with God's word, as He has better plans than we do. When we carry out intentions purely for our own gain, we're blind. But when we carry out intentions that are focused on God's word and His will, He opens our eyes to a world of new possibilities. God's plan and what He wants is the bigger picture.

ACTION

We often yell a loud yes to God in a church or youth meeting. But the quiet yes to God when you're on your own at school or in a quiet place with Him and He's asking you to stop sinning, that is important. What does your quiet yes to God look like today?

DAY 07

DO GOOD

JAMES 4:13-17 MSG

And now I have a word for you who brashly announce, "Today - at the latest, tomorrow - we're off to such and such a city for the year. We're going to start a business and make a lot of money." You don't know the first thing about tomorrow. You're nothing but a wisp of fog, catching a brief bit of sun before disappearing. Instead, make it a habit to say, "If the Master wills it and we're still alive, we'll do this or that." As it is, you are full of your grandiose selves. All such vaunting self-importance is evil. In fact, if you know the right thing to do and don't do it, that, for you, is evil

THOUGHT

Our minds are powerful and God wants to help us use that power for good. Not to allow our minds to be polluted with self importance and ego, that leads to evil. Instead His plan is to allow our minds to be submitted to God's will and surrendered to His ways, that's how we find unity with God - and heaven on earth.

ACTION

Is there an area of your life or future where you have got yourself ahead of Gods plans? Are you running in a direction He didn't set? Take a few moments to pray and ask God where in your life you need to seek His will and ways.

DAY 01

GOOD VALUES

PROVERBS 3:1-4 MSG

Good friend, don't forget all I've taught you; take to heart my commands. They'll help you live a long, long time, a long life lived full and well. Don't lose your grip on Love and Loyalty. Tie them around your neck; carve their initials on your heart. Earn a reputation for living well in God's eyes and the eyes of the people.

THOUGHT

This is the secret to a long and full life - remember and take to heart the teaching in the Bible. It's important and relevant for us to not 'lose our grip' on what this scripture talks about. Traits such as love & loyalty, taking commands to heart & living well for God are so powerful. Being loyal and loving to those around you is not just a good idea, it is an instruction from the word of God. As we weave these behaviours and the value of the word of God into our everyday life we can see our lifestyle begins to shift into one which is wise and honourable.

ACTION

What does it look like for you to practically live a lifestyle of "Love and Loyalty"?

DAY 02

LEAN ON GOD

PROVERBS 3:5-8 NIVUK

Trust in the LORD with all your heart and lean not on your own understanding; in all your ways submit to him, and he will make your paths straight. Do not be wise in your own eyes; fear the LORD and shun evil. This will bring health to your body and nourishment to your bones.

THOUGHT

When we read the scriptures, we can see numerous stories of people who have encountered God, trusted in Him and how that shifted their life into fulfillment. Let's work to build our trust in our powerful, loving and good God through daily relationship. This trust in God sometimes goes against our own emotions or understanding, but it is a choice to follow what the Word says and trust it is the right thing to do. This instruction even has a promise attached to it - health to your body & nourishment to your bones!

ACTION

Is there a place in your life now that you could trust more in God than your own understanding? If so, what is it?

DAY 03
FINANCIAL WISDOM

PROVERBS 3:9-10 NKJV

Honor the Lord with your possessions, And with the firstfruits of all your increase; So your barns will be filled with plenty, And your vats will overflow with new wine.

THOUGHT

Money can be a sensitive topic for people. Especially when talking about giving. But we have the power to shake that culture! Whatever wealth and resource we have comes from God anyway; that should shift our perspective. A good way to know money doesn't have an unhealthy grip on us is to give the first bit to God. This is another instruction given to us with a promise attached, we honour God with our finance and He will bless us to overflowing!

ACTION

Ask God this question - "How would you like me to honour you with my income this year?"

DAY 04
A WISE LIFESTYLE ALLOWS GOD TO SHAPE YOU

PROVERBS 3:11-12 AMP

My son, do not reject or take lightly the discipline of the LORD [learn from your mistakes and the testing that comes from His correction through discipline]; Nor despise His rebuke, For those whom the LORD loves He corrects, Even as a father corrects the son in whom he delights.

THOUGHT

Remember, when parents correct children it's because they know there's a better way or choice for their child, even though the child can't see that perspective. Discipline can be a bitter pill to swallow but we should know that God still delights in us; He just knows there's a much better option for us. God delights in our life and is interested in our journey, He will put things in place that can shape and change us to be more like Jesus. This may be an uncomfortable process but it is so important and worthwhile.

ACTION

Take time to choose how you will respond next time you sense God disciplining you.

DAY 05
NEW LIFE

COLOSSIANS 3:1-10 ESV

If then you have been raised with Christ, seek the things that are above, where Christ is, seated at the right hand of God. Set your minds on things that are above, not on things that are on earth. For you have died, and your life is hidden with Christ in God. When Christ who is your life appears, then you also will appear with him in glory. Put to death therefore what is earthly in you: sexual immorality, impurity, passion, evil desire, and covetousness, which is idolatry. On account of these the wrath of God is coming. In these you too once walked, when you were living in them. But now you must put them all away: anger, wrath, malice, slander, and obscene talk from your mouth. Do not lie to one another, seeing that you have put off the old self with its practices and have put on the new self, which is being renewed in knowledge after the image of its creator.

THOUGHT

It's incredible that we've been raised with Christ! Because of this, we now have a responsibility to try and live more like He did. We have the blessing of being able to look at the situations in our lives from a 'birds eye' or eternal perspective, rather than in their current context. When tempted, triggered or swayed in life, let's set our sights on things above and live in accordance with our new life!

ACTION

Reread these verses. Pause after each sentence and consider how it practically applies to your life today.

DAY 06
THE NEW YOU

COLOSSIANS 3:12-17 NIVUK

Therefore, as God's chosen people, holy and dearly loved, clothe yourselves with compassion, kindness, humility, gentleness and patience. Bear with each other and forgive one another if any of you has a grievance against someone. Forgive as the Lord forgave you. And over all these virtues put on love, which binds them all together in perfect unity. Let the peace of Christ rule in your hearts, since as members of one body you were called to peace. And be thankful. Let the message of Christ dwell among you richly as you teach and admonish one another with all wisdom through psalms, hymns, and songs from the Spirit, singing to God with gratitude in your hearts. And whatever you do, whether in word or deed, do it all in the name of the Lord Jesus, giving thanks to God the Father through him.

THOUGHT

When we read the scriptures, we can see numerous stories of people who have encountered God, trusted in Him and how that shifted their life into fulfillment. Let's work to build our trust in our powerful, loving and good God through daily relationship. This trust in God sometimes goes against our own emotions or understanding, but it is the right thing to do. This instruction even has a promise attached to it - health to your body & nourishment to your bones!

ACTION

Is there a place in your life now that you could trust more in God than your own understanding? If so, what is it?

DAY 07
IMPORTANT COMMITMENTS

COLOSSIANS 4:2-6 MSG

Pray diligently. Stay alert, with your eyes wide open in gratitude. Don't forget to pray for us, that God will open doors for telling the mystery of Christ, even while I'm locked up in this jail. Pray that every time I open my mouth I'll be able to make Christ plain as day to them.

THOUGHT

Even while he was locked up in jail, Paul could still see God in his circumstances. Paul recognised God in absolutely everything. Things may get difficult, but we'll always have the opportunity to give glory to God in tough times and to pray. Pray in all circumstances and with everything you have. In any circumstance - prayer and reliance on God is the best option.

ACTION

Is there a person or situation you need to pray for at the moment? Take time to do this today.

DAY 01
FORGET THE PAST

ISAIAH 43:18-19 NIV

Forget the former things; do not dwell on the past. See, I am doing a new thing! Now it springs up; do you not perceive it? I am making a way in the wilderness and streams in the wasteland.

THOUGHT

God's plan for the future is so exciting! As followers of Christ we have so much to look forward to no matter where we are at in life. In our 'wilderness' and 'wasteland' seasons we can know that God is making a way. In order to move forward with God we need to let go of the past and begin to forgive others and ourselves. We can remain hopeful whilst God does a new thing even when we do not understand it. Remind yourself of God's promise for your future.

ACTION

Take some time to talk to God and get excited about His plans for the future!

DAY 02
FAITH & WORKS

JAMES 2:14-19 ESV

What good is it, my brothers, if someone says he has faith but does not have works? Can that faith save him? If a brother or sister is poorly clothed and lacking in daily food, and one of you says to them, "Go in peace, be warmed and filled," without giving them the things needed for the body, what good is that? So also faith by itself, if it does not have works, is dead. But someone will say, "You have faith and I have works." Show me your faith apart from your works, and I will show you my faith by my works. You believe that God is one; you do well. Even the demons believe—and shudder!

THOUGHT

We have an opportunity every single day to meet the needs of those around us - to show God's love and share His word with others. This passage is beautiful because it is not saying that we must do good things to get to heaven, but it is an example of the fruit which we see from following Jesus. Our faith is not just something that we have, but something that fills us up to overflowing. Our faith is not just for us to enjoy but it is a means by which we can bless this world & live as Jesus did.

ACTION

Where in your life can you let your faith overflow to deeds more?

DAY 03
FULL COMMITMENT

JOHN 6:60-69 ESV

When many of his disciples heard it, they said, "This is a hard saying; who can listen to it?" But Jesus, knowing in himself that his disciples were grumbling about this, said to them, "Do you take offense at this? Then what if you were to see the Son of Man ascending to where he was before? It is the Spirit who gives life; the flesh is no help at all. The words that I have spoken to you are spirit and life. But there are some of you who do not believe." (For Jesus knew from the beginning who those were who did not believe, and who it was who would betray him.) And he said, "This is why I told you that no one can come to me unless it is granted him by the Father." After this many of his disciples turned back and no longer walked with him. So Jesus said to the twelve, "Do you want to go away as well?" Simon Peter answered him, "Lord, to whom shall we go? You have the words of eternal life, and we have believed, and have come to know, that you are the Holy One of God."

THOUGHT

Full commitment to the Word of Life is hard - it is challenging and oftentimes instructs us in a way that is in disagreement with our emotions and desires. However, when we read the word of God and listen to Jesus' instructions, we must have the understanding that these are not just wise words - they are words and teachings which are FULL of 'the Spirit and life'. We always have a choice, just as the people in this scripture did, to have full commitment to it or to walk away. Make the choice today to follow Jesus with the commitment of the Twelve - they knew the instruction of God was full of eternal life.

ACTION

Is there a part of scripture that you find challenging to accept? Pause and think about how it works from God's sovereign perspective rather than your current circumstances.

DAY 04

TAKE UP YOUR CROSS

LUKE 9:23-26 NIV

Then he said to them all: "Whoever wants to be my disciple must deny themselves and take up their cross daily and follow me. For whoever wants to save their life will lose it, but whoever loses their life for me will save it. What good is it for someone to gain the whole world, and yet lose or forfeit their very self? Whoever is ashamed of me and my words, the Son of Man will be ashamed of them when he comes in his glory and in the glory of the Father and of the holy angels.

THOUGHT

Jesus willingly picked up the cross and laid down His life for us. He took on the sins, guilt and shame of all humanity so that we no longer pay the price for our short-fallings. What a blessing it is that we get to be in relationship with the God who sacrificed so much for us! Whatever comes in between us and God in our lives is what we need to lay down. No matter how big it is, nothing is worth breaking our relationship with God. As it says 'What good is it for someone to gain the whole world, and yet lose or forfeit their very self?'. In order to pick up the fullness of life in Christ we must lay down our lives.

ACTION

What can you do today to lay down your life and pick up life with Christ?

DAY 05

TREASURES IN HEAVEN

MATTHEW 6:19-21 TPT

"Don't keep hoarding for yourselves earthly treasures that can be stolen by thieves. Material wealth eventually rusts, decays, and loses its value. Instead, stockpile heavenly treasures for yourselves that cannot be stolen and will never rust, decay, or lose their value. For your heart will always pursue what you value as your treasure.

THOUGHT

Every one of our treasures, except our relationship with God, is temporary. When we put Him at the centre of our lives and allow Him to be our biggest treasure we will be sustained. Earthly treasure can be things like money, possessions or even fame. All of this seems important now but none of it can be taken with us when we go to heaven. The greatest value should be in your relationship with God & bringing other people into relationship with Him.

ACTION

What currently has your heart's attention? How can you bring that into alignment with this scripture?

DAY 06

GREATEST COMMAND

MATTHEW 22:36–40 NIV

"Teacher, which is the greatest commandment in the Law?" Jesus replied: "Love the Lord your God with all your heart and with all your soul and with all your mind.' This is the first and greatest commandment. And the second is like it: 'Love your neighbor as yourself.' All the Law and the Prophets hang on these two commandments."

THOUGHT

Loving God with everything empowers us to love other people. We can show God's love to others, the same way He has shown us His great love. As we love God fully, we learn to become more like Him. While it is a choice to love others, it also begins to flow as a natural progression from our love for and relationship with God.

ACTION

What does it look like to practically love God with all you heart, soul and mind?

DAY 07

GREAT COMMISSION

MATTHEW 28:16–20 ESV

Now the eleven disciples went to Galilee, to the mountain to which Jesus had directed them. And when they saw him they worshiped him, but some doubted. And Jesus came and said to them, "All authority in heaven and on earth has been given to me. Go therefore and make disciples of all nations, baptizing them in the name of the Father and of the Son and of the Holy Spirit, teaching them to observe all that I have commanded you. And behold, I am with you always, to the end of the age."

THOUGHT

Jesus has called us to continue the work He started when He was on Earth. When we seek Him first and show others what it looks like to live a life for Christ we are fulfilling this call. We also know that we aren't going out into the world alone. 'And behold, I am with you always, to the end of the age'. In everything we step out in to honour God and lift His name high we can know that He is with us! We have the King of Kings & the Lord of Lords with us every single day, let's go out into the world and live in that confidence!

ACTION

Pray and ask Jesus what it would look like to live out the great commission for you today - then go and do it!

COPYRIGHT & ACKNOWLEDGEMENTS

THANK YOU

We want to say a massive thank you to everyone who contributed to this project. To the writers, editors, proof readers & designer – all of you played such an important role in making this happen and we honour you for your contribution. We also honour all of our leaders and young people – you are making a difference to this world and we love you.

ROCKNATIONS CONFERENCE

Rocknations hosts an annual Youth Conference for young people and their leaders every August. Thousands of teenagers gather for incredible worship and relevant teaching , interactive seminars, insane activities and heaps of fun.

THIS
IS
LIFE